The School Superintendent

Living with Conflict

The School Superintendent

Living with Conflict

Arthur Blumberg
with Phyllis Blumberg

Foreword
by Seymour Sarason

Teachers College, Columbia University
New York and London

Published by Teachers College Press, 1234 Amsterdam Avenue, New York, N.Y. 10027

Library of Congress Cataloging in Publication Data

Blumberg, Arthur, 1923–
    The school superintendent.

    Bibliography: p.
    Includes index.
    1. School superintendents and principals—
United States.   I. Blumberg, Phyllis, 1933–
II. Title.
LB2831.72.B55   1984   371.2′011′0973   84-14953

ISBN 0-8077-2764-4

Manufactured in the United States of America

90 89   4 5 6

To
Benjamin, Joanna, David, and Daniel

Contents

Foreword

Education has returned to the national agenda, a fact that engenders little optimism in me that the result will be improved public education—not because I am a pessimist who can only see the bottle as half empty, or because I am a spoilsport—but because the current discussion (hardly a debate) is suffused with rhetoric, slogans, and a "shape-up-or-ship-out" psychology. In addition, most of the participants in this discussion seem never to have been in the school culture, or, if they have been, to have forgotten how complex that culture is, characterized by a hierarchical structure; by ambiguities in role; by responsibilities coupled with ill-defined authority; by myriad conflicts deriving from formal and informal sources of power; by tensions among groups within and without the school; by dependence on local, state, and federal monies; and by struggles (sometimes muted, often not) among students, educators at various levels, and parents. We are hearing much about change today, but what is really being called for is change from the present to a past that hardly existed. But if that judgment seems unfair, it is not unfair to state that the current participants in today's discussion have been wonderfully successful in avoiding any suggestion about how their proposals will be reacted to, assimilated by, and transformed by those in the school culture. Nor do they offer anything other than oversimplifications about why in past eras similar proposals died in the process of change. Let me hasten to add that in no way am I suggesting that those who teach and administer our schools are mindless foes of change and innovation. But too many of those who make or influence policy seem to have no comprehension of what makes change difficult or impossible, or of what makes for a desired change.

In recent decades the conventional wisdom about the job of being a superintendent of schools has been that it is a thankless role in which one survives, if one survives at all, for only five years or so in one district and is then forced to go elsewhere to learn what one already knows: it is not that you cannot win, it is that you can do little more than nothing. The superintendency can be seen as an exalted role, but it can also be seen as an impossible role. It is surprising how few studies of the role have been carried out, and not many of those have particularly illuminated its public and private aspects, the contrasts between the "public figure" or "image" and the private person who, no less than any of us, struggles to rationalize these contrasts in order to feel that his or her values and actions are consistent with each other, that he or she is deserving of self-approval, and that the selfish and the selfless balance each other.

Professor Blumberg gives us a picture of superintendents and the superintendency that should earn him our deepest respect. When you finish this readable, often gripping, always informative book, the chances are that, like me, you will say, "I *really* have learned something." Professor Blumberg does not hide behind jargon; he lets his interviewees tell their stories, but all the time the author is painting a picture of the superintendency that contains both stark features and delicate shadings.

I wish that this book could be read by those participating in the current discussion on educational policy and change. At the least, they might resort less to oversimplification. It is also possible (I am a hopeful person!) that the policies they propose would contain some appreciation of the complexity of the change process and the fact that it inevitably causes conflict. This book demonstrates that "living with conflict" is a natural or predictable characteristic of the experience of all those who populate our schools. If it is a characteristic that the superintendent experiences in spades, it is through his or her eyes that we see how much of a feature conflict is for those who are directly or indirectly affected by what the superintendent does (or does not) do. This book is more than a splendid contribution to the educational literature. Social scientists, parents, members of boards of education, and any citizen with an interest in our schools will find it unusually instructive and rewarding. And, I must repeat, Professor Blumberg writes lucidly and engagingly. That in itself is no small feat. The clear writing is matched by clear thinking.

Seymour Sarason

Preface

Some years ago I had a conversation with a superintendent of schools whose district had just emerged from a bitter month-long teachers' strike. The conversation focused on the character of the personal and organizational trauma with which he had had to deal before, during, and after the strike. My professorial naiveté concerning the situation must have startled him. Although the conditions that attached to the strike were undoubtedly not typical of his ordinary working life, he told me that dealing with situations involving conflict was a constant part of the superintendent's job, and perhaps its essential feature. Some of these situations were trivial, and some were critically important to the life of the school district.

Viewed in retrospect, that conversation was the genesis of this book. Intrigued by his comments, I decided to investigate the subject further. As I read about the superintendency, talked with and simply listened to the talk of superintendents, and read newspaper accounts of the trials and tribulations of school districts, it occurred to me that the theme of "living with conflict," as it relates to the life and times of superintendents of schools, had not been explored in any focused and systematic fashion. It was not so much that issues of conflict are hidden from view—though some are—as it was that the superintendency seemed not to have been conceived of, studied, and extensively written about with that theme in mind. Though most accounts of public schools and their problems imply some sort of conflict involving the superintendent—sometimes rather openly, but more frequently hinting at it as lurking below the surface—the issue has not been confronted directly.

My preliminary investigation had suggested, then, that the essential meaning of the superintendency as a type of work and the meaning of that work *for the superintendent as a person* could not be grasped unless the role could be viewed through a lens that focused on its unavoidably conflictual nature. To test this idea, I checked it out with a number of superintendent friends and colleagues. I approached them with a rather simple question that went something like this: "If I have any understanding of what it is you do, underneath it all is the need to continually deal with and manage conflicts of one type or another. Is that it?" The unanimous response I received was, in essence, "You got it! That's where it's at!" Hence, this book.

The decision of just how to go about gathering information for my study was made rather quickly. I wanted to be able to present an image of the superintendency from the perspective of the people who did that work. The result would enable me and the interested reader to get some insight, in very human terms, into the ways that superintendents seem to think and feel about what they do; how they deal with conflicts involving individuals and groups; and how they deal with themselves.

This book, then, is based on interviews with 25 superintendents of schools. The interviews were recorded and later transcribed. Twenty-four of the superintendents were men. One was a woman. They ranged in age from the early thirties to the late fifties. Some of them were interviewed twice in order to go into more detail.

The primary criterion for selection of the people to be interviewed was not at all complicated. It was simply a matter of getting in touch with a number of superintendents who I knew would be open with me. I was not interested in whether or not the superintendent could be judged to be successful. I was interested in what it was like to be a superintendent—not in the superintendent's performance.

The school districts that were administered by these superintendents varied widely in character. Some were in rural areas, others in working-class suburbs, still others in affluent suburbs, and one was in a middle-sized city. In terms of pupil population, they ranged from a district of 450 pupils to one of over 23,000.

The first interviews were very much open-ended. I began by asking the broad question, "What is it like to be a superintendent?" Conversation never lagged. Shortly after each of the first three interviews was held and before the next one took place, I listened to the tapes and analyzed the conversations to see what aspects of the job had been consistently stressed. I then used the categories developed in this way as cue questions in subsequent interviews, if the respondent did not raise them of his or her own volition. After about the tenth interview, it became clear that no new categories would develop: the categorical world of the superintendency appeared to have been covered. The interview process was continued, however, in order to add richness of description to the study.

One part of the study that was unanticipated at the start developed directly as a result of the early interview analysis. In speaking of the time demands placed upon them by their jobs, particularly the numbers of evenings they spend at meetings, the superintendents interviewed frequently made reference to the problems the job posed for their wives. This led to a decision to interview wives of five superintendents and to include an analysis of these interviews as part of this study. The notion was that in order to understand the superintendency, one also needed to understand that job from the point of view of its potential effect on the superintendent's family.

After the interviews had been transcribed, I analyzed each interview transcript to see what categories and themes emerged. This procedure resulted in the chapter organization of this book. In looking over the table of contents, the reader will note that although this book is concerned especially with the theme of "living with conflict," not all the superintendent's work life is conflictual. Some of it is quite mundane and placid, and this will be reflected from time to time in the discussion.

Questions of generalizability always attach to studies such as this one, and legitimately so. The sample of interviewees was not random. All of them, with one exception, worked in New York State. However, their work experience as superintendents had not been confined to any particular section of the state, and two had been superintendents in other states before coming to New York. There was also a wide range of degrees of experience. While one was interviewed about three months after he assumed his first position, several had been superintendents upwards of 15 years. Nevertheless, despite the range of experience, age, and type of community represented among the group, no claim can be made that their responses adequately represent all superintendents everywhere.

There is another side of the coin, however, that leads me to think that the image of the superintendency that will unfold throughout the book is one that the huge majority of superintendents can relate to and understand as a valid one. First, of course, this is not a study of individuals. It is a study of an office, its role demands, and what work seems to be like for people who hold that office. As will be seen, although there was a range of behavioral reactions among the interviewees to these role demands, there was general agreement concerning the nature of the demands themselves. Second, my reading of the history of the superintendency suggests rather clearly that the underlying focus—living with conflict—is an appropriate and perhaps central framework for understanding the character of a superintendent's work life. Third, one only has to read the daily papers from almost any section of the country to affirm the central theme of the book. Finally, my conversations about this study with colleagues from widely separated locations have, without exception, reinforced the idea that this theme is central if one wishes to understand the superintendency.

While I believe this book makes a contribution to the literature on the superintendency, I do not intend it to be a reference book for scholars and researchers, although they may benefit from reading it. Rather, I have three other audiences in mind. First, graduate students, school administrators, and teachers who aspire to the superintendency ought to find its discussion of value. It presents aspects of the superintendency of which they may be only dimly aware. Second, superintendents themselves should find it of interest. Each should find a bit of himself or herself here and may enjoy carrying on a "conversation" with the book by comparing its themes with his or her own

experience. Third, members of boards of education, on reading it, will probably learn some things that they were unaware of about the school person
with whom they have the most direct and important contact. I think if school
board members read and discuss this book with their superintendent, that
discussion could be most interesting.

A question that I was concerned with in the writing of the manuscript
dealt with the extent to which it should be organized along traditional academic lines. The central issue here was whether or not I should include an
extensive chapter on previous research. Somehow it didn't seem appropriate
for this book. Thus, the reader, either to his or her dismay or pleasure, will
not find a time-honored "review of the literature" included in the text. For
those readers who may be interested and desire some guidance concerning the
literature in the field, I have provided at the end of the book a brief bibliographic essay describing some important books about the superintendency
("For Further Reading").

I have tried, as much as I could, to limit my use of academic jargon
throughout. I wanted to be able to communicate the experience of being a
superintendent rather directly—almost conversationally, I have been
told—without cluttering the text with undue reference to theory and research. Some jargon, though, will certainly be found. My use of masculine
terms for the superintendent throughout the book is regrettable but deliberate. There are women superintendents and very effective ones, but the huge
majority—well over 90 percent—of chief school officers are men.

Some final comments: First, the jobs people hold and the work they do
may be studied in different ways. For example, one may inquire into the
functions to be performed, technical skills required, or conceptual abilities
deemed necessary for effective job performance. One might say that this book
is about both all and none of these ways of understanding the work of
superintendents: all of these things are touched on, but the focus is always on
the human experience of being a superintendent. That is the meaning I attach
to the use of the term *work life* throughout the book.

Second, though readers may find that some of the things that superintendents go through arouse sympathy for them, this book is not a plea to the
public to be kinder to superintendents. Nor is it an apologetic—an effort to
defend them against what some people might think are their shortcomings. It
is simply intended to be an objective analysis of what it's like to be a superintendent.

Third, the reader should know that I have never been a school superintendent. Though some may think that having been a superintendent is a
necessary qualification for writing about the job, I think otherwise. In a very
real way, not to have been one frees me to write more objectively about
superintendents.

I am indebted to many people for their support of my efforts: to the superintendents who were my interviewees for their time and clarity of thought; to Professor Seymour Sarason for his close reading of my work and for writing the Foreword; and to Dr. Volker Weiss, Vice President for Research and Graduate Studies at Syracuse University, who provided financial help when I needed it most. Finally, my thanks go to Lindy Cirigliano for many things—her willingness to type and retype, her clear view of what I was doing, and her unfailing good humor through it all.

The School Superintendent

Living with Conflict

1

Introduction

Conflict: A Major Theme

"It comes with the territory." The "it," in this case, is what the people who were interviewed for this book told me was the essential and underlying character of the school superintendency: the necessity of having to live daily with conflictual or potentially conflictual situations in which the superintendent plays a focal role as decision maker, mediator, or simply as a human lightning rod who attracts controversy. Some of the conflicts take on major, systemic proportions, affecting the entire school district. Some are major but affect only individuals. Some are minor. Some relate to the superintendent as a person, some to his job and career, and some to his family. Regardless of the focus or substance, a seemingly absolute condition of the superintendency is that there are only rarely days when the superintendent is not called upon to make a decision that will create some conflict, or is not involved somehow in conflicts not of his own making. All of this seems to occur irrespective of the person involved: "It comes with the territory."

Interestingly, Callahan (1962), in his book *The Cult of Efficiency,* arrives at a similar conclusion, though he expresses it in somewhat different terms. He writes in his preface, "When I began this study some five years ago, my intent was to explore the origin and development of business values and practices in educational administration." He continues, "I am now convinced that much of what has happened in American education since 1900 can be explained on the basis of the extreme vulnerability of our schoolmen to public criticism and pressure and that this vulnerability is built into our pattern of local control and support." If Callahan is right, what may have occurred, certainly in an unplanned fashion, is that we have created a system to educate our children that sows the seeds of its own controversy. For our purposes, then, it becomes important to understand that though some superintendents may deliberately induce controversy from time to time in order to focus attention on issues that they think require it, the controversies with which they seem to be continually involved are more endemic to the system than they are a function of the person.

I do not mean to imply that superintendents are forever running around

1

with furrowed brows or with worried looks on their faces. Far from it—they seem to be a rather jolly lot, who, confronted frequently with very complex problems and a set of constituencies that are, more often than not, in disagreement, seem very much to enjoy what they are doing. What the opening paragraphs imply, however, is that one cannot understand what the superintendency is all about unless one also knows that the undercurrents that move the position and the person in it are almost always conflictual in nature.

While the "living with conflict" theme will be apparent throughout, sometimes boldly and sometimes subtly, in a larger sense (as I have mentioned in the preface) this study is designed to present a wide-ranging perspective on the role of superintendent and how it gets played out. This perspective will emerge, in particular, through discussion of the themes that seemed dominant in the interviews. These themes include the images that superintendents hold of themselves; the political demands to which they must accommodate; their dealings with teachers' unions; their perceptions of themselves as "public property"; and their feelings of loneliness, anger, success, and failure.

A caveat is in order lest the reader assume that the work life of school superintendents is characterized by one bloody battle after another. This is clearly not the case, though I know a couple of superintendents who would dissent. Despite these dissents, much of a superintendent's work is mundane; he performs his share of routine administration; he sits through many boring meetings; he attends many public functions and is a member of community groups in which he has no interest; and he "shows the flag" at high school football and basketball games when many times he couldn't care less. In these respects, the demands of the position are not unlike those affecting the executive officer of any sizable organization. Maintenance functions must be performed. Routine decisions must be made. Attention must be paid to institutional public relations. As we move beyond some of the basic facts of organizational life, however, it will be seen that the work of superintendents is anything but mundane. At its roots it contains opportunities for excitement, challenge, and a real sense of accomplishment, as well as possibilities for personal and professional failure.

In describing that challenge, I suggest that the opportunities and possibilities that confront a superintendent have less to do with the education of children per se than they do with maintaining the viability of the school system as a human organization, in its several dimensions—political, economic, social, and psychological. At first glance, this may seem like a curious position to take. Surely, if you ask most superintendents why they aspired to that position, the answer you will receive will go something like, "I wanted to get into a position where I could have a wider and more powerful impact on the education of kids." I think that statements like this are honest ones. They adequately reflect, for the most part, the motivation of people who want to become superintendents of schools. However, I do not believe they reflect at all adequately the dynamics of the demands of the job. This does not mean, of course, that superintendents are not concerned about the education of youngsters or that their decisions and organizing ability do not affect what goes on in schools. Their concern for youngsters, however, will be evidenced in matters that may be some distance removed from what is happening in school buildings, and further still (except perhaps in very small school districts) from what is happening in individual classrooms. Superintendents simply play in larger, more ill-defined, and, in many respects, quite different ball parks from those where principals or teachers carry out their roles. This is an obvious statement, perhaps, but one that is important to keep in mind.

The remainder of this chapter will set the stage for the rest of the book by introducing the reader to the broad theme of conflict in the superintendency. You will glimpse the tip of the iceberg here, so to speak, and will also start to understand that this theme is not of recent vintage—a point that will be dealt with in some detail in chapter 2.

A Historical Perspective

We start with excerpts from a couple of letters written by a rural school superintendent in 1922 and 1923 to his daughter, who was away at school. The district about which he wrote was located in western Massachusetts. The letters were published in the *American School Board Journal* in two articles entitled "Letters from a Country School Superintendent to his Daughter."

> The people of South Sandisfield are fine people. They will do anything in the world for a person, but if they are not busy doing something for you, they are sure to be busy fighting you. I remember one big fight I had over there. It was just after I first became superintendent. You were away from home at the time. Word reached me that the teacher was not a fit person to teach school, so I went over to investigate. I called the people together and we had a general confab, and as a result, this is what I learned. There was a widow over there by the name of Mrs. Clyde who had a son that fell in love with the new teacher as regularly as the new teacher arrived. And while Raymond was attentive to the new teacher, Mrs. Clyde was genuinely motherly to her. But when the question was popped, as it always was, just about the time of the Thanksgiving concert when Raymond was so busy helping to decorate the school, a sudden change always took place. The teacher ceased to be an angel. And this year was no exception.
>
> Ray says "Will yer?" Teacher says, "No thanks." Mrs. Clyde says "Vamp." (*American School Board Journal*, 1922, p. 36)

Mrs. Clyde, the letter then implies, was so angry at the teacher that she kept her son out of school and eventually had to appear in court on charges of allowing him to break attendance laws. Further, though the townspeople originally supported the teacher, when the court case developed they switched allegiance to the beleaguered mother. The superintendent, obviously, was left in the middle of it all. He continues his reminiscences:

> I recall another incident that happened in that district that amuses me whenever I recall it. I was over in Great Barrington. . . . While in Barrington, the Chief of Police told me it was dangerous to go to South Sandisfield without a revolver, and he gave me a permit to carry firearms. Of course I didn't own a gun, so the next time I went over that way I borrowed a revolver from Edgar Peck. But I was so much afraid of the blamed thing that I packed the cartridges in cotton wool in a little tin box and carried the gun empty. (p. 36)

On one occasion, the superintendent went on to tell his daughter, he actually did load the revolver in anticipation of a violent confrontation with a parent, but his concern proved groundless. He and the parent became friends, "and I never again worried about firearms."

A few months later this same superintendent wrote:

> I continue to be a leader in this district but to be honest, I doubt if I am leading by more than a few yards tonight, for Bill Richmond and his crowd are circulating their annual petition again. It is a little early in the season for this paper to appear, as January is its regular month. A year ago the petition secured four signatures, but I think it will be more than double that number this time, because it is written in more attractive form, the wording being the work of a lawyer. I understand that the paper last year was a wordy document and that the author of it was modest enough to admit it was of faulty construction, which he claims explains why more citizens did not sign it.
>
> But to be serious, I have not yet learned how many charges are to be brought against me, and I think nothing definite will be stated. I do, however, know what one of the charges is, namely, that by remaining here so long I have proven myself a second rate man. No other superintendent stayed in this district longer than was necessary while waiting for a better job. So all have the reputation of being too good for these towns to hold. But in my case it is different. I know the needs of rural school work and instead of looking for a position in a larger town, I have tried to become a rural school specialist with the results that now a few people are saying that I am remaining here because I cannot leave. This is what I call the irony of fate. (*American School Board Journal,* 1923, p. 34)

Much more recently (in 1980), and without amusement or a sense of irony, an Indiana school superintendent wrote in his district's newsletter:

I write this letter in one last attempt to make you aware of what the real issues are confronting your school board and superintendent at this time. Yes, your superintendent's image is at rock bottom. . . . I was informed when I took the position here as superintendent that I could not survive more than 2 years because no outsider has ever been welcome in the Northeast Dubois School District.

A few have put my family through hell on earth since I moved here by kicking in the side of my truck, knocking my mailbox over, breaking radio antenna, making snide remarks to my children, but worst of all sending anonymous letters to the school board and my wife[,] with the following excerpt taken from one last week to the Board: "Please, you represent us, the people, you are our voice and so far you are completely blind to this anti-Christ that is trying to destroy our school corporation. . . . But he is just a person who is out for his own gain. This man that we call our school superintendent is c mpletely insane." (Northeast Dubois County School Corporation, 1980)

One may react to the foregoing in a variety of ways: emotionally, for example, with amusement or a sense of tragedy. One can also view them, however, as historical statements about the school superintendency, illustrating Sarason's comment, in his discussion of the problem of change in the schools, that "The more things change the more they remain the same." (1971, p. 2). Though almost sixty years elapsed between the writings of these two superintendents, the picture is still that of a person who constantly finds himself on some sort of battleground. This is a very generalized statement, of course, and one might be inclined to question it severely, based as it is on very isolated data. But serious current inquiry into the role of school superintendents, as well as a review of the historical literature on the superintendency, suggest that the generalization holds. Indeed, as will become apparent in chapter 2, practically from its inception within the developing public school system in the United States, the office of the school superintendent has been one that has been constantly embroiled in conflict of one sort or another.

Some Modern Data Sources

Data of another sort come from the character of the conversations that superintendents have when they meet with each other in informal situations. A good bit of their time is taken up in the swapping of "war stories."

Indeed, the stories are referred to that way, which is a significant commentary in itself. The stories are serious and funny, at the same time. It is the humor rather than the seriousness that concerns us here. A great deal of humor, whether in the daily comics or informal bull sessions has an underlying base of hostility. It serves the function of enabling people to put problems in a livable perspective, and for many superintendents this is apparently a pressing need. Humor also permits people to express their anger and discomfort in a socially acceptable way. Clearly, the country superintendent of a few pages back was able to do that. The man from Indiana, though, at the time of his writing, found absolutely no humor in his situation. One would expect that over time he may have found something funny in it all that would enable him to smile about his trauma. But more to the point, the informal conversations that superintendents hold with each other create a montage of what it is like to hold that position. If one listens to what they say, it is clear that their work seems continually to put them in the position of adversaries to a variety of people, groups, and institutions.

Other cues that support this position range from stories in the daily newspapers, to articles in popular magazines, to reports of research, and to expository academic papers. Hardly a week goes by, for example, when even an imperceptive newspaper reader can fail to notice that a school district (read, superintendent) is involved in some kind of conflict—over budget, busing, sex education, union negotiations, curriculum, closing schools, or some other issue. Mostly, the messages in the newspaper stories are subtle, but sometimes they are direct. Witness, for example, the headlines that a *Wall Street Journal* article (Sease, 1981) gave to the story of the firing of the superintendent of the Mt. Lebanon, Pa., school district: "In the Line of Fire"; "School Superintendent, Once Pillar of Society, Now Is Often a Target." What gets published in the newspapers, of course, is deemed worthy of a wide audience—in this case a national one. But newspapers do not report the angry phone call a superintendent may receive from a parent at 11 P.M. Nor, as a rule, do reporters write of the personal and organizational trauma involved in trying to terminate the contract of a tenured teacher who is incompetent.

Some of the professional and lay educational literature deals with problems of the work life of superintendents in terms that are much more direct than the usual inferences one must draw from the newspapers. Some examples will make the point. *Nation's Schools* (1972) reported an interview with Mark Shedd, who had just been ousted as superintendent of schools in the City of Philadelphia. Shedd had come to Philadelphia in 1967 as a reformer. The character of the cross fire in which he was eventually caught can be described briefly as follows:

> While Shedd's supporters credited him with decentralizing the city's massive school system, streamlining budget management, recruiting of staff, introducing innovative learning programs, and establishing good rapport with students and their parents, his detractors claimed otherwise. They said he coddled students, alienated the Philadelphia teachers union by advancing black administrators over whites, and contributed to racial tension by giving in to demands of black students. (p. 66)

The detractors' opinions were shared by Frank Rizzo, who was campaigning for mayor. Rizzo had promised that if he was elected he would get rid of Shedd. He was elected, and fulfilled his promise in relatively short order.

Fascinating as the situation may have been for the detached observer, the primary issue for our purposes does not rest in the details of the political confrontation. Rather, what seems important from the point of view of this book is a brief comment that Shedd made toward the end of the interview when asked what advice he would give his successor. His response dealt first with the need to protect oneself and maintain one's own well-being: "Don't take the opposition personally. Try not to let it get under your skin. That's the only way you can keep from having ulcers." Then he said, "In the last analysis, with most decisions you make you're damned if you do and damned if you don't. These days it's a no-win game, so you might just as well make up your mind to do what you think is right and let the chips fall where they may" (p. 68).

If Shedd was right—that the superintendency today is an unwinnable game and that one is damned regardless of the character of his decisions—we are confronted with a no-exit situation (except out the door) for the incumbent. That is, according to Shedd, regardless of what the issue is, the superintendent's decision always leaves one or another group dissatisfied and perhaps angry. It is an unavoidable state. One can argue, of course, that these circumstances are not unlike those that any public official who is an institutional executive must face: presidents, governors, and mayors are in the same bind. In one sense, the response is correct. They are in the same bind. There is, however, a critically important difference. These officials, unlike superintendents, are elected for specific terms of office, and they have a partisan political constituency to which they can and do turn for support. They cannot be fired before their terms are up, regardless of the unpopularity of their decisions. (There are, of course, ways of removing them from office—through impeachment or, in some areas, a recall vote, but these methods are rarely used and even more rarely succeed).

The political conditions with which a superintendent must deal are quite different. He is a nonelected employee. He is appointed by the school board and is usually given a contract spanning two to three years. He serves at the pleasure of the school board, which may ask for his resignation at any time and over any issue. He has no formal supportive constituency. Whatever support he has, either on the board or in the community, he must cultivate through his own skills. While most elected officials would probably agree that the saying "You're damned if you do and damned if you don't" applies to them too, the consequences of making unpopular decisions are quite different. The worst that can happen to these executives personally is to become unpopular and possibly not be reelected at the end of a term of office. For school superintendents, as the Philadelphia situation illustrated, the consequence of making unpopular decisions, regardless of how morally and educationally correct they may have been, can be and not infrequently is the rather abrupt loss of one's job.[1]

If this comment seems to paint too dark a picture, consider the following: The primary conclusion of a study of the superintendency conducted in West Virginia by Martin and Zichefoose (1980, p. 3) was that "the superintendent is a political animal whose fight for existence is nearly always doomed to failure." They go on to say that in West Virginia over 90 percent of the superintendents who left their positions within six years of appointment were fired. West Virginia may be unique. But one must pause and wonder a bit.

Moving backward in time—to 1909, to be exact—we find some examples of conflictual problems that apparently affected superintendents of that era. In the light of the circumstances with which today's superintendent must deal, they may be read with amusement—to a point. Certainly, their seriousness seems to pale in the light of Mark Shedd's experience. Nevertheless, the very fact that in 1909 someone saw fit to write and someone else saw fit to publish what follows suggests once more that the phenomenon with which this book is concerned has been with us for a long time. The author was described as "an un-named battle scarred warrior in the field of public education" and produced a list of dilemmas that he had to confront:

1. There are two factions on the board; one has six votes, the other two. Which crowd should the superintendent favor in order to ensure his re-election and a raise?

2. The chairman of the teachers committee swears, attends political conventions, and knows about Fitzsimmons' record. His wife has inherited the total immersion theory and believes in temperance reform. What trend should the conversation follow when the superintendent takes tea with the estimable couple? Should he confine himself entirely to eulogies of the biscuit?

---

1. I am not suggesting, of course, that the character and magnitude of the problems with which major elected officials and superintendents have to deal are comparable but only that the potential personal impact for the decision maker is different.

3. The W.C.T.U. has asked the superintendent to address the organization on stimulants. Should he do this, or go fishing with two members of his board?
4. Two churches are equally influential and equally jealous of the other. Which Bible class should the superintendent attend?
5. Miss Primary Grade is pretty and interesting and lives with a maiden aunt. Miss Grammar Grade has overcome the birthday habit, talks shop and sings Ben Bolt. Her brother is one of the majority on the board. Which lady should the superintendent, if unmarried, take to the strawberry festival next Thursday?
6. Five different lodges are represented in the town. To how many organizations should a well-regulated superintendent belong?

And last, but hardly least:

7. How many irate parents does it take to create a vacancy? (*American School Board Journal*, 1976, pp. 24–25)

As was noted above, one may read this list with some amusement. But not with total comfort, for it can be suspected that many present-day superintendents have had to confront analogues of each item, particularly numbers *1, 6,* and *7*. But more important, to my way of thinking, is the description of the anonymous author as "battle scarred." My hunch is that there are any number of chief school officers today who would think that an apt description of themselves. It seems clear that to entertain the notion that the superintendency equals living with conflict is a recent phenomenon is an error. They have apparently been bedside companions for a long time.

The problem with which we are concerned is similarly raised in a satiric way by Heller (1978). In a tongue-in-cheek article, he proposes for school board consideration "Ten Sure-Fire Ways to Kill a Superintendent." He begins by stating that "boredom and complacency among school board members are the enemies of educational progress. A way must be found to generate excitement and create tension in your school district" (p. 25). He suggests that one superb method by which this can be done is to "assassinate the superintendent. . . . My plan would not actually cause the superintendent to be dead. It merely makes him WISH he were" (p. 25). The article then describes a number of things that school boards can do (and undoubtedly have done) to make a superintendent's life miserable and eventually cause him to resign. A flavor of them can be obtained by sampling a few: "Demand irrefutable proof for every administrative recommendation." "Put embarrassing questions to your superintendent in public." "Hold unofficial board meetings without your superintendent being present" (p. 26).

The substance of these "prescriptions," of course, is totally unimportant. What is important is the not-so-hidden agenda that can be inferred from the very writing and publication of the article. It is, in effect, a scolding of school boards for behaving in ways that are bound to disrupt a system by introducing inappropriate conflict into it and the life of the superintendent. All of which is not to say that relationships between school board and superintendent should be free of conflict. Indeed, that *would* be boring. Rather, the crucial issue is "Conflict over what?": community power politics or issues of educational policy, program, and management?

The several illustrations that have been discussed to frame the context of this book have been taken from publications whose reading public tends to be lay people and field practitioners. They do not represent the thinking of the academic community, nor are great numbers of that community likely to be found as regular readers of these publications (which may be a problem in itself). Academics, of course, are not unconcerned about the character of the superintendency and the problems that attend it. However, their approach to these problems, rather than being oriented toward action or toward "telling it like it is," tends to be reflective, conceptual, and analytical. Instead of being concerned, for example, with how school districts *should* be run, their intellectual focus is more apt to be on trying to understand and conceptualize how they *are* run. Academics and field and lay people approach problems of education differently. What they write is also different but, in the best of all possible worlds, complementary.

We close this chapter, then, by turning to an academic. Goldhammer (1977) analyzed the changes that had taken place in the character of the superintendency in the twenty years between 1954 and 1974. The major functions of the position, he thought, had not changed. They were those of serving as executive, manager, educator, and spokesman for the school district—that is, public relations man. But as Goldhammer saw it, that is where the similarity stopped. In 1954, schools were relatively placid institutions, as was American society as a whole. We had no teachers' unions, no clamoring for community control, no issues of desegregation or busing, no Sputnik- or blue-ribbon committee concerns about educational quality. There was no counterculture revolution and no Vietnam. Superintendents presided over an expanding enterprise, much as might any executive. They were not without problems, of course, but the problems seemingly were not those that called the very existence and efficacy of the schools into question. Since that time, however, the American scene, and inevitably the schools, have undergone great and fundamental, if not fabric-rending, changes. As for their cumulative effect on the schools, by 1974 "there could . . . be no question that the schools were a key public agency within an aggressively pluralistic society" (p. 154).

A radical and very much unplanned-for change had taken place in the role of the schools in American society. All of us confront the implications of this change in our daily lives, either in fact or vicariously through the newspapers. For our concern here, though, Goldhammer makes these incisive comments about superintendents of schools:

> School administrators had to learn to *live with conflict* on major issues, which could only be resolved by working in collaboration with other social and governmental agencies. (p. 154)
>
> The effective school administrator had to learn how to *contain conflict, how to manage conflict,* and how to negotiate and win compromise among contending forces (p. 154)
>
> As executive, the superintendent has to declare himself in spite of the inevitability of his becoming the *center of conflict!* (p. 160)
>
> The superintendency—Always at the center of some controversy, it is now at the *very core of controversies* affecting the schools. (p. 161)[2]

Thus, the outlines of the arena within which our analysis will proceed have been roughly laid out. Our concern will be to try to understand the underlying conflict dynamics of the working life of superintendents of schools and the superintendency itself. As we shall see, some of the conflicts in which superintendents become involved can be ridiculously petty. Others can be system- and community-shattering in their seriousness. Regardless, hardly a day goes by in the work life of most superintendents when they are not engaged in one tussle or another. It is the character of that life and, to some extent, of the people who live it that has our attention in this book.

---

2. All italics added for emphasis.

2
The Superintendency: A Developmental Perspective

Before the Beginning

In his book *The Creation of Settings* (1972), Seymour Sarason, in writing about the initiation of new social or educational programs, coined the phrase "before the beginning." He used it to suggest that an understanding of what has happened in the past is indispensable to our understanding of that which is new.

This book has a "before the beginning," not in quite the same sense in which Sarason used the phrase, but by way of suggesting that if one is to make conceptual sense of the work life of superintendents in today's world, one ought to have a "feel" for the broad flow and development of the position of superintendent over time. To provide the reader with that "feel," this chapter presents not a detailed history but a discussion of the development of the role as one around which some sort of conflict seemed continuously to center. What will emerge, at its conclusion, will not be a neat and tidy image. But this is precisely the point, because the superintendency is not a neat and tidy situation. It is, indeed, quite the opposite and may be conceived of as a conceptually "sloppy" office, if that term can be taken to mean a condition where nothing of consequence is really ever finished; where the unexpected has to be the expected; where the role expectations emerge from conflicting reference groups; and where the character of one's power may be, at the same time, great and miniscule.

It is, perhaps, this conceptual sloppiness that may be partly responsible for the title of Mosher's article, "Educational Administration: An Ambiguous Profession" (1977). Her focus is mainly on the superintendency. She leaves little doubt that the early faith, primarily espoused by Cubberley (1916), that educational administration would soon be governed by scientific principles was misguided. According to Mosher, Cubberley "depicted educational administration as coming of age in the 20th century, following a period in which many gifted amateurs and pioneers had struggled to create the conditions under which expert executives would one day rule the schools according to an emerging science of education, free of the kinds of politics that had crippled superintendents in the past" (p. 654).

Such faith does, indeed, seem to have been misguided. Today's superintendent will likely read Mosher's comment with a smile, wondering where they might find that emerging science of education that would free them in the way Cubberley foretold. It needs to be understood, though, that Cubberley was a child of his time, as are all of us. He wrote over a span of years when a belief in scientism—the trust that the methodology of the natural sciences could also explain social and psychological behavior and resolve pressing human problems—was starting to become popular in American life. Frederick W. Taylor's *Principles of Scientific Management*, for example, was published in 1911. If scientific principles could reign in industrial management, why not in educational management? Indeed, the subtitle of Cubberly's *Public School Administration* is "A Statement of the Fundamental Principles Underlying the Organization and Administration of Public Education." Hindsight, always a friend, suggests that this subtitle postulates a type of knowledge and a set of conditions that do not exist and never have; that whatever fundamentals may exist have so far eluded empirical confirmation; and that if they are ever discovered they are more likely to be of a naturalistic political variety than based on the findings of rigorous scientific inquiry.[1]

There was a beginning to the "ambiguous profession," of course. The cities of Buffalo and Louisville were the first to establish the position of city superintendent in 1837 (Knezevich, 1975). However, it appears that the position of state, county, and town superintendents of education, at least in the state of New York, goes back to 1813, the date of the first annual report of the Superintendent of Common Schools to the New York State legislature. The dates themselves are relatively unimportant except as they give us some sense of the time span within which the role has been in the process of development. What is important, however, is the set of circumstances and underlying conditions that prompted the establishment of the position.

Knezevich (p. 372) notes that the superintendency is "a position born of conflict" and that it came into being only because prior attempts to administer school systems had, in effect, failed. Not only had schools, in both cities and rural towns, being governed by lay boards, but these boards had also assumed responsibility for the day-to-day operation of schools. For example,

---

1. The reader should not infer that I am making light of Cubberley's work as being dated. He is well worth reading to learn about the thinking of a most influential educator in the early years of this century. Indeed, I suspect one problem that confronts us in education is that we lack a sense of our own intellectual and institutional history. I can't document this, of course, in any generalized fashion, but I do know that the two books of Cubberley's that I borrowed from our library have certainly not received any current study. One was last borrowed in 1971 and the other in 1948.

"lay committees often examined pupils, inspected privies, chose textbooks and methods of teaching penmanship, certified and selected teachers and decided on the myriad details of running the schools" (Tyack and Cummings, 1977, p. 51). Obviously, as the population grew the ability of such lay committees to perform these functions became very limited. Hence the need for assistance developed, and this took the form of appointing someone who was called the superintendent. It is very important to note, however, that the duties typically assigned to this position were more or less clerical, in the cities at least. As we shall see, there does appear to have been a difference in the duties of the rural superintendent.

One might ask, "Why the early reluctance to delegate executive and managerial functions to the office of superintendent?" Knezevich, referring to White's (1939) analysis, suggests that part of the reason for this reluctance may have been the tradition of antiexecutive feeling that had its genesis in the colonial period and found its expression in the various state constitutions. Americans, apparently, were willing to delegate executive powers, with appropriate limits, to an elected public official but much less so to an appointed one, and particularly, it seems, in the case of the schools. In addition, what the action of creating the post of the superintendent and the assignment of rather mundane duties to that post seemed to communicate was that no special expertise was needed to run the schools. All that was needed was some help in record keeping, and "Leave the driving to us." As will be seen, this attitude of lay boards of education was to become a source of major conflict concerning the role of the superintendent. To some extent, in some localities, it exists today.

Power and the Early Superintendency

We noted above that there appears to have been some difference, in the early days, between the functions of city superintendents and rural ones. We turn to the latter, not so much as to illustrate the difference as to provide some glimpse of their work lives. The source for this discussion is the *Annual Report of the Superintendent of Common Schools of the State of New York, Together with the Reports of County Superintendents* (1845). Up to about that time, the annual reports were essentially just statistical abstracts. They included data about money spent for teachers and books, pupil attendance, courses of study, sex of pupils, condition of school buildings, age and sex of teachers, and so forth. The particular volume used as a reference here, as its title suggests, also includes written reports of the county superintendents relative to their jobs, what they did, and the problems they encountered. Except for stylistic and situational differences, their format is not unlike an annual report today. Reading them gives the reader some insight into the times and also, if one has a sense of irony, a feeling of sad amusement.

Here is the way the state Superintendent of Common Schools presented to the state legislature the job description of the county superintendents:

> These officers are required to visit, either separately, or in conjunction with the town superintendent, all the schools within their jurisdiction respectively, as often in each year as may be practicable, with reference to the number of the districts under their charge; to inquire into all matters relating to the government, course of instruction, books, studies, discipline and conduct of such schools, and the condition of the school houses and of the districts generally; to advise and counsel with the trustees and other officers of the district in relation to their duties, particularly in relation to the erection of school houses; to recommend to trustees and teachers the proper studies, discipline and conduct of the schools, the course of instruction to be pursued, and the books of elementary instruction to be used; to examine and grant certificates of qualification to teachers, either generally, authorizing them to teach in any school within the jurisdiction of such superintendent, while such certificate remains in force and unrevoked, or special, limiting the candidate to a particular town, and for one year only; to annul such certificates for sufficient cause, and with his consent to annul any certificates granted by the town superintendent, whenever the teacher holding such certificate shall be found deficient. (p. 8)

Unlike what was apparently the case with the city superintendent at that time, the county superintendent, at least in writing, was an overseer of the school operation who had, particularly with regard to teachers, a great deal of power. It can also be seen that with regard to the school board ("trustees"), his prescribed role was not unlike the way we might conceptualize it today. He was "to advise and counsel" with them, "to recommend" to them, and so on. The notion of executive powers over the system as a system, however, seems not to be part of the job description. The fact that this is missing seems to reinforce Knezevich's thesis that the tradition of antiexecutive feeling was a factor that affected the superintendent's role. But note this one additional part of the county superintendent's job description. He was mandated "generally, by all means in his power to promote sound education, elevate the character and qualification of teachers, improve means of instruction, and advance the interests of the schools committed to his charge" (pp. 8–9).

It is not our purpose here to highlight the differences between the functions of city and county superintendents of schools as those positions were in the process of development. Rather, the purpose is to inquire, if briefly, into those early days to see if they can provide clues to our understanding of the superintendency today. They do, indeed, start to provide such clues. This is true, if only by inference, when one thinks about the last part of the job description that has just been noted. The statement mandating the superintendent "generally, by all means in his power to promote sound education," and so forth, describes a supraordinate goal, a goal with which no superintendent of the 1980s would argue. It is very general, in contrast to the very specific statement of job functions that preceded it. And it is, perhaps, in this very generality that the seeds of the role's development, with its concomitant conflict, can be found. That is, so long as what a person is supposed to do is quite specifically defined, is congruent with his skills, and is acceptable to him, the chances are that conflict over role relationships can be held to a minimum. On the other hand, when responsibilities are stated in general terms and when role boundaries are ill defined, if they are defined at all, the opposite condition may obtain.

These statements by the state Superintendent of Common Schools describe the superintendency in global terms. For more specific clues concerning the work of people in that office 135 years ago, we turn to the reports of the county superintendents in New York State. They are highly instructive and provide an amusing sense of déjà vu. For example, the superintendent in Albany County bemoans the apathy and ignorance of parents regarding their children's schooling:

> One of our intelligent and prominent citizens was descanting on the improvement of his daughter. On inquiry, it appeared that the father did not even know what she studied, but referred me to his child for information, who, to his utter amazement, gave a list of *thirteen* different studies, which she was then pursuing—and this child but twelve years old. And this instance but feebly illustrates that disgraceful, weak, and criminal neglect of admitted duty, which disorders and impairs the mind of the child, for whose advancement the parent toils unremittingly and spends unsparingly. (p. 67)

Present-day educators—superintendents, principals, and teachers—will have little difficulty in empathizing with the man from Albany and perhaps would use nearly the same language. Except when things are perceived to be amiss, the considered involvement of parents in the schools is a sometime thing. And as most people will tell you, the information that parents have is frequently inaccurate or does not include all the facts. But this superintendent goes on to make a statement that is almost mind-boggling, given the fact that it was written almost a century and a half ago and yet so closely parallels what appears to be the public's current attitude toward the schools. He wrote:

> *There is in the public mind an uncomfortable consciousness that the schools are not fulfilling their office—and that a vast amount of money is being wasted—*

that the prime of life is often lost; but a most obstinate determination
neither to investigate, or even to hear, closes every avenue against the
advocates of a better and higher culture. (pp. 65–66; emphasis added)

I am not merely making the intellectual point that on one level, at least,
we are dealing with conditions and attitudes that have been in place a long
time. Nor is the intent to convey to the reader the startled sense of
amusement—and sadness—that I felt as I came across that statement. I do
think we need to become aware that the office of the superintendency, practically from its beginnings and through all these years, has been confronted with
situations that repeat themselves. It is indeed clear that many superintendents
in 1984, using somewhat different words, could have written the above from
their own experience. One is forced to ask, "Why? Is there something endemic
in the system that provokes such reaction?" The answer is hard to come by,
but part of the intent of this book is to try to cast some light on it.

But let us go on. The superintendent of Chautaugue County found the
job to be too much for one person:

> I find the field of labor assigned to my supervision double what ought to be
> the charge of one county superintendent. I have gloomy feelings when I
> look over the great field of thought and mind assigned to my charge, and
> see how much ought to be done which I am not able to do. (p. 116)

A familiar lament indeed, and probably one that has good cause. I have yet to
talk with a superintendent, even one who would be judged as eminently
successful, who did not express some sense of weariness and, at times, depression brought on by what he sees to be both the problems and the opportunities that confront him, combined with his awareness of the human limits on
his time and energy.

In another vein, read what the superintendent of Allegany County had to
say about community conflict concerning the schools:

> It is to be lamented that on the part of many, very many districts there is so
> great a Want of Harmonious Action. The first sound that strikes my ear, on
> entering a district, is often that of contention, feud, and dissention; fre-
> quently engendered too by the most trivial causes—causes that are beneath
> the dignity and unworthy the attention of men—mere bugbears of the
> imagination—visionary grievances and borrowed wrongs. One man is
> afraid that he will *be* afraid. Another imagines that his *rights* are trampled
> on. Another would sacrifice the public interest to enhance his own.
> Another thinks his children, that are absent from school three out of every
> six, are neglected by the teacher because they "don't learn more." Another
> would have the district divided, and the old log school house removed to his

door. Another finds fault because "school laws and instructions" are too
complex and voluminous, ——. Another supposes there must be some
screw loose in the system, else he certainly could get redress for his wrongs,
——. The most fruitful source of dissention and broil seems to be traced to
the selection of school house sites. And in a new country like this, it not
infrequently becomes necessary to select new sites and change old ones.
(p. 80)

Again, there is a ring of familiarity to all this. Indeed, our Allegany superintendent was prophetic when he noted that the selection of school sites was
"the most fruitful source of dissention." We seem to be witnessing a similar
situation today in reverse, as controversy over school closings because of
declining enrollments has nearly torn some communities apart.

An early comment on community reaction to innovation in the schools
came from the superintendent of Essex County:

What now?—Something new again?—Let us look into this matter, a little!
It's not exactly what I was used to when a boy; yet there may possibly be
something in it! What do you propose to effect by this? What will be the
tendency of that? Indeed! I have my doubts! However, *try it*! And we'll see
how it will succeed! (pp. 159–60)

So we have attitudes about change in the schools expressed years ago—
and in almost the same words—that are familiar today. It is a little difficult,
because tonality does not accompany the written word, to know just what was
intended by the last sentence, "And we'll see how it will succeed!" The
superintendent, in the comments that followed, seemed to take it as a hopeful
challenge. And, if I'm not stretching things too far, he was also reflecting a
concern with what we now call "accountability."

One final comment has particular substantive relevance for us, as well as
helping to fill out an image of the superintendency in its early days, an image
that we have seen bears a striking resemblance in some of its forms to that
which we know today. The comment comes from the superintendent of the
city and county of New York. It has to do with politics, religion, and education.

Sectarianism in religion and partisanship in politics are both too little and
contracted to be allowed to mingle in the sublime and dignified work of
educational reform, and yet both are invoked in our June elections, and
both are alike influences in some of the wards in the choice of school
officers. In a few instances, these elements have already given the government of the local concerns of the schools to men of deficient qualifications
for the supervision of so important interests, and teachers have thus been

subjected to the dictation of officers immeasurably their inferiors both in intelligence and education. (p. 245)

Keeping partisan politics and religious sectarian interests out of education—a concern today—has, then, a long history. The argument advanced for this concern was that the education of children was too sacred a community responsibility to be affected by the narrow political interests of adults or the subjecting of school personnel to religious criteria for employment. The political argument is still with us, and perhaps rightly so. The issue of whether or not, and at what points of tangency, schools should move into the political arena is one that erupts constantly. It will be discussed at other points in this book. But one thing about today's superintendent is almost a given. Whether or not he is partisan in his politics, in order to survive he must indeed be a political animal—or behave like one, even if he is not so inclined.

The reports of New York State's county superintendents in 1845 were not, of course, totally devoted to the conflictual nature of the job. There were numerous comments about how well pupils were doing in school and about parental support. It is also interesting to note some of their additional concerns. They spoke about problems involving reading; textbooks; libraries; attendance; how pupils should be grouped; at what age youngsters should start school; corporal punishment (they seemed not to favor it, though they acknowledged its usefulness at times); the state of school building repair; the quality of teachers; in-service training of teachers; not having enough time for supervision; and teaching methods. In this latter connection, it may be that the superintendent of the Eastern District of Onondaga County can be acknowledged as one of the earliest proponents of what we now know as the field of media instruction or instructional technology. Crediting the improvement in "modes of teaching" to the experimental bent of "ingenious and skillful teachers," he goes on to say, "The blackboard is just beginning to be appreciated by some of our best teachers. It should be deemed an indispensable auxiliary in teaching every branch of instruction, from the alphabet to the most abstruse sciences" (p. 258). The superintendent then goes on to specify the desired quality and dimensions of a blackboard ("I mean a good one; which should be as long as across the end of one side of the school room, and at least six feet wide" (p. 258)), after which he joins the battle over teaching from textbooks or using a lecture-recitation method: "One of the teachers of considerable experience in Syracuse, has tried the oral instruction of grammar, without books, with the aid of the blackboard, and succeeded beyond his expectation. He informed me that he taught it to the whole school, in lectures, with explanations and examples upon the blackboard; and that the pupils learned more in that way in one quarter, than they did with their books, in the common mode in one year" (p. 258).

There is, finally, even a hint of the development of the field of educational research, as this superintendent closed his report by saying, "I doubt not that the Normal School at Albany will fully test the great utility of oral instruction in our common schools" (p. 258).

I have dwelt at some length on what these county superintendents had to say about their jobs for two reasons. The first, already mentioned, was simply to prove a historical frame of reference for our subject and to show that the problems of the superintendency did not suddenly emerge in the last half of the twentieth century. They have been with us, it appears, for a very long time—at least if any credence is to be put in the reports that have just been reviewed, other reports about the factotum-type functions of the city superintendents notwithstanding (Mosher, 1977).

The second reason is more conceptual and relates to the notion of "superintendent as factotum," only in the obverse. The point is this: If a position involves mostly clerical functions, any conflict that occurs is not likely to affect a broad constituency, certainly not a community's power structure. And this, apparently, was the condition of a city superintendent's work life early on. It seems that the lay boards of Louisville and Buffalo, for example, were interested in having someone to "mind the store" but not, to continue the metaphor, to engage in any new merchandising ventures. But as has been noted earlier, in New York State the county superintendents, although they certainly were charged with clerical functions, were also given a broad responsibility for development of the quality of the system. Recall the previously noted mandate charging the county superintendent to "generally, by all means in his power . . . promote sound education, elevate the character and qualification of teachers, improve the means of instruction, and advance the interests of schools committed to their charge."

Clearly, these words do not describe the job aims of a factotum. They describe a position in which the potential for the exercise of power and influence is great. And this is the conceptual crux of the problem. The development of the superintendency into a position around which controversy seems continually to swirl is directly related to the issue of power, or perceived power. If a superintendent has (or is seen as having) power, that power has the potential for affecting a community's value system, its pocketbook, and the welfare of its children—among a host of other things. No wonder, and perhaps luckily, an antiexecutive tradition was and still seems to be endemic to the American educational system.

From the middle of the nineteenth century until its last decade, questions about the superintendency and its function were apparently latent, at least as far as any public discussion was concerned. That decade, however, judging by letters, articles, and editorials that appeared in the *American School Board Journal*, was to witness a great deal of controversy over the role of the superintendent of schools, particularly with regard to the cities. Being a clerk was evidently no longer the rule. The following letter from the "late superintendent of the Omaha School Board," which appeared in the August 1891 issue of the *Journal*, provides some indication of both the diversity of the role and the change that had taken place over the years.

> The precise duties of the office are not so clearly defined as to make the work of city superintendent always the same. In some cities, he acts as secretary of the board and has charge of all accounts and records, but does very little with work that is strictly education. In some he guides the policy of the board in financial matters, and is rather a superintendent of business affairs than a director of educational processes. In this city, as in most others, he is known in the law and rules as the "superintendent of public instruction," and his duties are defined as of a strictly educational character. He is the head teacher of the city. He has no more to do with matters of finance than the humblest teacher or janitor. He contracts no bills; he fixes no salaries; he is not required to make recommendations affecting expenses, and he is responsible for nothing in the way of financial management. The rules hold him strictly and exclusively to the work of discipline and instruction.

The superintendency, then, seemed to be a many-splendored thing. There was something in it for everybody. All that one had to do was pick a school board and a city that were congruent with one's own expectation, another condition that appears to hold today. But then, compare the Omaha superintendent, who was apparently quite pleased with his role of "head teacher," with the superintendent of Flushing, N.Y., a Mr. John Clark, whose letter of resignation appeared in the August 1891 issue of the *Journal*. Clark's bill of particulars rejects his role as being that of a "mere passive agent of the board." He goes on to talk about the hiring and firing of teachers without his knowledge and the fact that "plans of organization, courses of study . . . have been passed upon by the board, or its committees, without consultation with the superintendent, and frequently against his judgment" (p. 6). He then wrote: "I have become persuaded that the theories entertained and the policy pursued by your honorable body in regard to school administration are inconsistent with the proper discharge of the duties of superintendent, and I must not continue to hold an office which involves responsibility to the people but in which I feel an increasing sense of powerlessness" (p. 6).

The issue of conflict over power is thus joined, and publicly so, perhaps for the first time. But it is important to note the change in locus of the problem and what the problem was about. The county superintendents seemed to have problems and conflicts aplenty, but for the most part they centered on their relationships with parents and community. They seemed not to be concerned with lay school committees or questions of role and power. All that appears to have changed by the time of Mr. Clark's resignation, and quite markedly so. The events that led to his resignation had little do so, so it seems, with education per se but with the question of "Who is running things?" That this theme of power and prerogative still pervades the superintendency will become apparent in later chapters.

Though the Flushing situation may have represented a first cry in the wilderness, it was reinforced by a resounding chorus less than four years later. What happened was this: At a meeting of the Department of Superintendents of the National Education Association held in Cleveland in February 1895, the superintendents attending gave their approval to a report prepared by a Committee of Fifteen. The thrust of the report was concerned with the power of the superintendent and the role of the school board, the former to be enlarged and the latter diminished. As might be expected, the *American School Board Journal* had an editorial heyday with this report, both through its written comments and through several graphic pictures on its cover that likened the Cleveland meeting to aspects of Shakespearian tragedies.

We will come back to this shortly, but a brief detour is necessary in order to help understand the *Journal* and its positions at that time. The detour involves the statement of purpose of the *Journal*. It reads:

> We are publishing the only Journal devoted exclusively to School Boards and executive officers. We furnish information on the doings of School Board committees, including important executive actions, best methods of heating and ventilation, textbooks, with prices and adoptions, school law decisions, models of school buildings, statistics upon salaries, publish engravings of leading school men, etc.: briefly, we keep *School Boards* and *Teachers* abreast with the time.[2] (Aug. 1895, emphasis added)

The most striking thing about this statement, it seems to me, is its last clause, "We keep *School Boards* and *Teachers* abreast with the time." It suggests that the current view was that the main adult actors in the schools were school board members and teachers. Superintendents were not part of the action. They are not mentioned and, though "executive officers" (perhaps meaning superintendents) are noted earlier, one does not get the impression that, whoever they were, they were of much consequence in the eyes of the *Journal*. Indeed, note the "furnishing of information on the

---

2. Current issues of the *Journal* include no statement of purpose.

doings of School Board committees, including important executive actions." The running of the schools is done in school board meetings, not in the superintendent's office. And teachers, of course, are also important. Clearly, as far as the *Journal* was concerned, superintendents are still just factotums.

With this background, then, let us move back to the Cleveland meeting. It is worthwhile to report the entire editorial comment printed in the *Journal* of March 1895.

THE "CZAR" MOVEMENT

The school superintendents of the United States gave expression at their meeting held at Cleveland last month on the organization of the city school systems. The Committee of Fifteen submitted a report through Prof. Draper, of Illinois, which, in substance, calls for smaller school boards and enlarged powers for superintendents. The school board to consist of a few harmless gentlemen with merely sufficient ability to audit salary accounts and a superintendent who shall have the arbitrary power to govern the entire school system.

A feeble attempt was made by some of the superintendents to combat the report, evidently only with a view to obviate the appearance of one-sidedness, or to dispel a "cut and dried" flavor. However, they were unanimous on all the essential points and the superintendent of schools was then and there in line of promotion to be *made the Czar of the American public schools*.

It was an interesting meeting. In the discussion of the organization of school systems, the school board was an unknown quantity. It was a clear case of Hamlet without the character of Hamlet. The melancholy Dane was left to wonder whether he ever existed. The educational destinies of the universe whirled around the superintendent only.

The slight reference to school boards, which could not well be avoided, were not complimentary. In fact, one gentleman hinted that school boards must not be mentioned. It was not well[,] he said[,] to play with fire. All went on the theory that school boards were bad things that must be dwarfed, and, if possible, legislated out of existence.

It seems incredible that a large body of intelligent men can assemble and deliberate in so selfish a manner, and with such utter disregard for the thousands of well meaning men who everywhere serve on boards of education, and who have loyally supported every measure in the interest of true education. The sacrifices, made by school board members, whose labors are not recorded on the salary list, should not be underestimated. The loyal and patriotic spirit of school boards has made comfortable school houses a fixed fact and high priced superintendents possible. They have been the mainspring of the wonderful development of the public school system.

We do not mean to underestimate the schoolmaster's labors, but we do question the propriety of attempting to legislate out of existence the very men who have made them, and to arrogate powers to superintendents which do not belong to them, and to relegate the school board to the function of a mere clerk.

The American people want to be in touch with their schools. They want to be represented. The school board is the only agency that can represent them. It can be made and unmade by the people. If it does not carry out the wishes of its constituency and keep abreast with educational progress it is retried, as it should be, by the people.

The public is not yet prepared for the "one man power" idea, and we predict that it never will be. (p. 8)

Given our earlier understanding of the role that city superintendents were expected by school boards to play in the day-to-day functioning of the schools, it is hard not to read this editorial without a sense of amusement. What the *Journal* interpreted the superintendents to be saying—and their interpretation may be correct—was that they wanted a complete role reversal vis-à-vis their relationships with the school board. Superintendents wanted to manage school systems, and it is obvious that the school boards were not about to buy that idea. It must be said, however, that not all city superintendents supported the Committee of Fifteen. Two months later, the *Journal* (May 1895, p. 8) reprinted a letter from a superintendent "presiding over the school system of a large city" whose position was completely reinforcing of its own and absolutely condemnatory of his colleagues'.

What we are witnessing here is part of a continuing struggle—a struggle that is by no means over, by the way—to establish a workable concept of what the superintendency is all about. This struggle, at its roots, involves questions of power distribution, expertise, deep-seated values, fiscal management, and ultimately, one might suspect, the character of a school system in American society.

Politics and the Early Superintendency

Problems associated with the effects of partisan politics on schools, the reader may recall, were mentioned in invidious terms by the superintendent of New York City and County in 1845. They appear again, this time in the public media, in 1896. G. Stanley Hall, writing in the March issue of that year in the *Atlantic Monthly* about a study he conducted of school people, referred to politics as "the bane of the public schools" (p. 406). And in June of that year, again in the *Atlantic Monthly*, L. H. Jones, superintendent of schools in Cleveland, published an article entitled "Politics and Education." He was nothing if not vehement in presenting what must be regarded as an unabashed polemic, and perhaps a justified one. For example, he charged that

> the unscrupulous politician is the greatest enemy we now have to contend with in public education. His high-spirited conception of the public school is that its revenues offer him the opportunity for public plunder. . . . He does not confine his depredations to the financial side of the matter, but pushes his corruptive presence into the school itself. He commits the unpardonable sin when he interferes with the rightful tenure of the office of teacher. (p. 810)

Jones's solution to the problem, particularly with regard to the selection, hiring, and terminating of teachers, was a simple one: "Selecting a capable man for superintendent, give him adequate power, and require results" (pp. 812–13). This advice would scarcely be disputed today, and Jones indicated that this was the system under which he worked in the two cities in which he had been employed as superintendent. As we have seen, it was a position concerning the role of the superintendent that most school boards seemed loath to take. Nonetheless, the seeds had been planted for a concept of the superintendency that would indeed take root. The transfer of power, despite political concerns, did take place, though there appears to have been no cataclysmic event that marked it.

One should note, finally, with regard to partisan politics and the superintendency, that the superintendents themselves and their own tenure were not immune from its effects. The *Journal* (August 1895) took note "that this year, more than ever before, have superintendents fallen the victims of political conspiracies and religious prejudices" (p. 9). And commenting further, "The superintendent is a ready target for unreasonable parents, disgruntled teachers and officious school board members" (p. 9). In particular, the *Journal* referred to the firing of the superintendent of Omaha, a Dr. Alfred P. Marble, which attracted nationwide attention. The *New York Post*, for example, is quoted on the cover of the September issue of the *Journal* as saying, "The recent defeat of Dr. A. P. Marble for re-election, has attracted attention throughout the whole country on account of the high rank of Dr. Marble and the peculiar circumstances of his defeat."

What is remarkable about this is not the particular circumstance of Marble's termination or even the fact that he was terminated. That happens all the time. However, given the difference in time and societal conditions that exist between Omaha of 1895 and Philadelphia of 1972—Alfred Marble and Mark Shedd—the similarities in the charges of their respective detractors are startling. Among other things, for example, Marble was accused of not knowing his principals and teachers and permitting the instruction and discipline in the schools to deteriorate. As we noted in chapter 1, Shedd was accused of alienating the teachers' union and coddling students, among other things. But in both situations, the roots of dissatisfaction and conflict seem to have been in community politics. Déjà vu, once more.[3]

The Modern Superintendency: Power and Its Price

There is little doubt, then, that by the 1890s a variety of forces had been set in motion that were to affect the character of the superintendency. Primarily, what was to occur was a shift in the relationships between school board and superintendent, particularly with regard to issues of executive power and management prerogatives. The shift was probably inevitable in any event, but it seems to have been hastened by changes in American society that occurred toward the end of the nineteenth century and in the first decade or two of the twentieth. These developments brought about what Mosher has referred to as "'the first revolution' in the management of public education." Mosher describes them neatly:

> Among these [changes] were the growth of the cities, the development of corporate forms of industrial management, and, within the intellectual community, an evangelical faith in scientific rationality.
>
> Concurrently, the public perception of education as a means of upward mobility in an increasingly technical society brought demands that the schools expand their offerings in quantity and quality. The corrupt and inefficient school boards of the cities came under attack from a loosely allied coalition of citizen activists, university professors, and concerned superintendents (Cuban, 1976). They agreed with the "public-regarding" philosophy of the Progressive reform movement which, in due course, brought wide adoption of the council-manager form of city government.
>
> To achieve similar goals of impartial and competent educational administration, the school reformers sought legislative changes which would make the schools more independent of City Hall, would retain the school board as representatives of the public but reduce its size, and would elevate the superintendency to a position of executive leadership.

---

3. In saying "déjà vu, once more," I am not throwing up my hands in despair. Instead I am reinforcing the thrust of this chapter thus far. That is, as we learn about historical images of superintendents and the superintendency we are not learning about isolated historical artifacts. Nor are we only engaging in an academic exercise that admittedly has some amusing sidelights. Most important, it seems to me, we are enabled to learn about ourselves as persons, about the character of the system we have built to educate our young, and about the way we, as individuals and as a society, react to and deal with that system and the people whose role it is to guide it. That, of course, is a large order, but I think the potential is there to do just that.

These initiatives, so reflective of the corporate image of organization, spread very rapidly. By 1920 the widely accepted pattern of overhead school management had become boards of five to nine members, elected at large on a nonpartisan basis with independent taxing and expenditure authority. Boards appointed a superintendent to act as an executive director of the school system. In many cities, he headed a sizable bureaucracy: central office management and education specialists, school site principals, their teaching staffs, clerks, and custodial workers. Agencies outside the school systems had entered the scene, such as state educational agencies with credential requirements, teachers colleges providing better trained entrants to the field, and the federal government with the first grants-in-aid for vocational education. (Mosher, 1977, p. 653)

Mere global description of developments, of course, does not reveal the conflicting attitudes and emotions that are attached to them. We can be sure that the process of change that Mosher described was not simply a rational progression of events. Many oxen must have been gored in the process, and the history of human events does not suggest that people and groups take kindly to the prospect of coming out on the losing side of a bruising fight. And even though superintendents, who had apparently started to mold themselves into a powerful pressure group, were by and large in favor of a changed role for themselves, there was no agreement among them concerning how this role should be conceptualized. Were they to be teachers, scholars, chief administrators, or negotiator-statesmen (Cuban, 1976)? What was the appropriate mix? Was their focus to be on academics or the business side of the enterprise? Suffice it to say, these are questions that today's superintendent implicitly asks himself daily.

Regardless of the particular aspect of the role that a superintendent's predisposition and skills led him to emphasize, one thing is sure: the executive powers relative to running a school system became transferred, over time, from the school board to the superintendent.

But everything gained costs something, and so it is with the present case. Superintendents became more powerful. In the process, however, they also opened up their work lives and their personal lives to the costs of having to continually live with conflict. To illustrate,

- Cuban (1976), in his study of the urban superintendency, entitles one of his chapters "The Vulnerable Superintendent: Insecure Expert."
- Wilson (1960), a professor and exsuperintendent, by inference refers to the conflicts inherent in the superintendency and suggests that the need to deal with them is "the major part of his role, or the part most likely to generate his ulcers" (p. xiv); and, in the same paragraph, he writes that "the superintendency carries with it acres of headaches,

long hours, family neglect, risk, loneliness, criticism, and good chances for a coronary."

• An anonymous superintendent, noting some years ago that the superintendency has always been characterized as a position in which there has been "open season" on the incumbent.

The point here, of course, is not to arouse the reader's sympathy for superintendents of schools. I doubt superintendents want anybody's sympathy. But I do want to suggest once more that as forces converged around the turn of the last century that effectively gave school superintendents what they wanted, they also paid a price. There are probably few superintendents today who are not aware daily, in one way or another, of having continually to pay this price.

And what is the situation today, when to speak of the superintendency "twenty years hence" is to speak of living in the next century? Mosher (1977) is again our reference. Under the heading of "A Profession in Turbulence," she suggests that a "second revolution" took place following the "baby boom" of World War II and the Korean War (p. 654). This revolution is still in progress:

> Its beginning is often said to be the 1954 U.S. Supreme Court decision ordering the end of the de jure segregation, but no single event set it off. Schools were just one of the American institutions shaken for two decades by the profound social and political changes stemming from their confrontations with the reality of pluralism. Challenges to traditional values have brought the demise of the "melting pot" myth and a quickening of the struggle for equality by various minority groups. (pp. 655–56)

We add that this "second revolution" probably spawned other facts of current school life that inexorably affect the superintendency and what it is all about: the lowered birth rate, with its concomitant effects of declining school enrollments and school closings; new federal and state mandates for specific programming; and the rise of militant teacher unionism. Clearly, what we have today is an office of the school superintendency that, though structurally similar to that which was brought about by the "first revolution," has to deal with issues that could hardly have been foreseen three-quarters of a century ago.

The Modern Social Setting
of the Superintendency

I hope that these few pages have provided the reader with a broader perspective on the superintendency as it developed over time. That perspective, of course, is an incomplete one, but it should suffice as a historical backdrop for the central concern of this book.

We need to look now for a moment at the social setting within which the superintendency must function today. One does not need to be a historian to know that the character of public schools and the problems of the people who work in them have changed within our own lifetimes. The changes, stemming from the "second revolution," have been radical and, in some cases, disquieting and depressing for many people. One may be sure that many superintendents have been among those so affected. And surely, these changes must have led Campbell (1966) to question what was happening in and to the schools and then write an article entitled "Is the School Superintendent Obsolete?" How curious that a scholar whose career has been devoted to promoting the study of school administrators and the administration of schools—always, it seems, with a hopeful outlook—would have cause to question the continued utility of the primary subject of his study and concern. He seems to have been prompted to raise his question by the growing turmoil in the schools, heightened public unhappiness with them, and his interpretation (perhaps widely shared) that the public was suggesting that something was wrong with the superintendency as we knew it. When things do not go well in the schools, Campbell says, "the superintendent is perceived as an obstructionist. His critics suspect that the wrong kind of people become superintendents, that training programs are out-of-date or even useless, and that professional organizations are attempting to protect the incompetent" (p. 50). Disturbing as Campbell finds this situation, he is not ready "to throw in the sponge" (p. 53). What is required is a clarification of the superintendent's role in the light of new demands that scarcely could have been anticipated before the "second revolution." There is a new setting for the schools, and new demands emanate from it.

The first characteristic of the new setting has to do with the change in the concept of the school from the traditional one in which the school is viewed as a place of instruction to one in which this focus is maintained but the school is also conceived of as a focal agent of social policy, deriving its mandates either from the courts or from the various state and federal legislatures. Second, a description of the new setting must include teacher unionism and its effects. Third, the growth of media technology, from computers to closed-circuit television, has created a changed school setting. Fourth, there is the demand for more rational decision making based on "hard" data concerning the assessment of results of schooling. Finally, the new setting is characterized, according to Campbell, by demands for the schools to collaborate with local, state, and federal agencies to a degree not experienced previously.

In the light of this new setting, are superintendents obsolete? It depends, says Campbell. "The superintendent is obsolete if he cannot accept the role of educational purposer, organizational designer, resource politician" within this new setting. "In short, the superintendent who is dull, inflexible, and tradition-bound is obsolete" (p. 58). True, but how much more so than when Frank Spaulding said, in 1895, that "what the school administrator has to do is . . . project ideas ahead and work up to them" (Cuban, 1976, p. 117). It seems to me that any superintendent at any time would be obsolete if he could be described in Campbell's terms—unless the community in which he worked supported dullness, inflexibility, and tradition-boundedness. And there are some today that do. But the crucial point is the new school setting. What Campbell is describing is a system that is much more open to pressures and forces, internal and external, than possibly could have been anticipated a few short years ago. We would take this a step farther to suggest that the more open the setting, the more highly conflictual the relationships within it will be. Perhaps the superintendent is obsolescent whose perspective of what the schools are all about is too narrow to enable him to understand, tolerate, and help resolve the conflicts that occur in today's school environment. But then, there is nothing new about that comment either. It would probably hold for superintendents in whatever "today" they were employed.

There is little question that the world of the public schools in the last half of the twentieth century has become far more complex and bewildering than it was in earlier times. In many respects the substance of the problems with which superintendents must deal is the same as it was before; in some respects, it is different. But I would suggest that the primary difference between the superintendency of today and that of yesteryear has less to do with substance of the problems and more to do with a change in the politics of the superintendency. By this I do not mean the partisan politics that early writers found to be so abhorrent, though that may enter into it at times. Nor am I referring to the sub rosa political machinations that occur in any organization. My point is that the superintendency today, if it is to be an effective office, must be conceived of in political terms, if by that we mean the ability of the incumbent to work with a wide array of conflicting forces so as to maintain the delicate balance upon which the vitality of school life depends. A future chapter will be devoted to a more searching inquiry into what one might call the new politics of the superintendency. Suffice it to say here that the rather recent and open acknowledgment of the priority that this part of a superintendent's work life has assumed constitutes a reconception of that role. It is a reconception that has not been easy for those superintendents to accept who thought that *politics* was a dirty word, beneath the dignity of their office, and preferred to think of themselves as educational experts.

Another social fact that has an important influence on the superintendent's role is that the office of the superintendent, and the person who occupies it, are conceived of as "public property." In a strict sense, this is true of any workers who are on the public payroll—policemen, firemen, teachers, social workers, trash collectors, and, of course, elected officials. They are all thought of as being responsible to the public in one fashion or another. But the case of the superintendent is different, and the difference is a qualitative one. The responsibility that elected officials and most civil servants have to the public seems to be more or less a collective one: to see that the community has adequate police and fire protection, that streets are cleaned, and so forth. In the case of the superintendency, the responsibility is more particular. Though parents may be concerned with the overall quality of the community's schools in some vague way, they are very focally and forcefully concerned with "my child" and feel that "you, Mr. Superintendent, are directly responsible for my child's welfare and learning in school. I don't want to hear about going through channels, to the principal or the teacher. It is *your* job!" This illustration may have been somewhat overdrawn, to make the point, but the point remains. With some exceptions—in very large cities with massive school bureaucracies, for example[4]—superintendents are seen as exclusively and particularly responsible to the public—a part of their job, incidentally, that is not in their job descriptions. And superintendents sense this, although they may not conceive of the situation in the same terms.

To conclude: The perspective on the school superintendency that I have offered in this chapter emphasizes the humanity of the position, not its technology—if such a technology exists. The rest of the book is designed to fill in the details of that perspective.

---

4. There is little doubt, of course, that the moves to decentralize large city systems and the pressure for "community control" were motivated by the desire to establish a more direct sense of parents' "ownership" of the schools and thus to make the school administrator more the property of the public.

3
The Superintendent's Role: Formal and Informal Images

Formal Job Descriptions

Formal images of the role of the superintendent at not hard to come by. Expressed mostly in functional terms, they are found in most textbooks about the superintendency. They can also be observed, quite explicitly, in the recruiting brochures that are published by most school districts when they conduct a job search to fill a vacancy for superintendent in their system. An example of the former comes from Griffiths (1966, pp. 70–71). He suggests that the superintendent's job can be divided into four parts:

1. Improving educational opportunity. All aspects of the instructional program are included in this part; such questions as what shall be taught and how it shall be taught are considered here.
2. Obtaining and developing personnel. The divisions of the job concerned with recruitment, selection, placement, and promotion of personnel are relevant here. All matters of personnel administration are likewise considered. Pupil personnel problems are considered under this head in addition to matters relating to professional and non-professional personnel.
3. Maintaining effective relations with the community. This part of the job is more broadly conceived than mere public relations. It includes interpreting the schools to the public and studying the community so as to further education.
4. Providing and maintaining funds and facilities. The business and housekeeping aspects of school administration are included in this part of the job. Included are budget planning, plant maintenance, construction and renovation of buildings, and similar functions.

This certainly seems not to be an unreasonable formulation of the job demands that are made on a superintendent of schools. He is, after all, the chief executive officer of a public educational enterprise, and the functions to which Griffiths refers would seem to include, broadly, all the responsibilities that might adhere to that position. He suggests further that attached to each job responsibility are a set of particular conceptual, human, and technical skills. For example, he states that "the major conceptual skills of the superintendent relating to obtaining and developing personnel are: (1) the basic personnel plan, and (2) the 'value set'" (p. 75). Superintendents need to have the ability to conceptualize and develop such a plan for their school district and "above all have a basic attitude of respect for the worth and dignity of others" (p. 75). The human skills concerning this function have to do with the development and maintenance of morale, and the technical ones with handling the specifics of personnel policy.

Boards of education, probably without the benefit of having devoted much time to formal study of the superintendency but frequently with the help of superintendent "headhunters," mention these same functions in their advertisements for superintendents. For example, in Central Square, New York, a small town near Syracuse, the Board of Education listed the following as important capabilities of a new superintendent: financial management; community relations; organization development; executive leadership; communications.

The list of the superintendent's responsibilities published by the Westhill Central Schools (a small suburb of Syracuse) follows Griffith's list quite closely, with some elaboration of subcategories. The Westhill Central Schools mentioned instructional leadership, financial planning, personnel relations, community relations, organizational planning, and school board leadership. And the City of Gloversville, New York, specified that "The new superintendent must have the skills required to manage and lead a complex public educational organization such as the City School District. Of great importance are skills in financial planning and management. Other such skills include educational program development, personnel administration, community relations, communications, school board leadership, and comprehensive planning." There seems to be nothing unusual in all this.

Metaphors for the Superintendency

The job skills that are specified represent a rational view of what a superintendent is held accountable for either through his own actions or through his delegation of responsibility to others. (One possible indication of the changing times, incidentally, is that two of the three school districts put financial management at the top of their list, and one put it second. Though Griffiths does not indicate the priority of the various functions, financial management was last on his list.)

The problem with such job descriptions, however, is that they do not tell us very much about superintendents, except, perhaps, that they are very busy people. But this we already know. What we don't know is how superintendents conceive of themselves as they do all that they're supposed to do. Do they see themselves as guiding lights, as kings, as servants, or what? The point is that neither academic analyses of the superintendency nor job descriptions tell us very much about how an individual superintendent conceives of his role. Knowing what superintendents are supposed to do does not help us to know what is central to their concepts of themselves as superintendents—the image they have of themselves relative to their work, the school system, and the people in it. Because enactment of their role centrally involves personal style preferences, the question of the images the subjects of this study held of themselves became a major focus.

This question was approached with the superintendents interviewed through the use of metaphor. Though metaphor frequently is used for lighthearted and comic purposes, it also has a profoundly serious quality. Eisner (1979), for example, suggests that "metaphor is the arch enemy of the stock response" (p. 260). He comments at another point with regard to educational program development, "The metaphors and images of schooling and teaching that we acquire have profound consequences for our educational values and for our views of how schooling should occur" (p. 261). When the appropriate occasion arises, thinking in metaphorical terms helps us clear away the fuzz of convention in a way that establishes a more elegant and artistic ground for our thought. Thus, toward the end of each interview, it was suggested that the person try to think and talk about his job in metaphorical terms.

What follows, then, is a description and discussion of the metaphors that the superintendents in this study used to describe themselves in their job. No pretense is made, of course, that the list includes anywhere near the universe of possible responses. However, it will be adequate enough to enable the reader to get a sense of the superintendency in terms other than the ordinary. It will also communicate more of a flavor about what it means to be a superintendent of schools than studying a list of job functions.

It is obvious, of course, that superintendents enact a variety of roles, depending on the problems they confront, during the course of a school day. And, certainly, they would characterize themselves differently at these various times. The metaphors that developed in the interviews, though, were the ones that centrally described the way these superintendents conceived of themselves as interacting with the job. They tended to form small, loose categorical clusters. For example, one cluster had a theatrical orientation:

> If you think about the job as it being a theatre, I find myself
> working the spotlights, and then once I've hit what I want, I run
> down onto the stage and start directing things.

> I see myself as being a sort of producer. Not a director who's really
> involved with the play, but more—let's produce this film, let's
> stage that event.

The subtle nuances connected with the leadership role of the school organization start to come through, then, in ways that are hidden, if not ignored, by
academic discussions of that role. In this case, the use of the theater as the
setting suggests that there is some sense of drama in it all. But it's important
to note, continuing the metaphor, that the superintendents here did not see
themselves as actors performing before an audience. On the contrary, the
image is of a role that is behind the scenes, yet very influential with regard to
what happens on the stage—that of director or producer. But here too,
within the idea of playing an influential role that is removed from the actual
performance, there is differentiation. Note, for example, how one superintendent sees himself very actively engaged in the whole drama. He not only
works the spotlight, focusing on parts of the play that are in need of adjustment; he also shifts roles and becomes involved in the directing of things. It's
as though he sees his skills as enabling him both to sense those parts of the
production that need to be improved and being able to prescribe the behaviors that will improve them.

On the other hand, the superintendent who used the term *producer*
conveys something different. There is a sense of disengagement from the
details of what happens on the stage and more of an inference of "That's a
good idea; I'll back it." But being a producer does not necessarily mean
playing a passive role. Though producers don't typically get involved in the
intricacies of actor behavior, they do indeed exercise control of the total
production. They can cancel it by withholding support or provide additional
resources in an effort to ensure its success. Or, if the production does not go
well because the director or actors were unskillful, the producer can refuse to
give support to future proposals from the same people. One's imagination
does not have to come into full play to understand some of the implications of
this point for a school district. In fact, without reference to the producer
image, at another point in our interview this superintendent spoke to the
point quite directly.

> I think the kind of thing that really gets me mad is when we have
> allowed a lot of time for planning and then we end up in chaos
> because someone has failed to implement as they were supposed to.
> You've laid out a time line and said, "Here's what needs to be
> done. Let me know if you need any additional support, and we'll
> break loose whatever you need." And then it doesn't get done.
> There's no excuse for that. The person just hasn't done the job.

Much as a producer of a play would be reluctant to back a loser a second time, then, it's not hard to picture this superintendent-producer being somewhat reticent about lending future support, at least without exercising more control, to people whom he has trusted to do something and who didn't perform adequately.

Another small group of metaphors for the way superintendents saw themselves had to do with symphony orchestras. Here are some picturesque examples:

> It's kind of like being conductor of the Philharmonic. The orchestra, a hundred pieces or so, plays a classic piece. You can't say you don't like the music itself, but you may end up not liking the way the conductor has arranged it or what he put the emphasis on. So, it's the superintendent—me—who winds up creating the style.

> I think my job involves me mostly as an orchestrator. And orchestration means taking all the dissonance, taking all the discordant things, and working with them. I listen for all the flat notes and try to know when something has to be fixed. Here's an interesting thing. When I was hired, one of the board members said, "We think we have a good school district. We just want the Stradivarius tuned." It was right at the interview!

There are similarities and also subtle differences between the metaphors of conductor and orchestrator. Both convey the need to be sensitive to the ways the various sections of the orchestra are playing—whether or not they are together and whether or not the particular arrangement itself produces the most desired effects when it is played in the way intended. But differences do exist. The conductor image clearly communicates the notion of someone being actively in charge of the musicians' behavior, while that of the orchestrator seems to focus on the more global arrangements of things, planning how different parts of the orchestra will fit together. Thus, the "conductor's" comment about style. Close involvement by the leader with the group seems more apt to communicate a desired style of behavior than that leader behavior that focuses on tuning the Stradivarius. This, of course, is not to say that the orchestrator, in this case, does not or would not get directly involved with people. Rather, it seems to be a matter of emphasis that depends on how one conceives of one's role. But it seems likely that the conductor-superintendent would attend more to the effects of his behavior on the system, while the orchestrator-superintendent would be less likely to be concerned with personalized style and more with the system as a system. Tuning the Stradivarius means listening to and adjusting the instrument—and letting someone else play it. Conducting means listening, too, but also telling the orchestra how the music should be played.

Though it can be inferred that each of the role metaphors that have been discussed above had some implication for inducing change in the system, others had the induction of change as their direct focus. For example,

> I'm a creator of crises. I love to create them, and I do so with a great deal of forethought. It depends on the time of year. When we're into budget time—May and early June—I do a little less of that. But when we're into the February-March doldrums, I really create them. Let's assume I have a department that has been rather stagnant, and I want to move it along. All of a sudden I create a crisis by recommending a change. Even though the situation might not move in the direction I recommend, I create a crisis, and get people all up in the air. I want them to stop and ask the question of why the change has been even considered. My day-to-day life involves looking for things I can hassle around with.

> I'm very community-oriented, and I frequently see myself as a bus driver. Let me give you an example. We had a group of representatives from five elementary schools that was considering the problem of reorganizing these schools. But they couldn't seem to get together on what they wanted. So I went up to the board, drew a picture of a bus, and I said, "I'm the bus driver, but I don't know where the hell we are going to go because this group hasn't given me a clear signal." So my job is to set it up in such a way that I will get a signal that says, "Yeah, let's go." But the question is, Do I simply take directions, or do I have the obligation to say it's much more beautiful in Maryland or Alaska than where you want to go, and should we fly, walk, drive, or ride a bicycle? In a way, my job is to be demand-creator. And then I drive the bus.

> I'm sort of the tone setter, a modeler. In a sense, I'm expected to do that, but no one but I would know if I didn't. But you know, sometimes it bothers me—the need to have to do things, set tones for other people. I don't want to spend my time reminding other people of what they should be doing.

> It's sort of like being a trout fisherman. You start out and just slowly bring it in. As you try to bring it in, maybe you lose over here, you don't bring it in today, but over here you bring it in two steps tomorrow. So eventually, every time you win, you bring it closer to what you want. You have to put up with a lot of momentary defeats, but in the larger battle, you've got all the resources to win.

In some important ways, I feel like a coach. "Hey, gang, let's go get 'em. We're really together in this." But sometimes, when I look behind me, I wonder about my coaching skills. I wonder how far the team is going to run. I have doubts.

I'm most effective when I can help set direction and then change roles to become an obstacle remover. Someone has to clear the channels. There are more damn artificial obstacles in education. I'm the one that arranges to remove them so that you can do the job.

That the creation of change in the schools is rather a many-splendored thing, then, seems to get reflected in the metaphors that some of the superintendents applied to themselves. It could scarcely be otherwise. Schools and school systems are different—sometimes radically so—reflecting as they do the interaction between their community context and the character of their leadership and school faculties. One senses in the things that superintendents said about themselves a rather wide range of styles, running from the active and demanding creator of crises to what on the face of it seems to be the rather quiet obstacle remover. The critical variable that accounts for the range seems to be the individual's preference for the kind of interaction he wants with people relative to changing the character of the system, parts of it, and sometimes individuals. For example, the creator of crises leaves little. doubt that he rather relishes pitched battles with people, preferably, of course, on ground of his own choosing. Notice, too, that though one might conceive of a bus driver as being more or less at the beck and call of people who ride the bus—stopping and starting at their bidding—bus drivers have also been known to drive by would-be passengers waiting on a street corner, as well as to stop in the middle of a block to wait for someone running to catch up. There is more information available in the metaphor, then, than one may appreciate at first glance. But we note as well that the same bus driver also saw himself as a demand-creating mechanism. We can reasonably suggest that creating demands is as much the ground for his "bus driving" as creating crises is for the other superintendent. In one fashion or another, he gets the system to place demands on itself, changes roles to help the people involved examine the situation, and then guides it to select the most appropriate destination and routes.

A different type of interactive preference seems evident in the metaphor of superintendent as trout fisherman. It is rich imagery, as one pictures the superintendent "playing the fish" in a delicate manner, putting tension on the line at one point and releasing that tension at another, depending on how he judges the fish's strength, position, and the various obstacles lying beneath the water's surface. It's important to note, however, that there is a distancing effect here. Most typically, the trout fisherman casts his lure some distance away and, having hooked a fish, gradually works it in close, so that it can be netted. This image suggests a removed and somewhat unobtrusive role for the superintendent, in contrast to the one who deliberately saw himself creating crises, center-stage, so to speak. One must also attend to the attitude set that is implicit in the fisherman metaphor. People who go fishing don't land every fish that gets onto their hook. Sometimes they lose their bait, and there are days when they catch nothing. But they always seem to go back, sometimes to the same spot and sometimes to another. They also change the type of bait that they use. They are patient, but know that if they are persistent they will end up with the catch they want or one that is, perhaps, not what they anticipated, but a catch just the same. This seems very much to be what is implied in the stance of our superintendent–trout fisherman. Finally, one cannot fail to take note of the manipulation and maneuvering that attends these activities. But of course, this is the case for, as we shall discuss in the next chapter, much of what the superintendency is all about: manipulation and maneuvering.

The use of tone setter or modeler as a metaphor for the superintendent role conveys a somewhat different interactive preference. It suggests that the superintendent is a focal socializing agent in the system, the setter and conveyer of norms. The processes of socialization run a range from activities that are highly direct, such as a formal indoctrination process, to those that are highly indirect and subtle, where the individual is more or less responsible for sensing out and conforming to system norms and expectations. The tone setter-modeler, by his words and behavior, seems to fall somewhere in between. For the most part, he is at some distance from people in the system, depending on his style and decisions to communicate through the system what he thinks education should be about. But it is apparent that with this particular superintendent, the process is not a passive one, particularly when he becomes aware that individuals are not behaving in ways he finds appropriate. He confronts directly and not at a distance, and as he said, he becomes bothered by the need to do this.

The "coach" presents a different image of the superintendent's role and the type of interaction the individual prefers. It conveys both heavy and close involvement (accompanied by cheerleading) with people while they are preparing for the "game," and then distance as they are sent out on the field to perform. It is this distance that, it appears, causes some difficulty for the coach and separates him from the conductor. Will the team perform the way he has trained them? Was he a good enough coach? Questions such as these must gnaw at every superintendent who conceives of himself in this manner, particularly when one thinks of the looseness of the control mechanisms that connect the superintendent's office with the schools and classrooms (Weick, 1976).

The image of superintendent as obstacle remover presents yet another view of a preferred interactive style. One is reminded of naval demolition crews whose task it was to remove obstacles in the water that guarded invasion beaches by whatever means, but mostly by blowing them up, so that landing barges could get to the beach unimpeded. But that analogy is quite extreme for our purposes. This metaphor suggests an initially close relationship between the superintendent and the school people who are working to solve a problem, and then a pulling back, not unlike that of the coach. The similarity between the obstacle remover and coach then seems to fade a bit, since the former keeps close touch, not as an observer of the game but as a player, working to clear away impediments to movement. Sometimes—rarely we suspect—an obstacle must be "blown up." More often, though, what is probably involved is a gentle nudging away of bureaucratic red tape or the provision of access to resources the need for which had not been originally anticipated.

While the two metaphorical categories that have been discussed—one having generally to do with leadership and the other with the induction of change—were the major ones that developed in the course of the interviews, there were other less dominant examples that provide colorful insights concerning how the superintendents conceived of themselves in their position. For instance, one superintendent said,

> I've always thought that being a superintendent of schools is akin to being a lightning rod. All of that emotionalism, all of that energy seems to get charged through you to someplace. You either find a way to transmit it into something effective in the system or deflect it in such a way that it doesn't contradict the directions of the system as you see them or as the board of education sees them.

There is an action-oriented quality to this description of superintendent as lightning rod that doesn't correspond to the actual instrument, which functions as passive receiver of lightning and then diminishes its destructive effects by conducting it into the earth. But then metaphors never are reality, though they do serve to give reality a more vivid and sometimes more vigorous character. So, one may picture this superintendent at times as waiting for a storm to engulf his district so that he can do something with the energy that develops. However, another image that is possible (and indeed, in another part of the interview he confirmed it in nonmetaphorical terms) is that at appropriate times he is instrumental in the development of storms. He then becomes a lightning rod and behaves in the manner he described. In this sense, he bears a resemblance to the colleague who described himself as a creator of crises. What seems to be ultimately important behind the lightning rod metaphor, though, is the set of attitudes upon which it appears to be grounded. It is the notion that schools and their effective operation are vital and dynamic enterprises. Further, it is this very vitality and vibrancy that are responsible for great stores of emotional and intellectual energy that frequently rests dormant in both the community at large and the professional community of the schools. To tap that energy is apparently the way this superintendent centrally conceptualizes his major task. But he also is discriminating in the way he handles it. He becomes the judge of what kind of "change" is useful and what kind must simply be rendered harmless.

Lightning rods are protective devices that come into use when a storm occurs. A more active concept of superintendent as protector emerged when one of the interviewees said,

> I almost feel I'm a watchguard [sic], a watchguard for the kids. It is very upsetting to me if the kids are getting a bad shake—if they're unhappy, if they're not being taught. That bothers me. I put pressure on people. First of all, I bring it up, and I demand that adjustments be made and [set] a time line for making those adjustments. It's got to be repaired. Things have got to be done. This gets you into problems with people, because they find out that I know the same things they know. They find out that they can't doubletalk me; that I know what it is to teach; that I know what it is to administer a building. It's almost like I'm one of them, but that I've turned on them. But I really get upset when kids get shortchanged.

The watchguard, then, is on the prowl. He listens and observes for indications that the system is not operating the way it should, particularly with regard to youngsters. But he appears to be more than just a sentry who might sound the alarm for reinforcements if he sees something amiss. He *is* the reinforcements, and the weapons at his disposal are of two major types. First, the obvious, is his authority as superintendent. The second may be more powerful because it tends to brush away the administrative and bureaucratic fuzziness. It is that he seems able to and does speak the same language as the administrators and teachers in his system. This weapon, then, disarms his opponents, because the superintendent knows excuses when he hears them, and his staff knows he knows them. As he said, they know he can't be doubletalked.

Interestingly, the use of the metaphor of watchguard introduces an image of the superintendent's role that we have not yet encountered. It is an image that has something of a militaristic tinge, one of being alert for the enemy. And the enemy, of course, is composed of individuals or groups who, for whatever reason, are behaving in ways in which "kids get shortchanged." It may seem odd to think of a superintendent conceiving of his professional staff as the enemy from time to time. But this superintendent does. Actually, it may be exceedingly productive to think in this manner. There are times when a superintendent's goals and those of the staff are opposed and the situation becomes adversarial. What this superintendent was saying, in effect, was that he was aware of when this opposition existed, and he was pretty well determined that it was his views that would prevail.

The next set of metaphors are of much interest because they come from a man who had just assumed the superintendency—his first—of a very small district, about three months prior to our interview. He was easily able to think in metaphorical terms and provided several interesting images.

> I tell my wife it's like working with a greased barrel, because some days you are on top, some days you are on the side, and eventually the barrel goes over on top of you.

> I am the sponge. I take it from the parents, the kids, the teachers, and the board. With a lot of luck, you can keep two of these groups happy so they are off your case while you are dealing with the other two. I tell everyone it's like a bunny hop. It's two up and one back.

In addition, this superintendent supplied a metaphor that originated with his wife:

> My wife calls me a prostitute. She says, "You make everybody happy but yourself." And I say, "Yeah, but I never gave it a name."

The difference between these metaphors and the ones that preceded them is startling. For the most part, the other images conveyed a sense of deliberateness and control. It was as though each superintendent knew what it was he was about and how he attuned his personal predispositions and values to the role demands as he saw them. This is clearly not the case for this brand-new superintendent. On the contrary, what we see is a person grappling with a total system for the very first time and trying to make sense of it. Thus, it's like working with a greased barrel. Where is the purchase? What does one grab hold of in order to lend stability both to the situation and to onself? How does one keep oneself outside of, not inside, the barrel? And how long can one tolerate being a sponge? When will the sponge be saturated and absorb no more water? And then what? Does one bunny hop forever? When does one stop being a prostitute?

One's first superintendency, in the early days at least, may well be a bewildering experience. It is quite unlike being a principal, as this superintendent had been and as many superintendents have been immediately prior to assuming system-wide responsibility for the first time. In the principalship, though it clearly has its ambiguities and frustrations, one's territorial prerogatives are fairly well circumscribed. One's responsibilities focus on the school building and what goes on in it, including, of course, the parent community. Not so with the superintendency, particularly if one gives credence to March's (1978) concept of school systems as "organized anarchies." Though this new, first-time superintendent didn't conceptualize the situation as anarchy, the metaphors that he used for his role suggest that he felt he was trying to deal with an anarchical situation. What's more, it seems clear that his personal survival in the position will depend on his ability to "degrease the barrel" and find its handle, so that he controls it, and not the other way around. (Subsequent conversations with this man indicated that he succeeded in the struggle for control.)

The metaphor that we include next is important because it provides a sort of developmental perspective on the superintendency. It arose during the interview with the "bus driver–demand creator," a man who had been a superintendent longer and in more communities than had any of the others interviewed. Reflecting on his over twenty years of superintending, he said,

> I really am a born-again superintendent, because I was brought up in the business literally as a manipulator. There was a kinder term for it. Superintendents were engineers of consent. That's the way it was in the late fifties. I really enjoyed the superintendency when I was the wheeler-dealer. I called all the shots. I was the quarterback, and the goddamn team did what I wanted. I still think it's probably one of the best jobs around, but I still have conflicts that are related to the way things have changed over the years.

Things, indeed, have changed, and for reasons that need no elaboration here. Along with those changes have come alterations in the role of superintendent. These people are no longer trained to be engineers who know how to gain the consent of others to their wishes. And, for sure, few of them today conceive of themselves as quarterbacks of a team that will "goddamn do what I want." But this is not to say that the concept of the superintendent has changed from that of a proactive educational executive to that of a community pawn. Far from it, as the list of metaphors has indicated. Rather, what we seem to have is a growing insight that the role of the superintendent involves an ever more sophisticated understanding of the community as an organism, of its political structure, of the need to deal with power centers outside of the superintendent's office, and of the wide variety of both human and technical skills needed to create a viable educational organization.

In presenting these metaphors, I have certainly not claimed that the examples used represent anywhere near the universe of metaphors that superintendents might use to describe themselves. Instead, I have tried to convey to the reader the richness and variety of imagery that can be associated with the superintendency (which is not to say, by any means, that this richness and variety cannot be developed in a host of other occupations). I wanted to use the imaginative value of metaphors to, as Eisner put it, step outside the "bonds of convention," so that the reader could start to get a coherent sense of the superintendency as a role that primarily focuses on the essential humanity of the person playing it. Conceptual, human, and technical skills are important, of course. But it seems to me that they assume secondary importance to the need for the superintendent to sort out what he is all about as the person responsible for the educational enterprise of a community.

The Fusion Process

What we are ultimately dealing with in this chapter is the "fusion process," described by Bakke (1953). This process involves the development of a satisfactory match between an individual's needs and those of an organization. It is a process that is probably continually evolving, since both the needs and goals of individuals and organizations change as the two place sometimes congruent, sometimes conflicting demands upon each other. This mutual demand-placing process, particularly with regard to the superintendent's role, is by no means overt. It is not a case of school systems advertising for a person who can perform certain functions and employing someone whose credentials imply that he meets the criteria. Instead, the fusion process is a subtle, complex phenomenon. It involves testing by both the individual and the organization so that each ends up creating a "good fit" for the other. In the case of superintendents of schools, this good fit is only rarely obstructed by a person's inability to perform the functions for which he was hired. The functions that superintendents are asked to perform do not require, for example, the skills of highly abstract thinking, nor do they require highly esoteric technical competence. The situations in which the good fit between superintendent and school system is likely to be upset are those in which the system's view of what the basic operating style of the superintendent should be conflicts with the view the superintendent holds for himself. These views are rarely the subject of open discussion and might not make much sense even if they were. They become apparent through the superintendent's behavior with various subgroups in the system and the reactions that behavior engenders. Life for a superintendent is filled with subtleties indeed.

4

The Superintendency and Politics

A Case of Total Immersion in Politics

The heading above is not my invention. This description of the superintendency came from an interview with a school superintendent, who said, at one
point,

> I see the superintendency, more than ever before, as just totally
> immersed in politics. It is very, very political. And what I'm really
> talking about is the entire political arena, not just the politics of
> education.

Not all superintendents would agree with this sweeping generalization, but
its very forthrightness is refreshing; there is no hedging. This person went on
to say at another point in our talk that he thought that the superintendent who
fails (i.e., does not survive on the job) is one who is not aware of the politics of
his situation and who sees himself as being able to isolate his problems and
decisions from their political context. Be that as it may, the point of overriding
importance in the comment is that the "ground" of the superintendency needs
to be conceived of largely in political terms if one wishes to understand its "figure"—what that role is all about and the behavior of those who occupy it.

Given this position, then, it is possible to recast the metaphors for the
superintendent's role that were discussed in chapter 3 in a different light.
They need to be seen against the more encompassing metaphor of "superintendent as politician." If conceived of in this way, then these images become
the personalized "figure" to the politician "ground." They were the ways
that the superintendents chose to see themselves acting within the broad
spectrum of events that require some type of political behavior. "Producer,"
"director," "fisherman"—all of these metaphors convey that essential meaning, for example, as do the other role images in one way or another.

The notion that the school superintendency is, at its roots, a political
venture and that effective exercise of the role requires keen political sensitivity combined with shrewd political skills is one that many people find distasteful, some superintendents included. Education is for children, the thinking goes. It is too important and sacred a societal function to be mixed up in

45

politics, whether that politics is public and partisan or involves the covert, astute manipulation of competing pressure groups in a community or on a school board. Educators should maintain a position untainted by the political battles that occur in the community and consciously seek to ensure that the schools will be unscarred by those battles. Decisions that are made about the schools should be rational ones based on what is best for children educationally, and not on the basis of any need either to satisfy special-interest groups or simply to keep the system functioning with a minimum of conflict.

This apolitical ethic of the superintendency has a long history, part of which has been discussed earlier. We have noted in chapter 2, for example, Jones's polemic, quite possibly justified, against the intrusion of community political influence into the schools, particularly with regard to hiring and firing. And we have also noted in that chapter the long-term and intense battles that took place between superintendents and school boards over the former's quest for more control over the educational enterprise. These battles were by definition, political, since they involved a struggle for power. In retrospect, one could take the position, as I do, that this conflict expressed the desire of the superintendents of the time to free themselves of community constraints so that they could be politicians in their own right—prime ministers of the schools, so to speak—or "educational czars," as the *School Board Journal* sarcastically termed them. Though the *Journal's* view is perhaps too cynical, it really doesn't matter which power-oriented label one applies to a superintendent or the way he performs his job. What is important is to understand that being a superintendent inevitably involves the manipulation and exercise of organizational power. This is essentially a political activity, as are, of course, the mobilization of community support and the management of conflict, activities that require a great deal of a superintendent's time and concern. If schools and their operation have ever been conceived of in apolitical terms, that is clearly no longer the case.

The image of the superintendency as being "totally immersed in politics," then, is an apt if broad metaphor for the position. However, further discussion is needed to make the details of the broad image clearer. Judging by our interviews, there appear to be three central facets of a superintendent's political life, and a fourth that though once somewhat peripheral is currently assuming more importance. The first three are

- The politics of local educational decision making
- The politics of being a nonelected executive of a focal public enterprise
- The politics of survival

The fourth has to do with those parts of a superintendent's work in which he deals mostly with centers of power and decision making beyond his immediate community, in both the state and federal legislative and bureaucratic establishments.

The Politics of Educational Decision Making

The fierce battles that developed over the emerging role of the superintendent shortly before the turn of the century, were, I have suggested, essentially connected to issues of power. Who would make the decisions concerning both the character of education to be supported in a community and the manner in which the system itself would be run? The prevailing views of the educators were (1) that it was of the utmost importance to keep the education of youngsters uncontaminated by community politics, and (2) that the proper schooling of children required a sort of conceptual and technical expertise concerning what was the best education. Such expertise, went the thinking, was primarily the possession of people who have devoted their lives to schooling youngsters. It was not widely shared in the community, and matters of education should therefore be left to the experts. Iannaccone, in *Politics in Education* (1967), put the matter this way:

> The preferred politics of pedagogues is the politics of the priest-craft protected by its putative mastery of the mysteries of educational expertise, supported by the public's response to sacred values, and proceeding within the privileged sanctuary of its private preserves. This pattern is not confined to dealing with "lay" persons; behavior characterizing the politics of education appears throughout the internal power struggles of educational associations as well. (p. 14)

It is important to note Iannaccone's extension of the "putative mastery" notion beyond the local community and into the educational associations that presumably influence the character of education in this country. His point is that if educators had their way, and at times they do, the decision-making system would be a closed one, impervious to outside attempts to influence decisions. Further, he suggested, the efforts to keep the system closed—to dampen any opposition or try to keep a "loyal opposition" from developing—have been ultimately damaging to the schoolmen's cause.

Iannaccone's point is that politics and education in our society are intertwined and probably always have been. This suggests that attempts to keep the system "sterile," or to preserve it from "contamination" with politics, are illusory at best, and costly in the long run. The costs become evident, for example, when communities start to withhold fiscal and emotional support from the schools and when they lay the failures of the schools at the feet of the people who said they knew best what the schools should do and how it should be done: the educators, from professors to superintendents to principals to teachers.

One meaning of the idea that the superintendency is "totally immersed in politics," then, is that the very fabric of the schooling function in American society, because of the nature of that society, is essentially political. Further, it means that this condition is an appropriate one; that, in Iannacone's terms, a loyal opposition in the decision-making process needs to be institutionalized, and that superintendents, like it or not, are part and parcel of the whole pattern.

The Political Dilemma of the Nonelected Public Official

There are, of course, countless numbers of nonelected executives of focal public enterprises. Each one of them must, from time to time, and some more than others, engage in the political processes that are necessary to the functioning of the organization. School superintendents, though, seem to constitute a set within this broader whole that is somehow different from the whole in important ways. For example, they have responsibility for an enterprise to which some of the most deeply held values in the American tradition are attached. The same cannot be said for the municipal director of public works or the executive in charge of parks and recreation. Superintendents assume their positions as supposed experts, yet their expertise becomes useless unless they are able to develop a supportive constituency among the school board, community, and professional staff. The organization that they are to lead and manage is composed of people who often have equal or more expertise in education than the superintendent. Because of this fact, they must deal with a lay policy board and with community groups in ways that don't apply, for example, to a director of public health or even of public welfare. The list of points of difference that separate the superintendency, conceptually and functionally, from the vast array of other public executives could go on and on.

The import of these differences in the superintendency as a public office for the work life of a superintendent has been nicely put by Boyd (1974). He notes, first, "the development of the role of the chief school officer as an *educational statesman*, a professional administrator who exerts extraordinary leadership and influence in policy-making primarily as a result of the weight his recommendations carry with non-partisan lay boards which are pursuing the public interest" (p. 1). Boyd then goes on to highlight the conflict, perhaps the most important one as far as the person of the superintendent is concerned. Starting out with a comment that echoes Iannacone's comment about the preferred politics of pedagogues, Boyd writes:

However much the role of the educational statesman has become central to the ideology of school administrators, and however much schoolmen would prefer to play that role, it is obvious that they sometimes face situations in which the role is not a viable one. Since the reform era, as well as before it, school superintendents have had to contend at times with boards which interfere in administrative matters and are reluctant to defer to expertise and delegate authority. Moreover, superintendents sometimes must deal with school boards and communities which are torn with factions and evince partisanship despite a nominally nonpartisan system. In such situations, superintendents find that circumstances seem to demand that, rather than the role of the educational statesman, they must adopt the more hazardous role of the political strategist, i.e., a leader who, because he cannot generally count on being given support, must instead win support through adroit maneuvering and persuasion based upon careful analysis of existing and potential coalitions on the school board and within the community. (p. 1)

The rose garden inherent in the concept of the educational statesman becomes, more frequently than Boyd suggests, a lawn full of weeds for the superintendent. Further, to continue the metaphor, the weeds are not all of the same species. The metaphor, of course, breaks down. Expert lawn care, using a variety of procedures, requires the eradication of all weeds. Expert "superintending," using any of a variety of procedures, requires the cultivation of many "weeds," helping them change form, and only occasionally if ever requires their outright eradication. There are superintendents for whom playing the political strategist constitutes the job's joy, excitement, and challenge. It almost presents them with their raison d'etre. For others, however, the role is distasteful, uncomfortable, and to be avoided whenever possible. Hess suggests the reason for this discomfort, commenting that when he engages in the political side of his job, "the superintendent . . . is a power-broker, a dealer in influence" (1981). Shades of Watergate and Abscam! Further, one can hear some superintendents reacting negatively to this description with "That's not the way it's supposed to be! The purity of what we're about is being contaminated, and me along with it." But that's the way it is.

The Politics of Survival

All of the superintendent's educational expertise—curriculum development skills, knowledge of the problems of teaching and learning, for example—comes to naught if the superintendent does not survive in his position. *Survival* may seem like too strong a term to use, implying as it does life and death.

Its aptness, however, comes from its common use by superintendents themselves. The very term and its frequent employment convey an image of the superintendency that is a curious one, setting it apart from other positions of executives in the public sector. One rarely hears, for example, overt concern expressed about the "survival" of district attorneys, police chiefs, or directors of social welfare. There clearly are such concerns among superintendents, however, and they are not only of recent vintage. Testimony to this can be found in both chapters 1 and 2 of this book. Recall, for instance, the somewhat humorous letter from the country superintendent to his daughter in which he said he was still leading the district, but he wasn't sure by how much.

Survival can be of many types, however. There is a wide range of conditions within which a person might survive in the superintendency, and certainly some of them are definitely preferable to others. The condition that is of interest to us here involves the variables of potency and activity.

It is not news to anyone in the field of education, lay or professional, that there are some superintendents who have survived for a very long time, the primary tools of their extended tenure being a lack of potency and activity. They have simply kept the system functioning through routine administration, kept the tax rate within acceptable limits, and have avoided irritating anyone in any but rather inconsequential ways. They are not bad people, of course, and the fact of their survival is probably indicative, more than anything else, of a good match having been made between them as individuals and the needs and desires of the communities in which they serve.

At the other end of the continuum are the superintendents who have survived for a long time, have retained their potency and activity, and are, in short, able to be the educational statesmen to whom we have referred. Not infrequently they are involved in controversy from which they seemingly emerge in a stronger position than they were previously. They have retained and enhanced their power. They have done more than just kept the system running. The politics of their survival has been less concerned with surviving per se and more with behaving in ways that permit them to have a continuing productive impact on the system, thus ensuring their survival and power. That is, they become a commodity that is valued because it is potent and active, and not because it is impotent and inactive.

Burlingame (1981) deals implicitly with the survival issue in a paper entitled "Superintendent Power Retention." The casual and naive reader may be shocked and repelled by his first sentence: "I seriously doubt that honesty is the best policy for superintendents who wish to retain power" (p. 429). Burlingame is not, of course, proposing a recipe for an immoral code of behavior for superintendents. Rather, what is at issue is that the schools, by both their organizational and technological character, are systems that elude an operational goal orientation, inspection, and control. Superintendents are caught in a dilemma. They

> must diligently seek to control both the internal reality and public image of the schools. In a very real sense, however, superintendents can control neither the internal reality of what goes on in the schools nor the public image of the schools. Under these conditions of relative powerlessness, superintendents become not only involved in processes of mystification or cover-up, but also become practitioners of tactical rules of survival. (p. 433)

These tactical rules of survival are

1. Act like a superintendent so that others can know how to act.
2. Anticipate that ignorance will produce more positive than negative results.[1]
3. Stifle conflict by denial, bolstering, and differentiation.
4. Provide simple solutions for human problems, complex solutions for technical problems.
5. Don't decide; help or hinder others to decide.
6. If you must decide, make the second best decision. (p. 438)

Again, the casual reader may be repelled by all this. Certainly, such a set of rules is not congruent with the values that our schools espouse. On the other hand, maybe they are, if one takes the position that the schools not only espouse the value of "honesty is the best policy" but implicitly one of "Let us try and understand how the world works." But my purpose here is not to argue the rightness or wrongness of Burlingame's point of view nor whether his analysis, though it is based on a deep and sensitive understanding of school organization life, is the most appropriate one. What is important for our purposes here is to understand that there *is* a politics of superintendent survival. It is real, and just how a superintendent chooses to make it function for himself will affect the character of his position and his ability to exercise leadership.

The Politics of State and Federal Relationships

The need for superintendents to be involved politically with both state and federal decision making and regulatory bodies is a relatively recent one.

---

1. Burlingame (1981) explains, "This rule anticipates that most people will not know what others think privately, only what others say publicly. People will then seek to fulfill public expectations in spite of private doubts" (p. 439). Further, "ignorance facilitates redundancy and deviancy—useful by-products not only for administrative survival, but also educational success" (p. 440).

Prior to the late 1950s, such involvement was infrequent, certainly as far as the federal government was concerned. Things changed, and radically, with the entrance—some would say intrusion—of the federal government into the field through federal monies for education and their accompanying regulations. And, of course, court decisions, starting with those concerned with racial segregation in the public schools, represented an additional force that influenced the way a superintendent might see his job. A third factor was the growing militancy and political strength of the teachers' unions. Teachers' unions are not only concerned with local issues. They are concerned and active, as they legitimately should be, with trying to influence decisions affecting education, particularly on the state level.

The interaction of these factors has had two major effects on the working life of school superintendents. First, and obviously, it has made their work much more complex. They perform their jobs under constraints few would have imagined three decades ago. New sources of conflict were introduced into their lives. Second, these circumstances meant a new form of political involvement for superintendents. They could no longer tend to their local business, with occasional goodwill visits to the state education commissioner's office. If they wanted to affect things, they had to become involved in the politics of power and influence, especially at the state level.

A superintendent's involvement in state and federal politics is less well defined and pervasive than the other parts of a superintendent's life that we have mentioned previously. A few superintendents are actively engaged in such politics. But most seem to limit their involvement to complaining about state and federal mandates that are handed down without accompanying fiscal support. The issue is raised here, however, not for intensive discussion but to indicate that the situation exists and that it will continue to play a part in determining how the superintendency gets enacted. An important effect of these circumstances is that the superintendency is inevitably inserted in one fashion or another into partisan politics. The teachers' unions, often opposed to the prerogatives claimed by superintendents, obviously don't share these feelings about inappropriateness. So it is probably true, then, that to the extent that superintendents avoid such a political role, they will probably lose control over their domain.

This somewhat extended introduction to the "total immersion in politics" concept of the superintendency was not intended to be an in-depth discussion of the "politics" of education, however that term is defined. It was designed to provide a backdrop against which the reader might think about the several comments that the superintendents in this study made about what they considered to be the "political strategist" focus of their role. The day-to-day meaning of the backdrop seems well summed up in the words of one superintendent, who said, "It doesn't make any difference what the decision is you have to make. When you make it, you are impinging on somebody else's territory." This comment is, perhaps, a bit too broad. There are certainly decisions that superintendents make that involve trivia or are encapsulated and that don't intrude on the territorial prerogative of other individuals or groups. But it is undoubtedly true, and this is our point of departure, that few, if any, of the decisions that confront a superintendent that have to do with the substance of education or the governance of the system can be dealt with on the merits of the arguments alone. Matters of whose territory is whose are almost always involved and must be taken into consideration.

The Superintendents Comment on the Politicalness of Their Jobs

The superintendents in this study, though they tended to describe the politics of their office in somewhat different terms, had no difficulty at all in relating to the concept. Here is a sample of the range of their responses:

> It's political, highly political. It's political because it's a human enterprise. I do things politically, yes. I am politically motivated. More in the sense of trying to get ahead of somebody. Sometimes I'll say to the administrative staff, "I don't want to be pressured into this, and, therefore, let's decide now whether it's a good direction to take, and if it's a good direction, let's beat them to the punch."

> It's a terribly political job. And I think it's increasingly becoming a measure of the superintendent of schools. In graduate school we took a course in the politics of education. What a joke! The whole damn thing is political. You always have to behave politically with the board. You can't ever believe you're going to have an off-the-cuff conversation. There's no such thing in my experience. And I think one of the unfortunate parts of it is that you hear of certain superintendents being put down as being really, really political. I guess the way I have always interpreted that is that these are people who are solely concerned about the image of the district, the job, the decision. They very seldom, if ever, will make a decision that costs them their chips.

> This is a very political situation. There's almost a Tammany Hall syndrome operating. People in the community, for example, think there's always someone "on the take." Or people get jobs because of someone they know. The president of the board happens to be chairman of the Republican Party. He's a very powerful political figure. At our first meeting I said, "Are there any sacred cows? You people want changes. You want all sorts of things. Are you aware of the implications of change? Are there any sacred cows?" And that's a way of saying, of course, "If you want changes, whom do you want to cover, protect?" And, of course, there are

absolutely none. And I know that will be the response. But that's my way of paving the way.

Here's how my job is political. What I do is to create demands and achieve solutions in meetings. The solution involves a constant set of trade-offs. I just went through one. We are going to reorganize our elementary schools. I had a solution which I think was probably the best one. Why wouldn't I think so. It was mine! The solution that evolved was, let's say, 35 percent different than mine. But it was still a good one. So the trade-off I made is okay because we built in a support system and are more likely to achieve it. So that you're constantly assessing what's achievable. And what you can do. You are constantly trying to assess what are the community norms and the staff norms and how far beyond them you can go and still be within a workable, acceptable framework of achievability. So you make trade-offs. You say, "What do I give up in order to get what I can get?"

I guess I've been active in the political sense in the community. I touch base with the power people. The county legislator, the state assemblyman, the village officials, the mayor, a couple of manufacturers, big property owners. I meet them in business situations and socially. The result is that people say you're doing your job, you've been accepted, and you get support.

The images of the politics of the superintendency conveyed in these comments carry elements of sameness as well as difference. Without doubt, there is agreement that effective performance, and probably survival, requires of the superintendent a shrewd sense of political imperatives. This involves, first, the need to keep one's personal or institutional "radar" continually scanning both the school and political community. One scans for both friends and foes. One also scans both for potential opportunities to achieve something and for potential sources of conflict. A superintendent said, for example,

> Being political means having a real sense of the workings of groups—power groups, pressure groups, decision-making processes. You're dealing with different constituencies, with people interacting with each other with their own special interests. And you really have to have that all sorted out so that you can anticipate their reactions. You have to be political!

What happens as a result of the scanning operation, it seems, tends to become a matter of one's own motivation and interactive style preferences. We have one person, for example, whose concern is "beat them to the punch." "Don't let yourself be 'one-upped' by the community," seems to be the message here. But there is another message that suggests that this is a strategy aimed at maintaining control and relative freedom of action. Further, if you can continually "beat them to the punch" you don't get pressured into doing things at a time and under circumstances not of your own choosing, a hallmark of an effective politician. Another superintendent tends to think of the politics of his job as putting behavioral constraints on him. In effect, when he said, "You can't ever believe you're having an off-the-cuff conversation," he was saying that he has to operate, at times, in an atmosphere of distrust; that he has to be careful not to say anything that he wouldn't want quoted. The waters in which the superintendent swims are occasionally dangerous ones, and he must be careful not to get caught in the undertow—or at least circumspect enough to avoid getting his big toe nipped by the fiddler crabs that abound in every school district.

For another superintendent, politics in his district exhibits "almost a Tammany Hall syndrome." The community is a distrustful one, and public officials are suspect merely because they are public officials. Behavior must be adjusted to meet the situation, and so, in his first meeting with his school board president, he raises the question of "sacred cows" that should be left alone, knowing full well what the answer will be. But the political game needs to be played out, and it is. Each takes the measure of the other, thereby enabling both of them to establish a satisfactory way of working together. And for yet another superintendent, the words with which he describes the political focus of his job might well have been spoken by the majority leader of either legislative house in Washington. The emphasis is on "what's achievable," and not on what should exist in the best of all educational worlds. Further, "what's achievable" is measured not by how much power can be mustered to force through a particular decision, but by whether or not the decision will be supported by the community.

The superintendency as a political office is revealed a bit differently by the comment "I touch base with the power people." But notice that this superintendent, too, is responding to community norms. His reading of the local situation told him that it was important in that community simply to be known as a person to the people in the community power structure. His willingness to be known and to reach out in order for others to know him was sufficient to garner community support. It was what was expected. His example presents a bland view of the politics of the superintendency. But an extremely important point is hidden behind the blandness. The community in which this superintendent works is, in itself, a rather bland one. An important point is at issue here: It is impossible to understand the politics of the superintendency simply in terms of the personal predisposition of any particular superintendent. Superintendents interact with, change, *and are changed by* the communities in which they serve. The political world view that a superintendent brings to one community, which serves him well there, may be counterproductive in the next. What is required, perhaps, is a *statesman's* view of *politics*, if the two terms, which Boyd viewed as opposites, can be joined. Such a view (though he did not use the term *statesman*) was voiced by one interviewee in the following way:

> So the superintendent must be totally aware of the changing pressure groups, and the changing potency of different pressure groups. That's the backdrop, and obviously that backdrop produces tremendous pressure and tremendous tension, in particular to those who have not been able to intellectualize it. They can't tell where all the pressure's coming from, and they're not sure why everything that is happening to them is happening the way it is. They're sitting in a pile of paperwork, yelling about it and criticizing it instead of trying to understand what it means.

Being "political," then, involves more than possessing personalized strategies and tactics for playing the politician's role. It also involves the ability to take a broad and (curiously) an almost disinterested view of the kaleidoscope of interacting forces that impinge on school system problem-solving and decision-making processes. First, one must have a comprehensive understanding of what is going on. It is not sufficient, for example, to sense that a particular group is mobilizing to defeat a school budget; that another group is organizing to protest a sex education program; that the community is in conflict over a prospective busing program; or that competing pressure groups are trying to influence a decision about integrating special education students into regular classrooms. One must understand the possible relationships that these groups may have with one another, their sources of power, and their potential influence. Only with these types of understandings can a superintendent think through appropriate strategies for action. But that is rather obvious. What is not obvious is the need to consciously conceptualize one's awareness of these various forces.

Conceptualizing the politics of conflicting forces in a school community is not merely an academic exercise for a superintendent. It is very closely related to his ability to create some sense of order in his work world. Unless this can be done, the superintendency becomes a hodgepodge of seemingly unrelated, distracting demands for action. Superintendents can become overwhelmed with what they interpret to be meaningless paperwork. They can also become organizational "firemen" and engage predominantly in management by crisis. In short, they can lose control of their work lives as they respond to situations randomly. It doesn't take much imagination to picture such a superintendent becoming angry and frustrated, losing his sense of perspective, and perceiving himself as victimized by the ignorance of others.

The need for order in one's work life also requires a superintendent to maintain a sort of detached sense of distance from the fray. This may appear to be a curious statement. Certainly superintendents are involved in what they do. Certainly they have an emotional stake in their plans, their budgets, and so forth. But they are also human beings, with wives, families, and very personalized needs. Just like everyone else, they have a personal world that makes demands on their intellectual and emotional energy. To prevent their work lives from consuming their personal lives, they must be able to stand back, intellectualize what is going on, and perhaps conceive of daily circumstances as some sort of drama that is being played out. They are involved in the drama, but they are also part of the audience. Thus they are able to maintain a sense of their own integrity and—if this is not too bold a statement—their sanity, in situations that some superintendents will tell you are absolutely insane.

To sum up: The highly political and conflictual world of the superintendency appears to be randomized, irrational, and uncontrollable. To the extent that a superintendent can understand the complex web of events that he confronts and subject that understanding to his own intellectual analysis, he is better able to order the world, control it, and maintain his own sense of self.

The imperative of "superintendent as politician," no matter how good a case can be made for it, does not sit well with all superintendents, however. In reacting to discussion about the superintendency placing strong demands for skilled political behavior on the person who occupies that position, one superintendent, a woman, said:

> I think it's important, but I'm not a very good politician. I am not a person who is inherently political, and perhaps that may be one of my weaknesses. I feel I am in this as an educational leader and to deal with what's right. If I were strictly a political type, I could come in here and do nothing. I could take my salary. I would just do what the board wants me to do. And there would not be the conflicts I have. So some people tell me that I should be more of a political animal than I am; that I should appease this group and that group. I've worked with people like that, and I'm sure it's a lot easier. I often say that people want a big fat marshmallow as a superintendent and not a big fat witch.

Another person, commenting that he finally found out what the politics of education was all about when he became a superintendent, said:

> Well, I discovered what I'm sure many superintendents discover. A lot of time is spent satisfying idiot board members and teachers. You have to do some of that, of course, but if you were to set your

own priorities it would be awful low on the scale. Most of it deals with petty issues. For example, we have some board members who are highly Title IX–oriented: no "his" or "her." I must have wasted several days rewriting policy to take out "his" or "her." It's garbage. It's pathetic. It's pathetic. And they're paying me thirty some odd thousand dollars a year to do that. Or, there are instances of an eighth grader playing JV soccer. Who the hell cares, if he's capable? Or, is it true that such and such teacher is being indiscreet? You trace that kind of garbage down in order to keep them happy. It all takes time, and it's petty.

I've had a couple of sessions with them about all that stuff because it makes me angry. I asked them where the hell they were. I'm becoming more of a risk taker. I guess I've discovered the more conflicts I have, the more I'm willing to do it. It's not that bad.

One thing becomes immediately obvious when these two comments are compared with those that preceded them. It is that the word *politics*, as it applies to the superintendency, triggers responses that seem to vary with the individual and with the perceptions they hold of themselves in their position. The earlier remarks seemed to be somewhat detached and analytical. They conveyed an image of a person engaged in an intellectual game—almost a chess game where one's moves depend not only on one's perception of the current situation but also on one's view of the future. The object of it all, of course, is to win.

This stance was clearly not foremost in the minds of the two superintendents whose comments were just quoted. Rather, they saw the "politics" of superintendency in negative terms. "Being political," in the first case, seemed to mean kowtowing to the board and placing the smoothness of that relationship ahead of the demands of educational *leadership*—whatever that term may connote. In the second case, the superintendent as politician seemed to mean engaging in educationally meaningless tasks that took a great deal of time, simply to avoid ruffling the feelings of one constituent or another.

It has to be true, of course, that both of these people also enacted behaviors that would be congruent with the broader political view of the superintendency that was expressed in remarks of their colleagues. But they did not see their role centrally in those terms. Both of them, in fact, perceived of themselves primarily as educators whose major thrust was affecting the quality of curriculum and instruction. The broader system view, although they functioned within it, seemed not to be a focal guide for their action.

Two other bits of information about these two interviewees reinforce the idea that the political focus of the superintendency was not central to the thinking of these two people. The superintendent we quoted first, indicated elsewhere in the interview that being a superintendent for the rest of her professional life was not necessarily a goal, either in the district in which she was currently employed or in another one. It would depend on how things worked out. In point of fact, she did not rule out returning to the classroom if the superintendency turned out to be a less than desirable circumstance for her. She would continue doing what she was doing as long as she could be an "educational leader"—or until she simply got tired of it. The second superintendent we quoted, I learned, was abruptly terminated by the school about a year after our interview for refusing to make an administrative personnel change that the board had demanded but that he disapproved of. Not sensing the potential fallout of his decision, he had taken one risk too many. He had thrown down the gauntlet and lost.

In addition to describing their general concept of the politicalness of their position, the superintendents also expressed some of the perspectives they held of themselves relative to the politics of their work world. Specifically, they discussed the topics of their own power, the notion of winning and losing, the balancing acts they perform, and their need to protect themselves.

The Power of the Superintendency

To speak of the power inherent in the office of superintendent of schools as if it was a one-dimensional concept is to oversimplify an extremely complex set of circumstances. Are we talking about the relationships the superintendent has to the school board, the community's political officeholders, teachers as individuals, principals, teachers' unions, pupils, the community at large? All of these, separately or in interaction with one another? Are we talking about legal power to make decisions, organizational power to allocate resources or to reward and punish, the power that is inherent in the ability to control sources of information, or what? It becomes glaringly obvious that when the global concept of power gets broken down in relation to the settings in which it may be exercised, questions related to power and the superintendency become both elusive ones to ask and almost unanswerable.

It also is true, of course, that questions related to the superintendent's power cannot be dealt with ahistorically. We have referred several times to the highly emotional conflicts that were waged almost a century ago between school boards and superintendents over the issue—baldly stated—of who should run things. Though those battles yielded no clear-cut victor—an impossible outcome in any case, given the American pattern of local control of schools and the idiosyncratic conditions existing in each school district—it is clear that over the years the balance of power has shifted from the school board to the superintendent. This shift was reflected in the graduate education of school administrators. Two of the superintendents interviewed, for example, somewhat older than the others, commented that their doctoral work in the 1950s clearly contained the message that (1) they were the experts, and (2) it was their job to run things, even if they became bullies in the process.

Pendulums swing both ways, however, and events in our society since the mid-1960s seem to have engendered a movement in the direction of diminished power of the superintendent. The growth of strong teachers' unions, community concern about costs and school effectiveness, and the focus on the legal rights of students are among the major factors that have contributed to a lessening of the prerogatives of the superintendent's office. This trend has, of course, been described in the professional literature. We noted earlier, for example, Burlingame's paper entitled "Superintendent Power Retention," as well as Campbell's expression of concern about the possibility of superintendents becoming obsolete. Another example, very directly to the point, is Nolte's article entitled, "How Fast Is the Power of the Superintendent Slipping?" (1974). Using biblical imagery, he writes, "School superintendents today, many complain, are like shorn Samsons whose source of power has been snipped away by numerous Delilahs" (p. 42).

What appears to be the situation, then, is that a state of flux currently exists with regard to the power prerogatives of superintendents. Indeed, the fluidity of the situation was testified to as the superintendents in this study reflected on the question of their power. They were asked to respond to the very general question of whether or not they felt powerful. Their reactions were varied:

> Yes, I feel powerful. Just consider it from the economic perspective alone. We have a multimillion-dollar budget, and it has to be administered in some way. The money brings people to you in terms of purchasing. And I'm powerful in terms of being able to solve tax propositions for better education.

> I think I exercise power over curriculum development. I can get things going. I can and do mandate that my principals give consideration to certain programs. And I can and do see to it that they stay on top of things in that area.

> I don't feel powerful. The question of power is a joke, because you're responsible to the board of education. That's where the power really is. The last thing I do is tell Mrs. Jones, "You gotta do it this way."

> Sure, I feel powerful. Especially in terms of dealing with the school

system and even with the community. Yeah, I feel that power, the power to change things, the power to change lives and to know that people react to that. There are times I certainly feel good about that, to have the opportunity to say yes or no, and they've got to do it. But that same feeling doesn't always carry over to the school board. Legally, they call the shots. Sometimes I feel a little vulnerable with them.

I don't really feel powerful. In some situations I guess that if I said something it would mean something. I know some people say my job is very powerful. I'm the head of the whole thing. It makes me smile. I can't change a teacher, really. If you look at what you can change, I don't think you can say you have a lot of power.

You have power if your timing is right. You keep people talking, and then, when you sense the situation has come as close as it can come, you move. You've got to make sure that everything has been played out so there's nowhere else to go, and then you gotta move.

Mostly I'm powerful in terms of personnel. Probably the strongest handle on that is through the power of appointment. The board cannot appoint someone without my say-so. The same thing goes for tenure. There can be no reorganization in the district staff without my approval. But I can't make that happen by myself, either.

I don't really feel powerful. I know it's there. I can move teachers around, and there's nothing they can do about it, but that would be wrong. The hardest thing I have to do is to avoid the use of power in this office. Sometimes I see something that is so stupid and so outrageous that I really want to react to the SOB with the power of my office. I have to stop myself.

It's hard to say, of course, what the reactions of superintendents to the question of how powerful they felt would have been had they been queried in the mid-1950s. Quite possibly the responses would have been different, reflecting the differences in American society between then and now. "Power to the people" has made an impact, even if in somewhat of a diffuse manner. At this time, though, the reactions seem to be "Yes," "No," and "It depends." If there ever has been such a thing as the "Imperial Superintendent," the comments alone indicate that that concept is no longer in vogue. Rather, even though there were affirmative responses to the question concerning feeling powerful, a pervasive tone throughout was one of a sense of limit, both personally and organizationally. Further, it seems as though this sense of limit is related to the territory in which the superintendent is operating. For example, a working hypothesis about the power of the superintendency might go something like this: To the extent that a superintendent's managerial duties (home territory) are involved, he is apt to feel powerful. When he moves outside the managerial part of his job, his power becomes diluted. That is, as he tries to exert influence across organizational and community boundaries, the question of having the power to get his way gets transformed into the question of having political acumen. He can recommend, set things in motion, and try to mobilize support. But as one superintendent said, "I can't change a teacher, really." Nor indeed, or so it seems, are superintendents able, for the most part, to propose decisions to the school board with an anticipatory attitude of fait accompli. Life, for superintendents, is no longer that simple, if it ever was.

Winning and Losing

The gamelike quality of much of a superintendent's activity has been previously noted. Games, of course, are a form of play, but unlike other forms of play—that of young children, or of parents or grandparents playing with young children, for example—they involve winning and losing. No adult plays a serious game with another adult in order to reach a tie.

On the whole, the superintendents in this study seemed to shy away from the idea that what they were involved in, ultimately, was a political game. The focus of their efforts, it seems, was much too serious for them to directly entertain the idea that their job had at its core the quality of very complicated play. However, in a way that suggests the possibility of efforts to repress the idea of the job as "game," they talked fairly extensively about the job in terms of winning and losing. It was not a job-unrelated concept at all, though the notion of "the superintendency as a game" seemed to be. Some of the superintendents dealt with the win-or-lose concept rather straightforwardly, coming down, of course, on the win side. After all, if one sees one's job in these terms, who wants to lose? Others hedged a bit and were more circumspect. But they, too, quite naturally wanted to win. Some examples of the unabashed "win" orientation follow:

> Yes, a lot of it is winning and losing. I put all my chips on the decision going my way. If my recommendation isn't supported, then I have lost, but I pick up somewhere else. I come up with another recommendation. The greatest loss of my whole career was the middle school foreign language program. But I'm going to tell you right now, mine was still the right recommendation. I wasn't angry about it, but I sure felt ineffective. There was a key to it that would have unlocked the door, but I couldn't find it. I felt very ineffective.

Yes, I see the job, I'm quite sure I see the job, as winning and losing. I would feel, for example, that if the budget went down when I thought it was reasonable, that would be a loss. I would personalize the loss. I would think that somehow it would be my fault.

I have to say that I do view the job as winning and losing. And I have to say it's unfortunate that I view it that way because I really don't like to be put in that position. I think I'm a pretty good loser. I get analytical about it and say "Why?" rather than getting frustrated by it. But during the fray, I'm damn well out there to win. I hate to say it, but it's true.

In the long run, I want to win, but I take a lot of temporary setbacks along the way. I absorb defeats and setbacks. I will not make a big deal about it today, but I'll be back next week, six months, a year later. I am persistent.

For some superintendents, then, conceiving of their job in win-or-lose terms is a central issue. Not that everything that comes across their desks is seen in this light; that orientation would be pathological. Nonetheless, one does get the image of people who have a design for things in their school district and who see the accomplishment of that design, or parts of it, mostly in win–lose terms. They don't win everything—particularly in the short run. But when they lose on a particular issue, they don't feel that the book is closed; instead, they make remarks such as "I pick up somewhere else" or "I'll be back." The picture bears so close a likeness to that of an elected public official having absorbed political defeats in trying to get a particular program approved that the resemblance is startling and probably, for some superintendents, a bit upsetting. A clue to that attitude comes from the superintendent who views his own win-or-lose orientation as an unfortunate reality of life. He sees himself as being "put in that position" by, one suspects, the changing perspectives of school district communities about who decides matters of school policy and budget. It's likely that this person speaks for many of his colleagues who feel "put in that position"—a situation where their success and, in some cases, their survival on the job, seems to demand that they be winners, when winning per se was not what they had in mind as an overriding career motivation. There is something sad about it: here are people who were motivated to seek a position from which they could apply their knowledge and expertise to create a better school experience for youngsters, only to find that the politics of winning and losing are more prominent in their lives than what may occur in the schools.

An interesting sidelight on the win-or-lose orientation came from a superintendent who, seeing himself as out to win, said,

> You also have to be willing to lose. Right now we've taken a gamble
> with one of our employees. She's a tenured teacher who happens to
> work for 11 months, and we've told her she can no longer do this.
> We want to cut her contract to 10 months. We know we don't have
> much of a case and that she can "grieve it" [bring a grievance] as a
> discriminatory action. But we felt it was the right thing to do, so
> we're going ahead with it and taking the gamble. We feel that we
> have enough chips in the bank so that if we lose one it's no matter.

A lay person, concerned with the quality of education in his or her community, might be surprised or shocked to hear the superintendent of schools speaking in these terms. They are not the words of an educational statesman. On the contrary, they are words that reflect the sophisticated politician at work. They are the words of a politician who wants to win, of course, but who recognizes that you can't win all the time; that sometimes it's all right to place a bet on a long shot, knowing you may well lose—if there are "enough chips in the bank." The point is that losing doesn't create a huge problem, if one still has enough residual leverage left to enable one to come back another time, perhaps on another issue—and win. The sophisticated superintendent–political strategist needs to be able to recognize which gambles he is likely to lose. Then, even if he loses, he still possesses a school management strategy for the long term. One doesn't doubt that if he loses this one, the superintendent will, in the words of one of his colleagues, "be back next week, next month, or next year."

While it is probably true, unless he is content with being a pawn of the school board, that he must have an overall winning average in the political battles in a school district in order to survive, there are superintendents for whom winning per se on all the issues that confront them is not the focus. Here are some responses that communicate something other than a straight win-or-lose orientation:

> If I thought of my job in those terms I'd have a loss score of about
> 500 to 1. I lose regularly. I lose on everything. I lose every day, but
> I keep coming back. All I have to do is win once. That's one of the
> advantages of being a superintendent. You can lose regularly on the
> day-to-day skirmishes, but all you have to do is win once. And then
> you've got the problem there, and you can hold it there.

> I try not to think of it as winning and losing, and I try not to think
> of negotiations, ever, as winning and losing. Sometimes I do have
> the feeling that I compromise myself; that what I would really like
> to do is to say, "No, damn it, this is the way it's going to be, and I
> don't care what happens, let the organization crumble." And there
> are times, in those situations, where I feel it was a real setback for
> myself.

There are certain situations that are winning or losing. I think with unions you win or lose. I try, however, not to create many situations in which I win or lose, because that's too black and white. It's negotiating, always negotiating. So much so that you don't even realize it.

Oh, there have been situations in which I really wanted to win, but I think it's unrealistic to conceive of the whole situation that way. What's important is to sense out the district's agenda and, if it's congruent with yours, try to help it move. If it's not congruent with yours, then you leave, but I don't think that's losing.

Before I became a "born-again" superintendent, I used to think it was all a matter of winning and losing. And I won most of the time, but it caused me some problems. I'd say to myself, "Why is it that when I fight like hell for a budget," and I used to get 99 percent of what I asked for, the board would say, "Well, you won again," or "We gave the superintendent what he wanted." I'd say, "Hell, it's what we *need* to run this school system." The problem is that when you win like that you also lose. You win five or six times, and the board says, "What the hell, we're becoming a rubber stamp for this guy."

The difference between these comments and those that came from the superintendents for whom winning and losing was a central concept is not attributable to situation. Though school districts and school boards certainly vary—and some are definitely more conflict-ridden than others—they vary along similar dimensions of organizational life. There is probably not a district that functions apolitically, for example, though the character of the politics differs from district to district. What we have observed, then, in these two groups of superintendents is different views of what the work world of the superintendent is like. This is not to place a value on one or the other, but simply to note the difference.

One senses, though, that a rather different organizational character would develop in districts where the superintendent's orientation is predominantly a win-or-lose one from that in a district where winning and losing is not focal to the superintendent's view of his job. For example, one can speculate that the approach of a win-or-lose–oriented superintendent to a conflict situation will differ from that of a superintendent who sees things as a continual process of negotiation, and thus of compromise. For the former, it would seem that "the aim of winning becomes a goal in itself, supplementing or even supplanting the original conflict of interest. This is a very personal matter" (Katz and Kahn, 1978, p. 634). Thus, a conflict, for a win-oriented superintendent, might become a zero-sum game or some slight modification thereof, and the district might experience itself as moving from one battle to another. After all, it is important for people for whom "winning becomes a goal in itself" to ensure that situations develop where one has the opportunity to test his mettle—and win. This is not to suggest, of course, that such a superintendent would consciously create these situations. rather, he would view the conflicts that arise in a school district as a challenge to his ability to win, and behave accordingly. In contrast, the superintendent whose attitude towards winning and losing is less polarized would probably see these inevitable conflicts as a challenge to is negotiating ability—and he would behave accordingly.

A final point is in order here. It is probably true that ideal types of these two orientations toward winning and losing in the superintendency rarely exist. More likely, they represent tendencies that superintendents have to move in one direction or another when confronted with actual or potential conflict. I have deliberately set the two orientations in juxtaposition to each other in order to contrast them. I also wanted to suggest that the behavioral tendencies inherent in each of them are real and that they affect both the work life of a superintendent and the school district he manages.

The Balancing Act

Regardless of a superintendent's orientation toward winning and losing, the situations he confronts in his daily work seem to require that he perform a continual balancing act. It is a delicate condition, its delicateness (to continue the metaphor) probably being related to (1) how high the tightrope wire is off the ground and (2) whether or not there is a safety net in place should he lose his balance. The height of the wire refers to how important the situation is to the superintendent personally or to the school system, and the safety net to the amount of support he has with the school board, the teachers, or the community, depending on the case at hand. The superintendents in this study made numerous comments about the balancing acts they engaged in. For example,

> Well, for instance, you know the union is going to be up in arms if I want to cut back staff. They're going to come out strong against it. "We need smaller class size, we need this, we need that." Okay. I understand that. Another group says we have to have more guidance people. Another wants more speech therapists. Another wants to cut the budget in half, and another says that we can't have any increase. So you have to do a balancing act. Sometimes you're in the middle, and it's kind of fun to be there because you have to keep things on an even keel.

> Yeah. For example, you have building principals who literally

detest certain teachers. I have one who detests the president of
my teachers' association. You name the adjectives. This guy [the
principal] will use them. Now I've got to live with this guy. It's a
political reality, and I'd like to have him in at least a decent frame
of mind. So I have to do a balancing act. I lean on him at times, but
then I buy him off by giving him something he wants. It's not
totally honest, but it keeps things somewhat peaceful.

Yes, it's a continuous balancing act, particularly when you're new
and until you've built up your credibility. After a time, though,
I've been able to build up my own power base. I become freer and
can tilt things in my direction easier.

It's always a balancing act because there are so many pressure
groups. More so than ever before, and the funny thing is that we
have made it happen that way. We have really pushed the idea that
everyone should be involved in the schools. So now I have so many
different constituencies out there with so many different interests
that my problem is to try and keep them appeased.

These are almost classical responses of people who understand that their
success and survival in their positions depend on their political acumen—
their ability to sense the character of the competing interests in a situation
and to behave in ways that keep these interests and themselves in balance. It
is important to realize, though, that merely keeping things in balance is not
what it's all about. Tightrope walkers don't want to maintain their balance so
that they can stand still—nor do most superintendents. For them, keeping
things in balance—and performing their own act, as well—is necessary for
movement, though there are times when the achievement of balance is of
positive value in itself, particularly when a system has been racked with
controversy. One superintendent reflected this idea when he said, "My problem is to keep them appeased." The district in question is a sprawling suburban one that includes a number of disparate socioeconomic and interest
groups and in which the teachers' union is strong and militant. Balance here
is indeed a desired goal in and of itself. There are undoubtedly times when
such a goal is appropriate for all school districts.

We note, however, that some other cues in the remarks just quoted that
cast a different light on the need to seek balance and to balance oneself. For
one superintendent, the politics of the balancing act are fun, particularly
when he finds himself in the middle. One senses that this superintendent
rather looks forward to those times when he must perform his own balancing
act so that he can "keep things on an even keel." These are times, and for
most superintendents they apparently occur frequently, that present a challenge to his political skills, thus creating a situation that for him is "kind of
fun." This comment suggests a somewhat different concept of the superin-

tendency as a win-or-lose game. To "win" in the arena of human affairs usually means to make one's views prevail in the conflict situation, and to "lose" is the opposite. There are certainly times, however, when one "wins" by being able to manipulate conflicting interests so skillfully as to keep the system in balance without major disruptions. Winning and the fun of winning, in these cases, has less to do with trying to ensure that one dominates a decision than it has with trying to ensure that the system remains in balance, or with keeping things peaceful, so to speak. Though he didn't suggest that it was fun, one of the superintendents just quoted specifically noted that a particular balancing act he had performed was designed to keep the peace—perhaps an armed truce—between a principal and the president of the teachers' association. That it wasn't fun can be inferred from the remark, "It's not totally honest, but . . .," with reference to his "buying off" the principal. Totally honest or not, keeping things in balance seems to require a sense of priorities, and there are probably times when one's ethical values take second place to the higher goal of keeping the system in balance and peaceful. It is probably true, then, as Boyd asserted, that on many occasions the need for a superintendent to be politically shrewd leaves little room for an open display of honesty. Burlingame, as we noted earlier, is most forthright (and courageous) in discussing that point.

Covering One's Tail

The phrase "Make sure you cover your tail" is not at all elegant, but it communicates a sort of folk wisdom about administrative life to which the interviewees responded knowledgeably. We were discussing the self-protective side of the superintendent's activity as he plays out the various scenarios of his role—as he tries to exercise power, to resolve conflict, to win or at least not to lose, for example. Superintendents of schools, of course, are not unique in their need to "cover" themselves—to make as sure as they can that when they emerge from a controversy, whether they win, lose, or draw, that their reputation for integrity and skillful management of the school district remains untarnished and that they have not been backed into a political corner from which it might be difficult to extricate themselves. Political and bureaucratic systems always seem to engender this need among those who govern or manage. It is more or less a fact of life, and that it holds for superintendents could be inferred from the very quick affirmative, and rather offhand responses they gave to the "covering one's tail" issue when it came up, as it did, in all the interviews conducted. For example:

> Hell, yes. There are certain issues, usually not of your own making, that arise. I can think of a recent one involving the placement of an

administrative intern. It wasn't a big deal, but it could have been embarrassing. Covering my ass in this case was simply a matter of writing a letter to the institution involved to let them know I was aware of certain circumstances. I got out from underneath it that way, on the record, and it became their problem, not mine.

I know there are times when I have said, "I'm going to make certain that I don't get hung out to dry on this one." For example, the first budget I inherited had overestimated revenues by about $130,000 out of a $6,000,000 budget. The board was never apprised of that, and I covered my own tail very quickly with a memorandum to the board. I didn't want them six months later asking what the hell happened. I guess, in my own mind, I've never done this kind of thing with the idea of feathering my own nest.

Well, I think you've got to be astute enough politically to know what's going to happen on things you propose and what the implications will be for you. There's no question about that. But do I spend most of my time covering my tail? I don't think so, and maybe I won't be around very long, because I don't!

Yes, I think all of us do that. A little bit. We try to keep things clean. The little things that bring about board–superintendent conflict are a buildup of those things that should have been taken care of. I think that if you can drop back and clean up your act a bit, it shows that you are trying to take care of things, as well as, quite frankly, protecting yourself. That's part of the game, and I think there's a part of us that's aware of that.

Yeah. You make sure you get there first.

What we seem to have, then, are some familiar images of the political mind at work—particularly the minds of executives whose occupational well-being and reputation for competence depend on developing and maintaining political support from various, and often conflicting, constituencies. It would be a mistake, though, to draw the conclusion that "covering one's tail" is a consuming preoccupation of superintendents. Rather, these administrators acknowledge pretty forthrightly that this concern is "part of the game." Part of the political equipment that superintendents apparently carry with them is a set of antennae whose function it is to warn them of those circumstances where wisdom dictates that they "clean up their act," "get there first," or "get out from underneath."

The need to protect oneself, or to survive, is not the sole motivation for this kind of behavior. Beyond the need to survive, if a superintendent is to influence the processes of education in his system, he must create the perception that he is "on top of things." It is important that he not be perceived as being easily caught by surprise or as embarrassed by not knowing what he "ought" to know. It's important that he not be seen as a person who isn't sensitive enough to small events that later prove to be embarrassing. This kind of competence—not technological expertise—is the stuff upon which confidence in political figures is based. Without such confidence, the person in charge is really not in charge, his potentital to influence others is severely reduced, and his ability to survive in the role of superintendent is in question. All this is not to say, of course, that "covering one's tail" is the primary strategy that superintendents use to build political confidence and influence. It is probably more accurate to say that if you don't do so, the building of such confidence and influence will be difficult, if not impossible.

Though the question dealing with the need to "cover one's tail" met with a generally affirmative response, there were some qualifications. One was noted by the superintendent who said, "I've never done this kind of thing with the idea of feathering my own nest." The implication, which he confirmed, was that he was aware of circumstances where colleagues of his had engaged in such covering activity for precisely this reason. Another person said,

> I know colleagues who tell me that whenever they make a decision they ask themselves, first of all, "How am I going to look? How am I going to come out of this?" That's not me. I don't go that way. I understand it, but I can't work that way. I can't just make myself look good, no matter what. I am just not that kind of person.

If one labels this discussion as concerned with "the ethics of 'covering one's tail,' " the issue can now be joined. *Ethics,* as I use it here, refers to the sometimes written, sometimes unwritten code of conduct that attaches to a profession. It includes both behavior and motivation. In the present case, what these two superintendents seem to be saying is that it is both all right and necessary to protect yourself—or as one person put it, "to watch your flanks"—as long as the motivation for doing that is aimed at keeping the system from being disrupted and, in the process, maintaining an image of competency. What is not all right is the motivation simply to look good, to create an image of the wise and infallible father or mother, as the case may be. I am not implying that the latter case is the usual one, though surely all of us, superintendents or no, have at times behaved in a manner intended primarily to make ourselves look good. I am implying that the position of the superintendency is one in which the pressures and conflicts sometimes act on a person so that he sees no alternative to trying to make himself look good— and the devil take the hindmost. We may not like to associate such self-concern with the role of superintendent of schools, the person who is supposed to model the highest values in the educational life of a community. However, it is probably part of the price that must be paid for the implicit demands that the character of our school systems place upon a superintendent of schools to be a politician.

5

The Superintendent and the School Board

A Historical Perspective

Here is the initial reaction of two superintendents when asked, "How about your dealings with the school board?"

> *Superintendent A:*
> The board is constituted to bring the absolutely necessary lay philosophy, whatever you want to call it, to the solution of technical problems. Without them, we would be in one hell of a mess, because I have a real inbuilt suspicion and distrust in experts in any field left totally unattended.

> *Superintendent B:*
> The board frustrates the hell out of me. I would say that running a school system is absolutely a pleasure, a delight—except for the board. I think the Board of Education should be someplace else and let me run the system.

We thus introduce a discussion of the most critical forum that exists as far as running a school system is concerned: that which involves the interplay of the superintendent and the school board. It is a forum in which both the drama of school decision making and that of the superintendent's professional and sometimes personal life gets played out.

Both the history of the superintendency and much of the research that has been conducted on the office have focused on superintendent–school board relations. For the most part, these studies have been concerned with trying to understand the broad sociopolitical character of that relationship and predicting patterns of interaction and decision-making consequences that might flow from one configuration or another. In this chapter, the approach is a narrow one as we attend to the variety of perceptions that the superintendents in this study had of the school board and their dealings with it. Although common threads appeared in the discussion, there were some sharp differences in the interviewees' attitudes toward the school board and in their analyses of the effect that having to deal with the board had on them.

First, though, a few general observations. On the face of it, with respect to their governance and day-to-day operations, school districts are organized for policymaking as are most other institutions, whether private or public, except for government bureaucracies. Corporations of any size have a board of directors whose role it is to set overall corporate policy. Hospitals, universities, and social agencies have their governing boards that have the same function. The organization, whatever its basic function, operates under the umbrella of general policies set by this governing group, and the chief operating officer of the organization is responsible to it. This pattern certainly holds for public schools, which have a school board, a school board president, and a superintendent. It is a very rational way to structure organizational life, at least in Western society. Further, because school boards tend to be composed of lay people and are typically, but not universally, elected, the theory is that they provide the means of community control of the schools.

What's the problem, then? Why does the history of the superintendency so frequently report conflict between school boards and superintendents? Why was it that the report of the Committee of Fifteen was viewed with such distaste by the editors of the *American School Board Journal* (see chapter 2)? And why has so much of the research on the superintendency been concerned with the superintendent's relations with the school board? Surely, one might think, there is much more to be concerned about in running a productive educational system than devoting one's intellectual and emotional energy to a group that meets once or twice a month for a few hours in the evening. The experience of the other types of organizations that have been noted above certainly does not suggest that their executives are nearly as concerned with their boards or that the conflicts between executives and boards of directors are as dramatic as the ones between superintendents and school boards. This is not to suggest that the governing boards in these other institutions are dismissed out of hand by the operating executives. On the contrary. But even a casual observer would acknowledge that only in a few, and rather isolated, circumstances have problems that attach to board-executive relations attracted much attention, and then certainly not the attention of the general public, historians, or social science researchers. How come? What's the difference? Why do issues of power and governance seem to be so much more important in the public schools than in other organizations?

The potential answers to these questions have been dealt with earlier, sometimes by implication and sometimes directly. Here we will try to summarize the underlying concepts to provide a context for the ensuing discussion.

You will recall Knezevich's statement that the superintendency was born in conflict and that a cause of the conflict was the antiexecutive attitude of the mid–nineteenth century. Schools were the public's business, and the public should not relinquish its power over them to any single official. Thus, in the early days it was the lay board and its many committees that were indeed running the schools. But as we have seen, the system grew in size and complexity and in the process became unwieldy in both its governance and operation. The situation was the other side of the organizational coin from that described in the Book of Exodus in the Old Testament. Much as the schools became too complex to be governed by many and large committees, so the numerousness of the Children of Israel presented similar problems for Moses as the only leader. It was at that point during the Exodus that Moses's father-in-law Jethro advised him to choose "rulers of thousands, and rulers of hundreds, rulers of fifties, and rulers of tens" (Exod. 18:21). This Moses did with dispatch.

The process of school boards divesting themselves of their power took much longer, and it was much more complicated. Part of the complications certainly had to do with the antiexecutive attitude to which Knezevich referred. American communities have long been jealous of their prerogatives, and the schools, as we are constantly reminded by school budget defeats, represent one of the last bastions of the community's control over its own destiny. Ceding public powers to a single individual is simply against the American tradition, and it is nowhere better symbolized than in the situations we are examining.

The increasing complexity of schools as social systems, however, was only one of the factors that contributed to the eventual alteration of the power relationships between school boards and superintendents. Two others stand out. There was the reform movement of the early 1900s, a reaction against the tendency of whatever political party was in office in a community to consider the schools its particular province for patronage. People were given jobs as administrators or teachers as rewards for party loyalty, without regard for qualifications. The spoils indeed belonged to the victors, but the reform argument was that the schools were too important a community institution to be subject to the personal preferences of whatever political party happened to be elected to office. Little is as sacred in American life as the education of children, and that all-important task should not be soiled with the profaneness of political influence. It was a powerful argument.

Second, there was the growth of the idea that educators are professionals and that they possess a body of knowledge and expertise essential to the education of children that is not held by members of lay boards. The message was that not only was the system becoming too complex as a system to be led by numerous lay groups but that the membership of these groups was by definition not competent for the task. They simply didn't know enough.

It seems, then, that the coming together of these three factors—the growing complexity of the system, the antipolitical reform movement, and the growth of educational administration as a profession—was the major circumstance that accounted for the shift in board–superintendent roles and relationships. It accounts for the character of school governance and the balance of power that typifies most school districts. But the situation, of course, is rarely an easy one for either school board members or superintendents. Issues of territory and office prerogatives tend to be ever-present. Further, although it is usually only in extreme conditions (such as during debate over whether to fire a superintendent) that these issues are publicly described in conflictual terms, few would deny that undercurrents of political conflict are nearly always present.

Implicitly, it is against this background that the superintendents in this study talked about their relations with their school boards. Their comments focused on their concepts of the board, the way they see themselves broadly functioning with it, the tensions and conflict they experience relative to it, their strategies and tactics for working with it, and their reactions to school board meetings.

Concepts of the School Board

Legally, of course, school boards are corporate bodies that derive their authority to organize and operate a school district from the state. They are responsible before the law for the district, its policies, its budget, and its program. The superintendent is typically seen as the board's executive officer, receiving his authority and responsibility from it. These comments, of course, serve no purpose except to put the concept of the school board into its legal framework, one that all superintendents would acknowledge as both a valid and appropriate one. But the framework says little about how a school board does or should operate, nor does it, except by very vague inference, define the character of the superintendent's relationship to the board. Presumably, the way one handles one's relationship to and behavior with a group depends on how one conceives the goals, structure, and processes of that group. With that premise in mind, we turn first to a sample of comments that reveal the way the superintendents in this study thought about the board as an entity.

> I think the thing with the board of education that the
> superintendent has to deal with, that I try to deal with, is to
> remember that boards are distinct people. They only come
> together, in my district, twice a month, and it is only at that time

that they are together as a collective body. And there are very few boards that are really totally cohesive. Most often, the members think differently on specific issues, so that conflicts occur. I have to work at reading that. You have to think about who is in the majority.

The board is seven individuals, and with every individual you have a different relationship. It's not a static thing. It's a moving thing as well. People change. Primarily, I see the board as the policy-determining body, with me as the chief administrative officer.

I think of the board both as individuals and as a group. But mostly I think about the individuals who make up the board, because it's through the individual that I establish my relationship and influence with the board as a whole.

There are two points in these comments, which echoed those that arose in the other interviews, that are of interest. First, note that none of these superintendents, nor any of those interviewed, expressed their concept of the school board in legal terms. Second, it can be seen that little attention was paid to conceiving of the board as a group with its own particular characteristics. Instead, the functioning of the board as a group, though it was acknowledged, was shunted aside, and the emphasis was put on the individuality of the board members and their idiosyncratic concerns. This does not mean that the superintendents regarded the board as a social entity, and its monthly or semimonthly meetings, as inconsequential. Indeed, quite the opposite is the case, as we shall see later in this chapter. It does appear to mean, though, that the political composition of the board, the personalities of the members, and the platforms on which they were elected stood out more in the minds of these superintendents than the degree to which the board functions as a group. Boards appear to be conceived of as political bodies, not as collaborative problem-solving groups. It is the politics of individual voting that counts. These politics, of course, may be related to the dynamics of the board as a group, but the focus of these comments remains on the individual board member. It is he or she who votes, not the group.

It is not surprising that superintendents have tended to think of the school board in terms of individual members rather than as a group. Both the superintendent's professional reputation and his personal welfare depend greatly on his ability to influence its decisions. Further, it is primarily through the one-to-one linkage between superintendent and school board member that attempts to influence take place. There is nothing necessarily underhanded about this. It is an accepted and legitimate part of the workings of our political institutions—and lest there by any misunderstanding, school boards definitely are political institutions. In addition, and most important to our discussion, the fact that school boards are political institutions mandates many dimensions of the role that superintendents play in relation to the board.

Functioning with the Board

On the face of it, if one takes a strict legal construction of superintendent–school board relations, the way in which the superintendent relates to his board, the functions he performs, and the roles he enacts might be seen as a relatively simple matter. The board makes policy, and the superintendent carries it out.

Would that the situation was that simple. But simple it is not, and for a variety of reasons. We focus on one. It will have a familiar ring and illustrates the complexity of the situation well. School boards are lay groups that exercise policymaking power over an institution the workings of which have, at least, a quasi-technological base. But then, everybody has been to school and "knows" how things should be done. Superintendents are hired for their expertise as educators and managers. They are assumed to really "know" how things should be done. However, leaders or not, they are employees, and, as has been suggested earlier, in a very real way their welfare depends on keeping the board happy or minimally unhappy. Some superintendents are hired rather explicitly with the mandate to preserve the status quo, and in those cases, if that mandate suits the particular individual, keeping the board happy may not be a big problem—except if a particularly militant teachers' union starts to assert itself. Most superintendents, though, do not see themselves as "minders of the store." They want to be known as people who influence the quality of education in a school district by using both their educational expertise—or whatever myths have been created about it—and their management know-how.

The bind, then, goes something like this: We have an expert—by definition, if nothing else—who cannot exercise his expertise on matters of any real substance without getting the support and confirming decision of a number of nonexperts (the school board) who are influenced by a host of other nonexperts (the community). This latter group, for many intents and purposes, are the same kind of people who are on the board and therefore also "know" how things should be done. Further, this global situation is not a stable one, since in many systems there is frequent turnover in board membership, presenting the superintendents with the likelihood of having to deal with a group of new nonexperts every other year or so, and sometimes more often.

What, then, do superintendents do under these circumstances? How do they go about establishing the type of relationships with the board that will enable them to develop the system in what they think is the best way? As in any other human relationship, no single set of techniques that can guarantee success is available; life is much too complicated for that. However, some overall propositions about how superintendents function in relation to school boards and the related problems seem to emerge from the following comments:

> I believe you can't have enough communication with the board. You can't! You can't! I think sometimes we forget that they are our immediate employer. This really influences me. I want to keep them informed of all major developments. I want them to know when I'm taking risks and when I goof up. I don't want them to have any surprises. I guess that's the catchword. No surprises. And I don't promise too much. It would be ridiculous of me to say I'm going to eliminate the use of drugs on the part of teenagers in this district, totally ridiculous. You've got to get them to set reasonable expectations. I level with them all the time. And you never divide the board. Never! If you have a 9-member board and there's a 7–2 split on an issue, whatever you do, don't communicate with just the 7. It's the biggest mistake a superintendent can make, and it's made over and over again.

> I get upset with board members who sometimes go out and speak about items they don't know anything about. They do it at board meetings, too. They'll talk about an issue and have it completely wrong. So I have to carefully manipulate this thing around so as not to embarrass a person and still get the point across. So I say something like, "Well, Mr. X was talking about one incident, but generally that's not so." I let him down very gently.

> There was an issue in which I made an administrative decision with which the board was starting to interfere. It was a gut decision, and I was either going to have 100 percent support or tell them to shove it. If they would have voted against me, I would have packed up that same day and left.

> Roles are different. You better watch out with a factional board, and with any board you can't become friendly with any particular member. You've got to keep yourself in a very open and honest relationship with the board. I was told once that I told them too much, but I don't believe that. Everything you get, you tell them. I send them a packet of things on Fridays. It's loaded with all kinds of information, including complaints and how they were handled. You've got to watch that you don't get too close to anyone connected with the board. And, on the outside, you've got to keep your mouth shut.

It's a back and forth kind of thing, and it's political, too. Every year, you get a new board, in the sense that there are one or two new members. In this community, we get a new president, too. So every July through October, there is a defining of roles. I tell them that if they want a go-fer, then they should hire a go-fer. But that's not me. There's a lot of jockeying back and forth to see where the power is.

I guess that I have tried to act as a teacher to boards of education, and I guess I teach myself and other administrators along the way.

I have it written in my contract that any issue brought to a board member when he's not functioning at the board table, which is the only place that individual can function as a board member, must come directly to me. No board member can go to any member of our staff without going through me.

Well, I have to train them; teach them. People who run for boards have no concept of what it's all about. They don't know that when they become a board member, they become a member of a corporate body and it is that body that makes decisions, not them as individuals. They have to learn that they don't go around snooping into things on their own. The big problem comes when we have new members who get elected because they are champions of one cause or another.

You have to make the determination early in your life as a superintendent that, okay, you can have board members as social friends, but if you do, you better have all of them as social friends. And it's the same thing with the operation of the board. I try not to splinter them in any way, shape, or manner.

What we have, then, is a brief primer of superintendent–school board relations. It can be read in at least two ways. One way is to think of these comments as suggesting some rules of thumb for superintendents: provide information, lots of it; never divide the board, either in a work sense or socially; be honest; don't be a pawn; let them know where you stand and what you're about; make sure the boundaries of responsibility are understood, and teach the board about them if you have to; understand that they come to the situation with their own interests and pressures. These all seem to be valid points, but there is nothing new or startling about them. They could be chapter headings in a "how to" book concerning methods of establishing an effective school board, a point which is not meant to denigrate their importance.

The second way of reading these comments is of more interest for our purposes here. We can read them as a set of ground rules to the *politics* of superintendent–school board relationships. In order to make the general point clearer, one must keep in mind the structure of those relationships. The superintendent—the expert—has no direct power over the group that can legitimate his expertise in the form of policy. But few superintendents want to be "go-fers," the term used by one of the interviewees. They want to have some impact on their district other than being seen as efficient caretakers. That impact comes primarily through their ability to *influence* the board.

Viewing superintendent–school board relationships this way, then, puts the ground rules in a different light. The superintendents' comments reveal some of the underlying factors involved in the politics of the situation. For example, providing the board with information—some of it critical of the schools—even when it's not asked for certainly serves the function of keeping members of the board informed about issues that confront the district. However, it also lets the board know that the superintendent is interested in keeping them informed and that having the district or parts of it criticized is not threatening to him. More subtle purposes are also served as the superintendent conveys a wide variety of information to his board. For example, he gains the reputation of not being secretive and of not trying to "pull a fast one." In addition, by supplying lots of information, he communicates that he thinks that (1) the board is entitled to it as the system policymaking body, and (2) its members are intelligent people who will use the information to make appropriate decisions. There is a psychological point to it all, then. As the superintendent behaves in ways that indicate his trust in the board, he no doubt hopes that he will be trusted in return. Further, as the superintendent gains credibility as a person who can be trusted, he also extends his sphere of influence with the board.

Another political ground rule was "Never divide the board, either in a work sense or socially." There are times in the larger political arenas of government when in order for the executive to get his program approved by a legislative body, he or she must indeed work to cause or exacerbate splits. Why isn't this good strategy with a school board? The reason is found, first, in the employee status of the superintendent. He is dependent upon the board not only for support for policy decisions that he favors but for his personal well-being and that of his family. And while it is true that he may achieve a short-term victory by actively working to splinter the board, it is quite apt to turn out to be a Pyrrhic victory: he will have won, but he will also have exacerbated conflicts among board members and certainly between the losers and himself. His future relationship with the board is apt to be clouded with ongoing conflict. Another reason to avoid splintering the board has to do with the superintendent's reputation as a professional. Superintendents develop reputations that go beyond their district, usually through informal networks. And these administrators do move from district to district, especially those who in Carlson's (1972) terms are career-bound rather than place-bound. Discretion, then, is the better part of valor for those who wish to move. School boards are understandably reluctant to hire a superintendent who has developed a reputation for having split boards, even though he may have won a few victories in the process.

The case for another of the ground rules suggested by an interviewee—being careful of one's social relations with board members—is less clear in its political implications. It would seem more an admonition to be aware of the fact that petty jealousies develop among board members as they do within any group. The superintendent would do well not to be seen as behaving in ways that might encourage such jealousies to occur. What is at issue, of course, is not that his personal life would become more complicated but that such personal conflicts might interfere with the functioning of the board.

Some of the other rules—"Be honest"; "Don't be a pawn"; "Let them know where you stand and what you're about"—are almost accepted virtues for an American executive. Even if we don't agree with the position the executive takes or if we think him misguided, we tend to respect the honesty. But as with other aspects of the superintendent's behavior with the board, there is more to being honest, forthright, and assertive than just exhibiting those virtues. They tend to inspire trust in the superintendent and build his credibility, and the lack of these two ingredients to the relationship—trust and credibility—makes for an untenable situation for the superintendent and the board, creating a situation in which, indeed, politics—using the term this time in the pejorative sense—becomes the order of the day. Ultimately, under these conditions, the superintendent will either be asked to leave or will see the handwriting on the wall and take his own departure.

Now at this pont the reader may recall that Burlingame said, "I seriously doubt that honesty is the best policy for superintendents who wish to retain power" (1981, p. 429). Burlingame is not a superintendent, but he is a student of educational organizations, and his position certainly is at wide variance from the one that has been suggested above. The issue can be made clearer, I think, by reference to a personal experience. I was impressed by Burlingame's thinking, so I sent a copy of the article to a superintendent friend of mine in another state who had the reputation for being honest, strong, politically astute, and highly respected by his community and his colleagues. He is also a student of the superintendency. After a week or two had gone by, I called him about another matter and, in passing, asked how he had reacted to the article. His response surprised me a bit. The article had made him uncomfortable, he said, and he had discarded it. When I asked him why, his response was that Burlingame's argument made him feel unmasked, and this was uncomfortable.

I am certainly not suggesting that the superintendents in this study were being untruthful when they talked about how necessary they felt it was to be honest with their boards and said that they were honest with them. But we have established the essential politicalness of the superintendent's relationship to the board and the corresponding tenuousness of that relationship. Since we know that in politics honesty is not always regarded as the best policy, we must raise the possibility that the superintendent's dealings with the board involve varying shades of honesty. I would assume, for example, that most superintendents do not deliberately lie to their boards. I would also assume, however, that the stakes and pressures associated with the superintendent–school board relationship are such as to induce the superintendent, as he sees the demands of the total situation to require something other than total honesty on his part, to engage in the various ploys that will help him to mystify or cover up, as Burlingame (1981) puts it. And he does this in order to maintain the system and his position in it.

I am not implying that superintendents are merely petty politicians whose only concern is to stay alive in the system by fair means or foul. That would certainly not fit with my knowledge of and experience with them, though that description would undoubtedly apply to a few. The correct inference, I think, is that political circumstances that govern a superintendent's relations with his school board are such that, at times, the virtue of honesty in all its forms is not the best policy.

Conflicts and Tensions

It would be highly unlikely, given all the foregoing, for the system that is created by the superintendent–school board structure to be free of underlying tension and conflict. One interviewee talked about the situation in some depth. He prefaced his remarks by saying that he felt comfortable and positive about himself in his role, that he was good at it, and that he felt he could be successful in practically any type of district. He conveyed a picture of a highly confident and competent person, and in fact his reputation among his colleagues is just that. But immediately following these comments about himself and his ability to do his job, he shifted gears, saying

> All these positive feelings I have about myself as a superintendent
> do not occur without a sense of insecurity that I have sometimes in
> the position. When I really put the position under analysis, the
> degree of incongruity, the degree of vulnerability that I'm exposed
> to sometimes generates waves of insecurity in me. As good as I
> think I am and as good as I think I've done my job—all of that can
> be blown away very quickly. Here's what I mean. I could do a real

good job, but if the board, or a cluster of the board, feels it is not good, I don't have any impartial court to stand in front of to defend myself. The board is both judge and jury, and that makes me insecure at times.

Boards tend to do their job in a very spotty way. I get concerned about how much they are listening and believing and trusting. I always feel like I'm a hired gun. And sometimes I feel like I'm a carpetbagger. I'm here to do a job. And I say to myself, "What else am I buying while I do the job? Maybe I want more. It's a vague thing." But boards are capricious. They turn over. They like what you're doing on one hand, but maybe they don't like your style on the other. And sometimes I sense that some board members think I'm too uppity. I'm too secure. And if they are insecure people, I know I don't make it with them. I know I don't! I didn't make it as a kid with insecure people. If I get a majority of them on the board, then I know I can have a problem. I have had individuals like that, and I have tended to stomp on them, and I've gotten away with this so far. I have a very aggressive demeanor. I am in control, and it's worked for me so far. But when I go out and meet with colleagues and I see guys who have had their asses creamed, I say, "Wait a second. When is it going to happen to me?" That's your insecurity. Because you say, "Hey, this guy isn't bad, and look what happened to him." You know, you hear stories about guys who go to the AASA [American Association of School Administrators], and when they come back there's a letter on their desk requesting their resignation because they spent public money to go to AASA. So you think, "That could happen to me." I worry about that. Not every day, but it's there.

What we have, then, is a sense of the yin and yang of the superintendent's relationship with his school board. Regardless of one's personal feelings of competence, there are basic insecurities connected with the job, and they revolve principally around the superintendent's relationship with the school board, both in its interpersonal process dimension and in its political struc-ture, fact-of-life dimension. School boards are not by definition mean or capricious, though they are subject to influence attempts from the political and vested-interest breezes that blow in a community—as they properly should be. The superintendent's relationship with the school board seems to reflect the continuing conflict concerning how schools should be run in American society.

The question seems always to be one of power and authority, and clearly, when these are issues in a relationshp such as we have been describ-ing, it is the full-time jobholder to whose position the underlying insecurities are attached—not the part-time governing board. Superintendents, after all, are not tenured in their office and probably shouldn't be.

There may be readers who will react to the comments of this particular superintendent by saying, "Well, to listen to the way he talks about dealing with his board—stomping on them occasionally—he ought to feel insecure. That simply isn't the way to treat people who hire you and can fire you." Certainly, the element of one's personal behavioral style may take on a central focus in all this from time to time. But it seems to me that is not the underlying concern in superintendent–school board relationships. It misses what is truly essential to the understanding of the condition, and that is, to repeat, that it inevitably involves subsurface but sometimes open conflicts of power and authority. The question that continually confronts school boards and superintendents but that seems to be addressed only during times of conflict is "Who's boss?" It's not surprising, then, that the position has some peculiar insecurities attached to it.

One may take the viewpoint, of course, that life as a whole is a fairly insecure matter and that most jobs have elements of insecurity attached to them. Why make a special case of the superintendent of schools? The response is that the problem is raised not as a means of offering our sympathy to these people. Quite the contrary, sympathy is not the issue except when a superintendent one knows gets fired, not because he was an incompetent educator but because he was a less than skillful politician. The real point of the discussion is that one cannot understand the behavior of superintendents, and thus the character of the decisions and the decision-making processes that occur in school systems, unless one also understands both the ongoing conflicts and the tentativeness of the situation in which practically all superintendents must operate. One superintendent framed the circumstances in rather down-to-earth terms as he recalled part of a conversation he had with his board president on a personnel employment matter. He said, "I told the board president very candidly that one of the things that was going to happen long range was that either I would give up and the board would overpower me, or I wouldn't give up and they would throw me out on my ear." This seems to be a simple and rather straightforward comment, but it cloaks what we have come to understand is a very complex relationship.

Other types of pressures develop between superintendents and school boards that are sometimes more subtle but ultimately still boil down to the question of role and power. It will be recalled, for example, that one of the early cries that was raised to remove politics from the schools was motivated by what was seen as unabashed political influence in the hiring of school personnel. Schools were too important to be subject to such practices. The public, applying pressure through the school board, has not given up the ghost on these efforts. However, they seem not to be crowned with success, as the following two remarks illustrate:

> I think somewhere along the line I have always, on occasion, been pressured to hire people. And I have been very careful of that. I tell them, "Thank you. I appreciate your recommendations. We'll certainly look at the candidate because you, as a board member, recommended him. But because you recommended him, we will also interview him, which we don't do with every applicant. But that's all we'll do. If he doesn't make the grade then, we're sorry." I think they have begun to accept that, because I haven't deviated from my position.

> Pressure from a board member to hire a person is a common experience for me. I try to be up front about it and voice my concerns. What I try to do is to control the situation so that it occurs in a more formal setting, rather than having an individual come in and say, "I know so-and-so would be a heck of a teacher, and she's a friend of X." And it goes for custodians as well as teachers. I always feel tremendous pressure at those times, and what I would like my response to be to the individual is that it's unfair. I rarely say that, first, because I recognize the person is a board member. Second, although they may be a little insincere, they're also trying to help a friend. But they're applying pressure, and they know it. I try to be straight with the person about our procedures, but I'm always careful. I don't want to put a little fragment in that guy's mind that may block me in the future.

One supposes that these comments simply reveal another "part of the territory" that goes with the job, and apparently that is precisely the case. It also appears that these situations get handled with relative ease. The superintendent stands on rather solid institutional and procedural ground to which board members themselves have assented. But one should also note that these situations are not simply cut-and-dried affairs, and each of the men who commented gave clues to that lack of directness in his response. For one, it was a promise that a candidate would indeed be interviewed. For the other, it was sublimating his feelings about being pressured and being careful about how he responded.

Circumstances such as these do not constitute major problems for superintendents. But even when there are cut-and-dried procedures that effectively negate influence attempts on the part of individual board members, the circumstance itself is not cut-and-dried. Instead, the rule seems to be "Fragile Relationship. Handle with Care."

School Board Meetings

This chapter opened with the idea that the interplay between the superintendent and the school board constituted the critical forum as far as running the schools was concerned. We turn now to the setting of that forum, the monthly (or, in some cases, semimonthly) school board meeting. Our object here is not to analyze these meetings, but, as before, to inquire into the meaning they may have for understanding the work life of superintendents. Here is a sample of the reactions that the interviewees had when they were queried about their school board meetings.

> The day before the board meeting is a tough and busy one. I want to make sure I have all the material ready. The time that's most difficult for me with board meetings is immediately after they're over, as I'm lying in bed trying to sleep. I think about the things I didn't say and that I might have said, and things like that. I replay the board meeting before I sleep, and sometimes it takes a long time.

> Yes, there's tension connected with it, especially on the day of the meeting. It's not because I anticipate conflict, but because it's the most important meeting I go to, month in and month out.

> The biggest pain in the neck with the school board is preparing the meeting agenda on Friday before the Monday-night meeting. And then I have to sit with them, sometimes till 2 A.M. listening to them discuss minutiae. It exhausts me.

> There are certain of my board meetings that have created tension for me. It's when you get to a decision point on a major program, when the issue is going to be put to the test, and you can say you've got it or you don't.

> In this district, board meetings have tended to be almost dull affairs. The most difficult problem I have is getting them to hold adequate discussion on issues. Maybe they trust us too much. If the meetings go beyond 11 o'clock, it's unusual. A couple of weeks ago, one lasted about an hour and a half and then they just sat around and talked because they didn't want to go home too early.

> The day of the board meeting is usually not a good day, but it all depends on the items that are on the agenda. I usually anticipate the stressful ones, especially from the public. But I've always found they're more stressful for the board than the superintendent. So I tell them to stay out of it and let me take the heat. But you know, we fantasize a lot, always the worst, and it doesn't happen.

That forum, then, takes on a variety of colorations. There was the tensionless, dull situation that seemed to be more of an aberration than the rule. (It was reported, significantly, by a superintendent of a fairly small and relatively encapsulated community.) The other superintendents reported that the meetings and anticipation of them tended to be tension-producing. For some, it was simply the knowledge that it was an important time, a time in which decisions could be made or when a hostile public might be present. For another, it was a "pain in the neck" that involved endless, and probably mindless, discussion. And for another the board meeting may well have been the high-tension point of the month, since he replayed the board meeting and his role in it sometimes for hours before being able to go to sleep.

These reaction patterns seem to be ongoing; when the superintendents spoke about them they weren't actually thinking about their last board meeting. The question is, How do we account for the individual differences? Why would one superintendent be primarily concerned with the way he played out his role, another with the character of the meeting itself, another finding tension associated with board meetings only at important decision times, and so forth?

It is tempting to respond that the question is primarily related to personality differences. That response would suggest that the superintendents reacted differently because they are different people, as indeed they are. They have different needs, tolerance levels, and emotional predispositions. However, if one takes this position, one also says that a superintendent's behavior (or any other person's) is precisely equal to his personality and that he will behave and feel similarly regardless of the situation. Obviously, this is not the case. We need no better evidence than our own experience, which tells us that though we carry our own personality within us, unchanged from day to day, we do change our behavior and emotionality in congruence with the different social settings in which we find ourselves and our perceptions of the characters and demands of that setting.

We are led, then, to suggest that the differences in superintendent reactions to school board meetings can be accounted for by thinking of these reactions as functions of an individual personality and the character of the board and the community it represents. For example, the man who played back his role for hours before he went to sleep is superintendent of a district in which there has been a large amount of board and community conflict. His position is a bit tenuous there. One would expect him to be tense about meetings and to focus his thoughts on what he did right and wrong. A different setting would quite likely yield different reactions on his part. Likewise, the superintendent who seemed only to experience tension at important decision points serves in a district that is not noted for being highly conflictual. It would be expected that if he moved to a different district—one that was marked by unrest—his reactions would also change. Or, if the man whose board engages in discussion of trivia until the wee hours of the morning became associated with a board whose concens were with major educational issues, one would presume that he would not refer to his preparation for meetings as the "biggest pain in the neck." In general, then, the point is that school board meetings do seem to constitute a source of tension, but not a universal one, for school superintendents. The specifics involve both the individual—his needs and tolerances—and the complexion of the board and its background community.

In this chapter, the aim has been to sketch out the broad outline of a superintendent's relationships with the school board, his primary reference group. Though it may be that with this group he is best able to combine his roles of educational statesman and political strategist, we have seen that the balance of thoughts, behaviors, and emotions appears to weigh in favor of the latter. The relationship, at its roots, does seem to be characterized by some basic elements of insecurity for the superintendent. Superintendents *have* been victimized by vagrant political breezes that waft through the board. The message for superintendents and would-be superintendents is the need to treat the board and its members somewhat gingerly, while at the same time maintaining one's sense of oneself as a person and respect for oneself as an educator.

6

The Superintendent
and the Teachers' Union:
Issues of Organizational Control

There is little question that the superintendents derive their authority and power from the school board and that the board is thus their most important reference group. There is also little question that their authority and power, in this day and age, is diminished in great numbers of school districts by the teachers' union. If there ever was a time of the "imperial superintendent" it certainly has passed, even in that dwindling number of states where teachers' association or unions have yet to be sanctioned as legal collective bargaining units under state labor relations laws.

In this and the following chapter, we examine some dimensions of the superintendent's relationship with the teachers' union. We will focus on a range of attitudes that superintendents have toward unions in both formal and informal settings. We will also discuss problems that a couple of superintendents—our sample here is very limited—have experienced under the condition of a teachers' strike.

Some Historical Notes on Teachers' Unions

A brief bit of background is necessary. Though it may appear, perhaps because of the media publicity that has been given to teachers' strikes, that the idea of teacher unionism is of relatively recent vintage, this is really not the case. Articles, editorials, and essays concerning teachers and labor unions appeared as early as the 1920s. Indeed, a dispute over salary in Seattle in 1929 was motivation for its high school teachers to try to organize themselves into a union. The board of education of that city denied that organizing a union was a right of teachers, and their position was sustained by the court (*School and Society*, 1928). The teachers there did, however, affiliate themselves with the American Federation of Labor. Their organization was called the Seattle

High School Teachers Union No. 200. Though not directly connected with the Seattle situation, some indication of the public view of teachers' unions 50 years ago is evidenced in an article by McAndrew (1932, p. 131) in which he suggested that their members were "soreheads, publicity seekers, Bolshevists, the educational underworld," and that this was not "the time to irritate the public."

Whatever was the form of the teachers' union movement after that time, it seemed to slumber its way through the next three decades. Several reasons may be advanced for this inactivity. First, of course, is the fact that the right of public employees to organize and bargain collectively had not received legal sanction. In fact, there does not appear to have been much concern about mobilizing political power or public support to enact such legislation. Why this was so is open for speculation. One might assume, for example, that the Great Depression years were inauspicious times for such efforts. Jobs were too hard to get, and school boards and superintendents held unchallenged authority over hiring and firing. There was no such thing as "just cause" in those years. The decade of the forties, with World War II and its immediate aftermath of striving for recovery, and that of the fifties, where the nation seemed to be relaxing, also did not seem to provide fertile ground for the development of widespread teacher unionism. Not only were the times not right, but there was also the pervasive and widely held notion that somehow it was not appropriate for teachers to organize themselves in labor union fashion. It was unseemly and not professional. Teachers were teachers because they loved to teach children. Matters of working conditions and remuneration were secondary. At least, that is part of the myth, and it probably had some substance.

The 1960s witnessed a change—a radical one—that was possibly inevitable. The nation's economy was booming, and it is probable that teachers saw themselves as not sharing in the prosperity. Additionally, it seems clear that both the legal and legislative system had begun to take a more liberal view toward the rights of public employees to organize themselves and bargain collectively with their employer. Probably the best-known statute that reflected this change as far as the schools were concerned was the so-called Taylor Law, which was passed by the New York State Assembly in 1967. One may be sure, of course, that that law was passed less out of the goodness of heart of the state legislators than because the teachers' organizations were starting to become a cohesive and powerful force in state politics. Significantly, though the Taylor Law gave teachers and other public employees the right to organize and mandated that school boards bargain collectively with them, it did not sanction the right to strike. On the contrary, it provided for both individual and collective financial penalties that could be levied on teachers and their unions at the discretion of the courts upon petition of the school board.

At this writing, about 40 states have enacted legislation that permits the legal existence of teachers' unions, including, of course, the right to bargain collectively. One need not know that in order to know the extent to which organizing has taken place all over the country. One need only read of the whereabouts of teacher strikes that seem, in the last few years at any rate, to have greeted the opening of school in September.

In addition to the obvious power that has accrued to teachers' unions in local school districts, they have become politically powerful on the state level. In many states, they have developed highly active and influential lobbying groups, and there are few state legislators who can afford to utterly ignore their influence attempts. For example, in New York State the strength of the movement for enacting a licensing statute for teachers is almost entirely a function of the pressure of NYSUT: New York State United Teachers. Without this pressure, one can be sure there would be no such move. One should not interpret these comments, incidentally, to be any sort of negative or, for that matter, positive, evaluation of the political activities of teachers' organizations. All that is intended is an observation that teachers, through their unions, have assumed a political role in our society that has gone far beyond the everyday concerns of salary and working conditions. In this respect, they have become part, and an important part, of our way of government.

Finally, it hardly needs to be said that the growth in numbers and power of teachers' unions has had a less than enthusiastic response from school boards. The reasons are not hard to find, and we mention a few. Unions tend to be seen by boards as intruding on their power prerogatives; as partly responsible for the increased costs of running a district; as engaging in unseemly activities for people who would call themselves professional; and, sometimes, just as a plain nuisance. Regardless of the extent to which these perceptions are grounded in fact, it is probably fair to say that there are few school board members who would not fantasize a happier condition of school governance if there were no teachers' unions. But the fantasy is just that. Teachers' unions will not be wished away, nor should they be, since they constitute a legitimate voice in the political arena in which school systems exist.

The Superintendents Comment on Unions

School boards, of course, rarely get involved directly with the union other than during the period when collective bargaining negotiations are in process. Even during those times, their involvement is typically not face-to-face. They may, and frequently do, work through a negotiator without any direct contact themselves. Quite the contrary condition holds for superintendents. Though in larger districts, a director of personnel may be responsible for dealing with the union on daily problems that arise, it is the superintendent who must ultimately deal with it on the institutional level. It is also likely that his stance toward the union determines the type of emotionality that pervades the relationship between the union and the district. His stance, of course, becomes obvious to union members through his behavior. For example, does he distance himself or reach out to the union? What kinds of issues does he consider legitimate for discussion and what kinds illegitimate? Whatever he does vis-à-vis the union, the superintendent is continually throwing off cues concerning how it should regard him. These cues set the tone of the relationship, and they, in turn, are a function of the general attitude set that the superintendent has toward teachers' unions in general and toward the one with which he is currently dealing. It is with that attitude set that we start our discussion.

Here is the way a number of interviewees thought about the teachers' union as a system with which they have to deal:

> I think that as I'm looking at it now rather than [as I did] seven or eight years ago, that, basically, they're good things. At the beginning, I would have said, "No." I think I would have been completely correct in my evaluation then. I really think they have gone beyond the question of dollars and turf. They are concerned more, now, about larger problems of education, the curriculum, etc. As a matter of fact, if I were to pick the point that I thought I could make an impact on education in a good way, I would try to get a job with a teachers' union.

> I think they're inevitable. I think collective bargaining is inevitable. The old notion that public servants have no right to bargain collectively will disappear. I do not feel that teachers should have the right to strike. If I had my "druthers," I would wish the unions weren't there. But they are, and I think we have to face that and be willing to deal with them or get out of the business.

> I don't really have any experience without it, first as a teacher and now as a superintendent. I tend to think the unions really are not that bad, especially with the state being so tough on us about funds. They put pressure on the legislature and they certainly put pressure on the board. It all helps us pay them fairly decently.

> I would say there was a need for collective bargaining. There were needs for clear definitions of working conditions. There is no question that board members and representatives of the community were, at times, arbitrary and officious. What bothers me, though, is the movement they have made in the curriculum areas. I truly see the control of education being wrested away from the public. I see this as incompatible with the purpose of the institution. And I

don't believe the justification of "what's good for the kids." Too often, interests of comfort, convenience, and security take priority over the kids.

It is absolutely a good thing. For one thing, teachers are no longer beggars. They don't have to go with their hat in their hand and ask for a raise. I hear of superintendents who want to go back to the fifties. It's a very naive attitude.

It's a good thing and a not-so-good thing, I suppose. I think unions have done some good. Certainly, they've brought up salaries for the teaching profession. And I think maybe they've improved communications. And they certainly have made teachers a force to be reckoned with in community affairs and politics. But there have been negative effects, too. Where does dedication come in? Where is that extra mile that people in the profession should give? I think kids are starting to come in second and third compared with the union's demands for its teachers.

I guess teacher unionization had to come. But I'm not so sure about it all. I would like to think that there ought to be some alternative. I guess it's a necessary evil that I have to live with.

I'm a staunch supporter of the union and collective bargaining. For years, I've felt that teachers didn't have a piece of the action in any matters pertaining to curriculum, working conditions, and practices or anything.

What we have, then, is a mixed bag of attitudes about teachers' unions. There are superintendents for whom teacher unionization was not only something that had to take place but also a welcome development. For one man, in particular, his memories of his teaching days when teachers had to "go with their hat in their hand" was enough of a humiliating experience to make him cast other considerations aside. If it took the union movement to make teachers no longer beggars, then, according to this person, whatever price has to be paid is well worth it. This thinking can be pushed a bit by suggesting that a system that has the effect of making beggars—a strong descriptor, and possibly a hyperbolic one—out of its employees when it came to matters of salary is a system that has something wrong with it. No one can truly be adult when that kind of dependency characterizes the employer–employee relationship.

Another superintendent, however, tended to place a negative value on that part of the union–school board relationship that placed emphasis on matters of "the dollar and turf." Had the unions made this their only motivator, his evaluation of their appropriateness on the educational scene would have been consistently negative. It was when, from his experience and perspective, they became concerned with other matters—curriculum, for example—that his attitude started to change to the point where he saw teachers' unions as a potentially very powerful force for upgrading the quality of education in the public schools. His position, though, is opposed to that of the superintendent who is supportive of the union's focus on working conditions and all that entails. What bothers him is precisely what excites two of his colleagues: the movement into curricular areas. His concern here seems quite clearly not to be a matter of substance but one of form. The issue is one of control, and the question is, Who should control the content of what goes on in the schools: the teachers or the public, through its elected school board? He comes down, of course, on the side of the public and takes it as a philosophical issue. To whom do the schools belong, the public or the teachers? Perhaps, at a deeper level, this superintendent was raising the issue of the proper place and influence of professional expertise when it comes to running the schools. As we have seen in chapter 2, this was one of the central questions that was in the background, and sometimes very prominently in the foreground, of the long and continuing conflict over the appropriate role of the superintendent in the scheme of things. A long-standing argument of superintendents was that education was becoming too complex to be left to ill-informed lay people, and they appear to have won the argument. It seems that teachers' unions are making a similar argument, but without the support of this particular superintendent.

Teachers' unions are also seen as mixed blessings by another man, but for different reasons than were just noted. The questions he raised had to do with the formalization of the rules of work, to the extent that they may dissipate the feel for and dedication to teaching as a type of work that people engage in for its own intrinsic rewards. If I am correct, he is suggesting that this formalization at times mitigates against the overt display of such dedication on the part of teachers. There is a grain of truth to this. It is evidenced by subtle pressures that are placed by teachers on other teachers whose work pattern is consistently to stay in their classrooms and work for an hour or two at the close of the official day. It is also very much in evidence in those situations where there has been a teachers' strike and where some teachers have, for reasons of their own conscience, not supported the strike and continued to work. The history of these situations is typically that the nonstrikers, after the conflict has been settled, have been isolated by their fellows and not spoken to for many months. Solidarity with the union, at times like this, apparently becomes a higher virtue than the exercise of one's conscience, a state of affairs that this superintendent finds professionally inappropriate for a teacher.

If several of the superintendents noted—with some reservations—the positive value of teachers' unions, two spoke about them in terms of the inevitability of their development, an approach that certainly does not convey strong support. "They had to come," said one, and described the union as "a necessary evil that I have to live with." Said the other, "If I had my 'druthers,' I would wish the unions weren't there," but we have to be "willing to deal with them or get out of the business." To grossly understate the matter, dealing with the teachers' unions for these two people obviously is not a part of their job that they find attractive. Though they might wish them away, both of them acknowledge the union as a fact of their work life, but a distasteful one.

These superintendents obviously held a variety of attitudes toward teachers' unions. Since one's behavior and the way one confronts situations are partly a function of one's attitude toward a situation, it is possible to conjure up a variety of scenarios of superintendent–union interaction from the comments made by these men. Some might have a sort of open-door and open-agenda policy in which they reach out to the union—to co-opt it, perhaps. For others, though the door is open, the agenda may not be. Boundary lines may be put around the type of discussion that is considered appropriate. And for others, it seems, the teachers' union is likely to be held at a distance. A person rarely invites a guest into his or her home if it can be anticipated that the conversation will not be enjoyable, or, perhaps more to the point, if the guest represents something that the host wishes didn't exist in the first place.

Adversaries—but Not Enemies

Regardless of the particular view a superintendent may hold concerning the desirability of teacher unionism having become a fact of his work life, he must ultimately confront and deal with the structure of their relationship. That structure, of course, as all the people interviewed agreed, is adversarial. It is not true that the legalization of the teachers' right to organize and bargain collectively suddenly made adversaries out of teachers and superintendents. Superintendents and teachers have always been adversaries, sometimes friendly ones and sometimes not so friendly. The conflict was simply a fact of school organizational life, though rarely acknowledged publicly. Superintendents had a great deal of organizational power and control; teachers had little. What the legal sanctioning of teacher unionization did was to acknowledge this conflict and to lift it from the undercurrent of school organizational life to a place of publicly acknowledged, if not publicly supported, legitimacy. In the process, of course, it altered the power relationship that existed or, at the least, it contained the potential for doing that.

Practically any decision that restructures organizational relationships—and the development of teachers' unions is certainly one of those—contains the probability of creating a backwash of unanticipated consequences. Legislative acts may seem rational on paper, but the human beings who must abide by those acts supply their own idiosyncratic rationality as they interpret them. So it is that the superintendents in this study supplied their views of the legally legitimized adversarial relationship between them and the union. For example:

> I was talking to a union president who was trying to convince me of the ultimate goodwill of the union and its concern with kids. He said that if I didn't believe that, I would force the union into a hard line. That's the union's whole thing—"You're forcing us. We really want to be with you" and "We are together." That's bullshit! We're not together. The structure pushed us apart, much as I wish it hadn't.

So we have a basic conflict. No one would deny that teachers, for the most part, are interested in kids. None would deny that the most productive relationship that might exist between a superintendent and teachers would be one that is based on professional collegiality. But this superintendent is suggesting — reasonably I think — that the legal structure of his relationship with the union now makes this condition difficult, if not impossible, to achieve. The two do talk with each other about educational matters and problems relating to the schools, but, he suggests, the power of the union is always lurking in the background. And we hardly need to be reminded that when relationships between two or more parties are characterized predominantly by power, they give rise to suspicion. Clearly, this superintendent did not believe the protestations of the union president.

The adversarial relationship between superintendents and teachers' unions was approached somewhat differently by another interviewee, but his view had subtle undertones of similarity to that of the one just discussed. He acknowledged that he and the union were pitted against each other. It was the appropriate control of the conflict that concerned him.

> I think the days are gone when you can talk about the union having as a primary interest the betterment of education. I don't think that's been true since day one. It is an adversarial relationship. I think the question will become: What's the substance of it? It's not inconsistent to be adversaries when you're talking salaries, benefits, etc. I think it's totally inconsistent when you're thinking about curriculum development and instructional strategies, for example. There, you've got some problems.

First, notice the similarity between these comments that stress the adversarial relationship and some of those in the preceding section that were concerned with attitudes toward the union movement. In the latter, the issue tended to be a philosophical one: the superintendents thought that union participation was not appropriate to the concept of public control of public schools. In the comments just quoted union participation in educational policymaking was rejected on the pragmatic grounds that the character of the relationship makes cooperation in policymaking impossible.

Underlying both views, though, are two related ideas. First, you can't have it both ways. You can't play adversary today over issues such as working conditions or grievances, and colleague tomorrow over curriculum problems. The underlying quality of adversarialness just doesn't permit that. The second idea is related to the forum in which disagreements are hammered out: the bargaining table. Such a forum, one would suspect, is seen as inappropriate for educational matters but quite appropriate for bread-and-butter issues, the proper concern of the union. The question ultimately involves a theme that has been apparent throughout this book—power. Who has responsibility for educational matters—the superintendent or the union? The fact that the two are, legally, legitimate adversaries suggests, to the superintendent just quoted, that the prerogatives are his and that he would fight not to relinquish them—that is, more adversity.

One final point: Note that these superintendents are not saying that teachers should play no role in resolving educational problems or planning curricula. This would be a foolhardy stance, to say the least. Rather, it is the union, as an institution, that is the issue. Teachers as *teachers* are considered indispensible to the planning, development, and implementation of new programs. It is the *union* that is not. Perhaps this is drawing too fine a line of distinction. Nonetheless, it is a distinction that superintendents have to consider.

Another problem caused by the adversarial relationship has to do with the superintendent's personal and job security and is related to the image the board has of how a superintendent deals with the union. One man put it this way:

> First of all, boards don't trust superintendents. It's the professional–layman thing, you know. And the teachers are professionals, too. So when I told the board I was going to try to comanage the district with the union, they became very threatened. They saw an unholy alliance in the making, and they were being left out of it. That's one thing. The second thing is this. If the union said about me, "He's great. He takes care of us," I'm dead! I'm dead! But, if they come out and say, "He's a sonofabitch. He's a devil. You can't trust him—he'll beat us out of this and that," the board says, "That's perfect." I know a guy in another town where he upset the teachers so they wanted to buy out his contract. His

response was, "I must be doing something right. The teachers are mad at me." Boards like that.

The example is probably overdrawn a bit, but the point is well taken. There probably has never been a school board, just as there probably never has been any other corporate management group, that has welcomed the idea of its employees being unionized. Management, feeling that it has the right and responsibility to manage, and union activities are seen as potential or actual intrusions on that right and responsibility. Further, as we saw in the preceding chapter, the superintendent's first obligation and loyalty is to the board. He is *their* man and must represent and support them and their positions before the entire school community. If he doesn't want to put his job in jeopardy, he cannot play on both sides of the line, at least not publicly. If the board is hostile to the union, the superintendent must be tough in his dealings with that body. And more than that, if the superintendent just quoted is right, the more a superintendent of a hostile board gets bloodied in his battles with the union and the tougher his stands, the more he will be seen by the board as an appropriate choice for a chief school officer. It is not exactly as if he were the board's hatchet man, but the analogy at times is a close one. Some superintendents have indeed been hired by school boards precisely because they have developed a reputation for not being pushed around by a teachers' union.

What we have, then, is a neat bind in which superintendents find themselves because of the adversarial relationship in which they must function. They are the men in the middle, and this means they always need to keep an eye on the power politics that surround their job—if they wish to hold onto the job. Sometimes, of course, playing this game, even if you win, is not worth it, and the superintendent resigns. This was exactly the case in a school district with which I am familiar where the superintendent, in the eyes of the school board, had "given too much to the teachers." The pressure became too great, and resign he did before his contract was up, much to the delight of the school board and the dismay of the teachers. It was a relatively extreme case, perhaps, but not so extreme as to preclude the distinct likelihood that his fellow superintendents "went to school" on his experience.

Interestingly, the superintendent's need to maintain an image of distance and toughness vis-à-vis the union seems to have its counterpart on the union side. Consider this description:

We had a situation last year where an officer of the union would occasionally come to my office to talk with me by himself. We chatted, we'd bullshit, we'd have a good conversation. Well, what happened is he started to get flak that he was getting too friendly with me. So he quit. He quit his office because he couldn't "buy" all the paranoia that was running rampant. Like they were saying to him, "You're trying to cut your own deal." So he quit. And this all makes you feel that when you're talking with people, you don't want to get too close. In fact, since that happened, a couple of union people told me that they've got to maintain their distance.

Each side learns its lessons, and in such cases the learning may be painful.

Constraints on the Superintendent's Power

Obviously, the growing strength of teachers' unions has put constraints on a superintendent's power that were not present formerly. But, of course, at its roots, that is what unionism is all about. While the issues raised most frequently involve economic matters and conditions of work, at a more basic level one must infer a continuing struggle for power and control. As was suggested previously, and as will become more apparent as we proceed, one of the things that seems to set teachers' unions apart from those in the industrial sector is that this struggle has reached beyond questions of working conditions and salary. In many cases it is focused on questions related to the control of the form and context of the educational enterprise itself. How one evaluates this situation, and one's opinion as to whether or not these are appropriate concerns for a teachers' union, depends on one's values. Certainly, there is disagreement about the matter among superintendents.

Another thing that is certain is that superintendents are very much aware of the ongoing power struggle between them and the unions. Given the nature of their position and the fact that they see their role in highly political terms, it could hardly be otherwise. This is the way one man put it:

I'm convinced in my own mind that the whole union movement is predicated on a search for power—who is going to manage a number of the operations in the schools? The union can only survive if it becomes a strong advocate for its members, and that advocacy can only become manifested through demonstrating that it can control the conditions of their work. The more influence or power they have, the more they can provide a service to their membership, and the stronger they become. The major problem I have is that I have observed them recently wanting to gain control of things beyond working conditions. They are moving, as a union, into such things as instructional and organizational processes. And those are areas in which management has a certain kind of orientation and the teachers' union a different kind. We are certainly in conflict.

Another superintendent echoed these remarks:

> The union is certainly becoming a major factor in the power
> structure of education. We have to realize their first interest is for
> themselves, for their constituents, and for the total amount of
> power they can obtain.

In these comments the issue is confronted directly, analytically, and, on the whole, dispassionately. They also provide a brief lesson in the dynamics of viable unionism and describe the aim of teachers' unions as analogous to the implicit aim of organizations in the private enterprise corporate world — though most unionists would probably reject that analogy. Each type of organization has to grow in strength. They do this by trying to exercise more control over their relevant—life-giving—environments. For the corporation, this means getting a larger share of the market through any of a variety of means at their disposal—producing new products or cutting costs, for example. Or it may mean increasing their financial leverage and profits through the merger process. Regardless, the goal is to increase their power and control over those factors that contribute to their strength. It is a never-ending process.

Teachers' unions—or any union, for that matter—are not in business for profit, but they must attend to the same basic organizational problem as corporations. They must continue to grow in strength, if not in numbers. And because their local environment is severely circumscribed, this growth, for the most part, must come from within the school district. (It is, of course, true that teachers' unions have moved into the wider sphere of state political action, but that is typically not a high-level concern for local union members). The obvious strategy in this situation is for teachers' unions to attempt to gain control over a larger range of elements related to school life so that it can be demonstrated to the teacher-members that the union is a strong and growing organization that is worthy of their membership and support. The two primary ways it has available to display its concern about power and control are through the collective bargaining process, and through its unwavering and militant support of teachers during grievance and arbitration procedures. These are the basic facts of union viability. The teachers' union that does not attend to them will become weak and ineffectual, and in essence will have little reason to exist.

It is important to note that most of the superintendents in this study seemed to have little problem with the need for unions to assert, through the bargaining process, control, or at least a high degree of influence, over basic conditions of work. Indeed, this was not only seen to be legitimate but was viewed positively. However, the specter of the inappropriateness of certain union activity arises once more in the first interview excerpt noted above. It has a familiar ring, reminding one of the "philosophical" view of the superintendent who felt that the union's concern for curriculum and instruction was outside the legitimate boundaries of union activity, threatening the traditional right of the public to control the schools.

The superintendent quoted in the second excerpt had a more pragmatic concern. The true situation, as he viewed it, was that as unions search for powers that have historically been held by the school board, and the superintendent as its agent, the result will be conflict, but of a different order than that associated with bargaining over salary and benefits. This conflict will be openly focused on power, and its substance will be, Who has the legitimate right to control the form and content of public education? Disagreements of this nature have much more potential for changing the fabric of American education than do disagreements over next year's salary increment. Lest the reader think that I am making too much of this, let me note that the massive teachers' strike in New York City in 1968 was conducted over educational decision making, not over salary issues. In one account of it, the strike was characterized as "the worst disaster my native city has experienced in my lifetime—comparable in its economic impact to an earthquake that would destroy Manhattan below Chambers Street, much worse in its social effect than a major race riot" (Meyer, 1969, p. 15). Somewhat closer to home for me, the only teachers' strike that has occurred in the county in which I live was conducted over the question of who has the right to make what kinds of decisions in the schools.

But teachers' strikes are not our focus here. Let's now examine some comments in which superintendents describe the severity of the constraints under which they work.

> So, you're feeling kind of increasingly more in a bind as your freedom of action is becoming more constrained. It's not only that. You have to weigh almost every word you say. I hesitate giving any major address without a prepared statement because I know I'll be misquoted without it. So I get to the point where I'm very, very technical, careful, and positive, wherever possible.

> I see myself being more and more hamstrung. And I guess maybe the longer I'm in this, the more I am sensitive to it. Initially, I was very naive about the things I could do, and, until I was reined up, I didn't realize how few things I could do. For example, it used to be an unquestioned prerogative of a superintendent to transfer teachers from one building to another. I made such a transfer not long ago, and there was a lot of tension and trauma. "How dare he be so presumptuous as to do that."

There's no question that the process of having to work through the union takes a lot longer. It's a restraint in many cases.

Well, the issue is the contract and what's in it. You are absolutely bound by contract provisions. If you violate them, you're subject to a grievance procedure that will correct that abuse of power or authority or whatever.

In the final analysis, the union impinges upon those prerogatives we want to keep to ourselves only when we've given them away in the contract. I want the ability to adjust class size in special needs. I want the ability to increase class size when economic factors tell us we'd better do that. I don't want to give that stuff away, and so far we've successfully avoided those things being included in the contract.

It's not as though I feel terribly constrained, but working with the union certainly means that at times you pay attention to things that maybe you didn't used to. You kind of walk a narrow path. You give a little, and you take a little. You keep your feelers out. You're careful to be careful.

Perceptions of the severity of constraints under which these people felt themselves put by the union ranged widely, then. In one case, the superintendent simply felt that the decision-making process is more time-consuming when the union is involved. At the opposite extreme was the superintendent who saw himself as being more and more in a bind over what he could say or do. His concern about being misquoted is not unlike that of political figures in much larger arenas of national life. This sense of constraint was also expressed in the last comment quoted, where the superintendent said that although he didn't feel overt constraint from the union, he did indeed walk a narrow path at times and was "careful to be careful." But certainly the most negative sense of constraint was expressed by the superintendent in the second excerpt who described himself as being "hamstrung," as having been "reined up," and as having lost his naivete in the process. There is sadness in these words, but it is probably good for us to hear them. As should be crystal clear, by now, the superintendency is not a job for the naive among us.

The interview excerpts that refer to the contract, rather than the union, as the primary constraining agent have a slightly different focus. Notice the sentence, "You are absolutely bound by contract provisions." The obverse is the superintendent assumes that whatever is not included in the contract is his decision-making territory, free of union constraints. For example, one interviewee said that his reply to teacher demands would be, in essence, "If it's not in the contract, don't bug me." But, of course, things are not that simple. The power that the superintendent assumes he has today may be up for grabs on the bargaining table tomorrow, as the union continually seeks to expand its power.

A basic strategy for maintaining the superintendent's prerogatives was implied in the statement of the superintendent who said, in referring to his control over class size, "So far, we've successfully avoided those things being included in the contract." The most fundamental way for a superintendent to maintain control of those parts of his job that he sees to be essential for him is to keep them out of the contract. Once given away in contract form, they are exceedingly difficult to get back, since such a retrieval would imply the diminution of union power. But, as a caveat, we must note that this superintendent said, "So far": the future is far from certain.

One superintendent summed up his place in this conflictual setting as follows:

> You know, a superintendent is in a rather strange position. He's in the middle of it all with responsibility for the total enterprise. If you have responsibility, you also have power. But there's a continuous struggle for power, and you have to draw lines. The decisions still have to rest with the board of education, elected by a populace, who choose a chief executive officer to carry out the wishes and wills of the community. In that struggle, you're sometimes in a no-man's-land. You almost have to walk on a tightrope, because if you go too much on one side the union's going to attack you, and if you go too much on the other side the general public is going to attack you. And you also know that occasionally you get shot at, you get lambasted, blackmailed, whatever it has to be in order that the union gets the things they want.

This superintendent summed up the difficulties of the situation for the superintendent rather neatly. In describing those difficulties in this chapter, however, I have not meant to imply that teachers' unions are evil social inventions. The unions represent a recently legitimated and proper constituency in the political life of public education. As such, and because of their obvious power, they become a focal concern of a superintendent's work life. It is true, of course, that the general welfare of the schools does not always flow from union activities. The same can be said for activities of school boards. It is equally true that each would have us think otherwise. So the superintendent, executive agent of the board and also the educational leader of the system, seems to be the man in the middle whose role is to help the two groups manage the conflict that, by definition, is indigenous to the situation.

Positive Aspects of Having a Union Contract

There seems to be little doubt that the advent of teacher unionism has made the superintendent's life in many respects much more complex and worrisome than it was before. It is also true that this same development and the substance of the bargaining agreements that have resulted have had the effect of making the superintendent's work life a little easier at times. The data from the interviews suggested two ways in which this can happen. The first stems from a broad organizational perspective on the complexities of school life. The second deals with day-to-day personnel decisions.

Viewed from a broad perspective, a union can be thought of as facilitating the superintendent's functioning within the system by providing a readily observed center of power. Speaking from this perspective, one interviewee described his feelings about the union this way:

> You know, if superintendents sat down and thought about the alternatives, they wouldn't feel so bad. Sure, there are times when I get very angry and very uptight because of something that's not going right with the teachers' association. It's not all peaches and cream, as it isn't with any kind of human relationship. But supposing we had no disciplined, organized group—supposing we had six, as well we could have. Or supposing it was a situation where there was no organization and a clique of teachers (it used to be the jocks) and the town would run the school district. They ran good football and soccer teams, and they had a lot of public support. But there was no discipline for dealing with them. There was no contract with them. It was all strictly under-the-table kind of political. I'd much rather deal with an organized group that has some discipline and has some control.

This comment provides an insightful perspective on the problems of managing a complex political work system, regardless of size. The superintendent acknowledges, of course, that the union is a force with which he has to contend and that contending with it is not always an easy matter. But, he asserts, the existence of the union gives coherence to the system and makes it easier to plan strategy. To elaborate, a school district can be conceived of as an interactive network of competing power centers. A central problem for the superintendent is to keep the pressures induced by the power centers in balance so that things don't tilt too far in one direction or another. It is obviously a job for a skilled managerial politician, and such people know that in circumstances that are basically conflictual, life is made less complicated when there are fewer competing interests than when there are many. It is not exactly a condition of "know your enemy," but it comes close. More conceptually, it is simply a case of reducing the complexity of the situation. One can plan strategy and think through tactical leverage points when there are fewer power centers with which one has to contend with than when there are many, and one thing is for sure: teachers' unions have had the effect of gathering in a number of loosely knit forces into one central one.

This may seem like rather faint praise for the way in which the union movement has changed the character of school district organization. One might argue, for example, that unions have created conflicts where none have existed previously, that they have made mountains out of molehills, and that, in general, they have simply made life much more difficult for superintendents and school boards. There is a grain of truth in this argument. The other side of it, though, as was suggested above, is that the union has forced the conflicts into the light of day and mandated that they be dealt with openly, in a formal setting, in contrast to preunion times when problems were often dealt with covertly, in informal settings. It would be naive to think that such things no longer occur. However, the intrusion of teachers' unions into the affairs and political network of school systems has indeed provided a point of structural focus with which a superintendent can deal directly. One must balance the cost and benefits of the argument out in one's own mind, of course. But for one superintendent, at least, the preference is clear: better fewer than many power centers in the system.

This broad perspective on the value of the union to the superintendent involves a particular theory of management, and thus is open to argument. But judging by the comments made in the interviews, it seems to be beyond argument that certain aspects of a superintendent's daily work life have been made easier by the union. A few excerpts will illustrate:

> Well, one thing that has happened is that it's reduced the patronizing manner in which many of us used to administer. We must treat everyone covered by the contract equally, and it relieves us of having to make personalized decisions. It gets us off the hook. There are fewer decisions to be made. It's all in the contract.

> The contract makes my life easier in lots of ways. You bet it does! Sure it does! I don't have to fret over a lot of little things, personnel things, personal days, and that sort of thing. All that I say when special requests come in is, "What does the contract say?" But that creates some problems, too, because sometimes things happen and a variance from contract provisions is requested. You have to be careful not to create a precedent, because sure as heck it will come up in the next round of negotiations. In a way, though lots of little decisions are easier or they don't even arise, there are times when I can't act as humanely as I would like to do.

> What the contract really does is that it helps you by giving some

firm guidelines on how to handle personnel matters. Like a teacher says, "I want this afternoon off." Well, the contract eliminates the decision because it says either you can have it or you can't. It eliminates favoritism, it really does. It's made us better managers. It's helped us keep better control of the situation.

Not all superintendents, of course, particularly those in larger districts, need get involved in the type of decisions referred to here. They are, after all, fairly small kinds of things when set against the background of the problems that confront the schools. But before collective bargaining and contractual agreements existed, superintendents were frequently called on to make decisions of this type. Now, for the most part, they don't need to: it's all in the contract, or if the circumstances aren't covered in the present contract, they will be up for negotiation the next time around. Union contracts result in a codification of working conditions. Such codification removes the need for superintendents to make numerous minor discretionary judgments that have little importance in the larger scheme of things but may loom large in the eyes of individual teachers. Today, it's all in writing. If he follows the contract, the superintendent cannot be accused of favoritism or of being inhumane. The rules have been agreed to by everyone.

There is another side to this, though, that is a bit more subtle and possibly more important in the long run. It is true that at one time, and to some extent today, the ability to grant favors to teachers in response to a wide range of personalized requests was used by many superintendents as a source of power. Such power, possibly because it was so individualized, had the side effect of building personal loyalty to the superintendent. It also encouraged the development of submissiveness among teachers. The situation was ideally made for benevolent autocrats who were not averse to giving, but made sure they got something in return—a very normal inclination among humans. The point is, though, that the giving was frequently used to control—a rather inappropriate relationship among people who saw themselves as professionals. The union contract removes those prerogatives from the superintendents, for the most part. Though there may be some who wish they still had them, there would seem to be little question that they and their organizations are better off and healthier in their absence. Adults—not children—agree to the contract, and adults have to abide by it.

In this chapter, the purpose has been to present some broad perspectives that superintendents have on teachers' unions and the manner in which unions affect their work lives. Some view unionization as a very positive development and some regard it as a distasteful part of the educational enterprise. But as one of them said, superintendents have "to be willing to deal with unions or get out of the business"—irrespective of their personal tastes.

7
Working with the Union: Negotiations, Meetings, and Stress

While the last chapter focused on general perspectives that superintendents may hold of teacher unionization, this one has more specific concerns. Our subject here is the issues and strategies that superintendents confront in the formal negotiations process; their dealings with the union outside formal negotiating sessions; and the emotional fallout that results.

A couple of prefatory notes are necessary. First, it appears that in the early days of collective bargaining in the schools, superintendents were actively engaged as negotiators at the bargaining table. In many school districts that role has been taken over by attorneys with expertise in labor relations or other people who specialize in this field and have negotiating skill. However, even in these cases superintendents have not lost their role as advisor to the school board on strategy, and they frequently sit in on negotiating sessions as well. They are still very much part of the bargaining action, though in some situations they may be somewhat less visible.

Second, active trade and industrial unionism has a relatively long history in this country, but, as we saw earlier, active teacher unionism does not. Though there seem to have been some rather feeble and unsuccessful attempts to incorporate teachers into the labor movement more than fifty years ago, teachers' unions did not emerge as a vibrant and powerful force in school life until the mid-1960s. They were Johnny-come-latelies in the world of organized labor. But when they finally made their appearance on the scene, their presence became known quickly. As is not hard to imagine, and as we suggested in the last chapter, this presence was greeted by most school boards and many superintendents with less than unbounded enthusiasm. Nevertheless, the legal sanctioning of the right of teachers to organize gave impetus to the very rapid growth of the movement, such rapidity probably giving testimony to the idea that the social, political, and economic time for teacher unionization had come and that possibly it was overdue. Things were bound to change quickly, and change they did.

Learning to Negotiate

The swiftness of union growth meant more than just a change in the organizational relationship among school boards, superintendents, and teachers. For the academic, this changing relationship might constitute an interesting phenomenon that he or she might observe in a detached manner and record at a distance, at leisure. For people who were actively involved, no such leisure was available, nor were they terribly concerned about observing and recording. The demands were for action, particularly action around the negotiating table. And a major problem connected with this was that the parties involved had little experience and skill in collective bargaining. One superintendent who was a teacher negotiator at the time when teachers' unions were legitimized had this to say about these circumstances as he reflected on his early experience with collective bargaining:

> At the beginning, the teachers' associations were very, very
> unskilled in negotiations. They conceived of them strictly as a
> power confrontation, and that caused problems. At the same time,
> boards of education were equally uninformed and unskilled and
> were asserting their rights to be at the negotiating table. Many
> districts, including my own at that time, had the superintendent,
> another administrator, and a couple of board members at the table.
> And across from them would be four or five teachers. There were
> just too many people, and they had no skill in the matter. All hell
> would break loose. You'd just about get consensus on one point
> when someone would say, "Well, I just thought of . . . ," and
> they'd be off again.

Three things were needed, then, in these new, strange, and probably at times somewhat threatening and frightening circumstances. First, all parties had to develop realistic perspectives of what they were about and what was the legitimate function of collective negotiations. Second, and quite dependent on the perspectives that were developed in each case, new role relationships had to be conceptualized, though, in all likelihood, not in a formal manner. Teachers had to learn, for example, that their new role was not simply a legal sanction to do battle, in a protected environment, with the superintendent and school board. But more specific to our purpose, superintendents had to learn a new role as they found their behavior becoming circumscribed by the need to negotiate a contract and then live by it. Third, stemming from all this was the fact that superintendents had to learn a new set of skills for which their training and experience had ill prepared them. One interviewee put the situation in these words:

It's a whole new ball game from what it was, and that means there's a whole new set of skills involved. First you that you have to sit down and negotiate. There are no two ways about it. Then you've got to learn to anticipate that the things you're going to put and write down in a contract have a price to them. And you're going to have to learn to say, no, if the price is too much. The skill is to anticipate the consequences of it all.

Of course superintendents were already accustomed to anticipating as best they could the various effects that any single decision could have on their school system. In a way, they made their living by being able to do this. But the "new ball game" involved the skills of learning to negotiate, anticipate, and strategize within the boundaries of a legal covenant in which decisions were put in writing and to which the superintendent knew he would be held. The game that had to be played by the superintendent, then, was characterized by caution. He (and the school board, of course) were the ones of whom things were demanded across the bargaining table, and the skill of weighing the costs and benefits of union proposals had to be cultivated, sometimes in a most deliberate manner.

There were other things to be learned about this "new ball game." A legal language, rather foreign to most superintendents, had to be understood. The meaning of such terms as *impasse, fact-finding, mediation, grievance,* and *arbitration* no longer was academic. These terms had direct implications for a superintendent's work life and for the positions he took during and after the formal negotiating. And there was a language connected with the actual bargaining, and the planning for it, that entered his vocabulary. He began to use terms like *caucusing* and *throw-away items.* Additionally, and equally important, superintendents had to learn new behavioral skills connected with meeting one's adversary at the bargaining table. This meant, among many other things, knowing when to bluff, when to threaten, when to back off, when to act with disbelief, when to become angry, and so forth. If these points sound like guidelines for manipulation, that is precisely what they are. The aims of collective negotiations are typically fulfilled by strategic and tactical maneuvering and manipulation. The object, from the point of view of management, is to give up as little as possible, as long as your adversary can find some satisfaction in the outcome. Sometimes, of course, this means the skill of creating believable illusions.

I am not suggesting that the process of collective bargaining is a sleazy one unbefitting the educational world. On the contrary, no value orientation is intended. We are simply observing that the advent of teacher unionism, with collective bargaining as its primary instrument, made it necessary for superintendents of schools to confront a new reality. If they were to survive, they had to learn new ways of thinking and behaving, because one thing was certain: this new reality would not go away.

The Superintendents Comment on Negotiating

The superintendents in this study tended to have vivid memories of bargaining experiences with the union. These memories were reflected in the general way they thought about upcoming bargaining sessions and in the way they thought about their behavior in these sessions. The quotations that follow give the flavor of the negotiating process from several points of view. For example, here is the way one man contemplated the upcoming negotiations in his district:

> Well, it's time for the balancing act to start again. The balancing act is trying to keep a reasonableness from the board's point of view, and being able to say to teachers, "Listen, you're just going too far on these issues. You can't do that." And you also have to negotiate with the board. You gotta make them be reasonable, too, because sometimes they get mad at the union and want to insist on an article that will only create bad feelings. It's January now, and I always have a negative attitude about it all. That's because informal negotiations will start soon, and the union will start to draw a hard line. In April, they're going to ease up a bit.

In chapter 4, we discussed the balancing act that the superintendent performs as a sort of premier school district politician. It is evident here as well and illustrates one of the binds in which the superintendency puts the occupant of that position. In a very real way, he must deal with the interests of both sides of the bargaining process. He is the board's representative, and he is hired, overall, to promote and implement their interests and decisions. However, he is also the leader of the educational establishment in his school district. After the contract is signed, it is he and his staff, not the board, who must live and deal with teachers on a daily basis. So there is pressure, and it comes from both sides. This fact, incidentally, is one among many that differentiates the role and attitudes of superintendents, who are, after all, the chief operating officers of a sometimes large fiscal enterprise, from that of their counterparts in the private sector. The latter, for example, are rarely in contact with their first-line production workers. Superintendents, except in very large systems, are apt to have such contacts frequently. For this reason alone, their freedom to take certain positions during negotiations is circumscribed.

The superintendent's comment, in the excerpt just quoted, that he had a "negative attitude" toward the start of informal negotiations suggests his strategic stance about the bargaining process. The scenario goes something like this: It was January at the time of our interview. Preliminary and informal talks were soon to start between him and the union as a prelude to formal ones, which would commence in April. He was predicting, based on his experience, that the union would take a hard line. He, of course, would have to take an equally hard line. He felt negative about the whole business. In April, things would ease up, and the problems would become more amenable to solution. But we can almost hear his thoughts: "Why do we have to go through this charade? We both know how things will happen over time. Why do we have to go through our posturing with one another? It's phony, time-wasting, and I don't like it." The answers to his questions are not hard to come by. That is the way the game is played, and who knows: sometimes through all of the posturing, one side or the other gains an advantage. All games that involve some deception, and collective bargaining is one, consider that such advantages may be gained at times.

Another superintendent, whose comments follow, also was irritated with the posturing in negotiating, which he called "prancing." He saw the root of the problem, though, in a somewhat different light than the ritualistic softening of unreasonable demands over time. For him, the problem was his inability to cut quickly through the myriad union demands—distracting ones, from his point of view—to the basic issues, which he interpreted as economic.

> We had 40 different things on the table last year, and when it came
> down to the wee hours, it was money. Everything else was
> discarded. The bottom line was money. Well, there's nothing
> wrong with that. I can accept it. There's nothing immoral about
> it. But what they do is go through all the prancing of all the
> educational baloney to develop a kind of lever so that they can say,
> "We'll drop all these other demands if you give us the money." So
> that's called that prancing you go through—the promenade for
> money. And that's what you have to understand and build yourself
> up to.

Several points emerge here. First is the patterned use of what are known as "throw-away" items in the union's (and the school board's) bargaining package. These are items that are included in the package in order to create the illusion that when they are discarded something important has been given up, thereby creating the expectation of a reciprocal giving on the other side. The problem, as this superintendent sees it, is that such items are inconsequential and everybody knows it. Why bother with the ritual? Why not cut to the heart of things, which he sees, almost without variation, to be money?

There might be many superintendents who would disagree with this view-point, but there are many who would heartily agree that most labor strife in the schools could be avoided if there was enough money, even when the focal issues being bargained over are not monetary. One superintendent told me that he could have averted a traumatic strike over management rights if he could have found enough money in his budget to "buy them off." Perhaps the view that money is the heart of any negotiation is too hard and cold. Perhaps, though, it is the ultimate reality of the problem.

From the standpoint of this book, however, the most important point in this superintendent's comments is contained in his last sentence, when, hav-ing described the situation, he says, with reference to the prancing and the "promenade of money": "And this is what you have to understand and build yourself up to." That is, we have a set of circumstances that are distasteful to be part of, but which the superintendent must deal with. One can almost picture him insulating himself against them through one means or another. But it may well be that the ability to insulate oneself from the posturing and prancing that occur during the negotiating process — and superintendents engage in posturing, too—is an integral part of any superintendent's survival kit in today's school world.

The survival kit, to push the metaphor a little further, contains some other guidelines for superintendents concerning negotiating a contract with the teachers' union. A very important guideline has to do with the fact, noted earlier, that the superintendent's organizational position mandates that he function in a condition involving split loyalties and responsibilities. He is clearly the "board's man," but he is also the titular leader of the schools. He must protect the managerial integrity of the system as the board sees it, but he must also behave in ways that will entitle him to the respect of the teach-ers, upon which his influence with them in matters of school program-ming and other educational problems ultimately depends.

If a superintendent wishes to have an impact on the character of educa-tion in his district, he cannot do this without the cooperation of the teachers, which he achieves through his ability to influence them in ways that they find palatable. Use of his authority alone will have little effect. For example, he has the right to convene as many curriculum committees as he wishes, and teachers will attend their meetings. But if they hold him in low regard or if they see him as having "put it to them" too heavily in their last contract negotiations, the chances of their being willing to work on projects that he deems important are minimized. There are simply an infinite number of ways that teachers can subvert a superintendent's best intentions if they so desire, and he needs to be continually aware of this possibility as it relates to the split-loyalty conflicts that are part and parcel of the bargaining process. One superintendent reflected on this conflict in the following way:

Now, how the hell can I be expected to step on their heads all the time? Just to demonstrate that I'm my own man or that I'm the board's man, and I don't have any indebtedness to them? But then I'm back in the middle again, 'cause I'll need them later. The board pulls you toward themselves, and what you're expected to do is not betray their interests because—well, you'll lose your job. But, the teachers know they have leverage on you, too.

Well, whose man is the superintendent in these situations? It is a question that has no easy answers. But the answers, if and when they are found, probably depend on the superintendent's ability to balance, in a very delicate manner, the conflicting pressures in what is by definition an adversarial circumstance. One interviewee framed the balance that was needed in win-or-lose terms. "Of course," he said, "I can win in a particular case, but the winning, and they know I have won, generates a whole host of problems on the other side." In his opinion, one generally finds out when it's all over that nobody wins and nobody loses.

He does not go into a negotiation thinking about what he's going to *win*. Rather, it's a question of where you want to be, and where you end up. The basic idea is to end up with a "good deal," as he put it, with both parties feeling that nobody's hurting and that "we're still working together." But the words, easy to say, cloud the delicateness of the superintendent's position as he tries to manage his image well for both parties. When contract negotiations are over, the board must still see him as its loyal representative who has upheld its interests well, and the teachers must feel he has not deserted them in order to reinforce his position with the board and hold onto his job.

Another superintendent also reflected on the win-or-lose, gamelike character of the bargaining table process. Bothered by it, his idea was somehow to get the teacher negotiating team and himself into situations where each could acknowledge openly the nature of the game they were playing with each other. If this could happen—possibly in a conference divorced from actual negotiations—then the two sides could build trust in each other, he thought. The result would be a great deal of time saved when they became involved in the actual process of negotiating. The negotiator for the teachers thought that this was a good idea, but then

> he said, "Yeah, we could probably do it. But we would still have to go through the game so far as our constituency is concerned, so that they wouldn't think we're being taken into camp by the administration."

So once more we confront the fragile and highly political nature of problems that attach to the process of collective negotiations. It is a curious situation. It must be assumed, for example, that all parties to the negotiations —the school board, the teachers' union, and the superintendent in the middle — are people of good will. Further, it must be assumed that these same parties have a similar ultimate goal, the provision of a high quality of education for youngsters in the school district. (This latter factor is quite unlike the situation in industry, where management's ultimate goal—to make a profit— is quite divorced from the union's, as a rule.) These assumptions, though, seem to fade so far into the background as to be of little importance when people engage with each other across the bargaining table. What seems to have happened is that a structure has been created that encourages suspicion and distrust—sometimes justified—and almost mandates the "prancing and promenading" that was referred to earlier. One of the superintendents, as he reflected on his experience of negotiating with the union and his wish that things were otherwise, summed up the situation by saying, "We're still dealing with a tradition where you've got to play 6 up, 3 down, 5 up, 2 down, so that the people in the field can see that their leaders are fighting for them."

We should not forget that the necessity for the superintendent to engage in this type of political game is created as much by his need to convince the board that he is on their side as it is by the union leaders' need to impress their membership. One superintendent, who characterized his relationship with the union negotiator as "extremely good right now," said,

> We both agreed that we could do this whole thing in a matter of
> hours or days. But my board would feel that I gave away the store
> if I did it that fast, and his union would figure that they got the
> short end of the stick.

There is a bit of tragedy—or irony, at least—to the situation. Some of those who are engaged in the theatrics might not agree. There are people on either side of the bargaining situation who look forward to it as a test of wit and skill. A union negotiator once told me that he was anticipating his next bargaining encounter because he would be called on to test himself against a board negotiator who had a wide reputation for toughness. If he could "beat him" at the bargaining table, it would be a feather in his cap. And for a superintendent, too, particularly if he is actively involved in the negotiations, the situation represents an opportunity to test and prove himself as a skilled bargainer and a man who is strong and can be depended on by the board not to be pushed around by the union. But both sides are still being forced to engage in a charade that both acknowledge to be just that. The real issues do not emerge until after the charade is over, and both sides acknowledge that, too. So the tragedy, or irony, for the superintendents is that they are drawn into situations over which they have little control and in which they must conspire to produce some unrealistic images of themselves. For the superintendent who is not hardened to this reality and who is sensitive to this dynamic, the prospect of the next round of negotiating presents conflicts that go beyond reaching a contractual agreement. They are conflicts associated with one's self-image, the way one wishes to conceive of himself and he conceived of by others.

Sitting Across the Table

Every superintendent, every negotiator has his own style and his own ground rules for behavior in face-to-face negotiations. What follows does not have the purpose of creating a litany of rules and tactics. Rather, the purpose is, through the use of just a few interview excerpts, to illustrate some concerns that superintendents seem to have as they engage with their adversaries across a table. For example:

> It can't be like two people in a fight, and the hell with the loser. It
> has to be more like two lawyers who fight a case on trial. There are
> limits beyond which they don't go. They recognize there's going to
> be another year. What this means is that I have to be aware that I
> have an obligation, in a sense, to protect my adversary. I can't put
> my opposing person in a position where he can't possibly deliver to
> his constituency. He has no option . . . but to match you head-on.
> I can't create this situation for him, because I know that the next
> time he's going to try to do the same thing to me. I always try to
> provide a situation which allows him to save face and negotiate with
> his constituency. I never want him to feel beaten.

> It's a mistake to get in an embattled position. I want them to
> believe that after it's all over, we can go out and have dinner
> together and be able to talk with each other. I think it's part of this
> business to be aware of the adversary's position and never drive
> him into a corner where he can't escape and then has to lash out.

These two comments present a broad view of negotiating sessions. They are strategic, but also have direct tactical implications for the superintendents who talked about them. They deal with the need to be continually aware of the broader context in which collective bargaining takes place. For example, to feel the obligation to protect one's adversary is an interesting way of thinking about it. Why should one feel this obligation? The answer is provided: If you don't do this, you create a cycle of conflict. Further, if you create such a cycle in one situation, you are also planting the seeds for the same thing happening in the next round. Also, to return to a point that was made earlier, superintendents have to live with more than the substantive results of the contract to which the parties agree. They have to live with how their behavior is perceived and interpreted by their opposition not only in the negotiating sessions but in the school system as a whole. Being seen as tough but reasonable and open to compromise is one thing. Being seen as out strictly to win and having an eye for the jugular is quite another. There is always a tomorrow, and this superintendent suggests that both he and his colleagues had better be aware of it.

Part of that tomorrow, as evidenced in the second comment above, involves the need simply to maintain cordial and civilized relationships with one's opponent when the conflict is over. And, of course, this condition is not likely to occur where one or the other of the parties feels soundly beaten and leaves the scene licking his wounds. What this superintendent seems to be saying, then, is that a guiding principle for him during actual negotiations is to try, by his behavior, to ensure that the discourse is one between friendly and civilized enemies, not mortal ones. In addition to the strategy implied by "There is always a tomorrow," then, there is also the notion of helping to create a situation where adults can simply behave like adults.

One could scarcely think of finding a person who would not agree that collective bargaining ideally ought to involve rational, adult discussion among people who are seeking reasonable ways to resolve their differences. There are times, though, in the stress and anxiety of it all, when what occurs makes that ideal seem very remote. One superintendent discussed such times:

> Sometimes I get really irritated; mad. There always seems to be a time in negotiations when I stand up, slam my fist a couple of times, and walk out. But I've got to be careful when I do that to make sure they don't walk out, because I might be at an impasse before I want to be. But sometimes I raise my voice, pound the desk, and scream and holler. But it's all with the idea of getting something back for what I'm giving.

It would be hard to imagine a superintendent who has not become extremely angry, at one time or another, during bargaining sessions. Some are obviously better able to control their overt emotions than the man who made the above remark. And this is not to suggest that he is less effective than they or a less competent administrator. Indeed, he may be better off than they because he can give vent to his anger openly. At least the opposite negotiating team has little doubt about the strength of his convictions, and something must be said for that. But notice that even at those times, there is what might be called a "strategic gleam in his eye." He becomes angry, slams his fist, and walks out—but not on pure impulse, regardless of the state of the negotiations. It is too touchy a situation to act on pure impulse, much as one might want to. "I've got to be careful," said he—careful that his behavior doesn't move the other side to walk out as well. It sounds highly manipulative, and perhaps it is. But it takes us back to our previous discussion of the need to avoid creating a cycle of conflict. Angry though this superintendent gets, and much as he might like to strike out, his deepest need is not to behave in such a way as to encourage the cycle's beginning. What we have here is a conflict between one's emotionality and one's rational thought processes. Some of us are better than others at resolving these kinds of conflicts.

The Rest of the Year

Negotiations do end, and contracts are signed, though the process may be and frequently is long and drawn out. Most of the time, contracts are agreed to before the close of school in June, but sometimes teachers work without a contract well into the next school year. And there are some situations, a tiny minority, in which the ultimate weapon of a teachers' strike is used in order for the union to gain what it conceives as an acceptable contract. Regardless, the relationship between the superintendent and the union is an ongoing one. The business of the schools does not stop during contract negotiations — though, if I may anthropomorphize, sometimes it holds its breath.

On the face of it, one might have a reasonable expectation that superintendents and the president of the teachers' union (or other members of its hierarchy) would hold regular meetings with each other in an attempt to deal with problems that arise over time or to prevent problems from arising. Reasonable expectations do not always match reality, however, especially when that reality develops in different school districts with different superintendents, school boards, and unions. Thus we find that some superintendents meet with the union leadership on a regularly scheduled basis and see these meetings as necessary and productive; others are tentative about the prospect of holding such meetings; and others would simply prefer to deal with the union only when problems arise. Here are some examples:

> I hold monthly meetings with the executive committee of the union, and they have been very productive. They are tremendous sounding boards. It gives me an opportunity to take care of things before anything builds up to the point where someone feels seriously grieved. It's been so successful that I've encouraged building principals to do the same thing with their building reps. Also, periodically I will share certain confidences with the union president, and he does the same with me, with the understanding that it's for our ears only.

> I meet with the head of the teachers' association every week. My
> assistant is there, and so is the vice-president of the association.
> There's no agenda. We each come in with a folder and talk about
> what's bothering us. We get together regularly by virtue of what we
> call the consultation clause. It's a pressure valve, and it allows
> things to be resolved in practical fashion before they blow up. But
> in spite of it, we've had our share of court proceedings and so forth.
> We also have an understanding that if either one of us calls the
> other, there's an issue that we need to get together about.

There seems to be nothing startling here. After all, superintendents and
unions do have a common overriding interest, which is to try to see that the
system runs as smoothly as possible. Of course, they may and frequently do
interpret the means of pursuing this interest in conflicting terms, but what
better way to resolve these conflicts than by frequent meetings? It is so
reasonable that one would have to ask why it isn't a universal practice,
whether or not such regular meetings are mandated by the contract, as was
noted in one of the comments above. But as we shall shortly see, this is not a
universal practice, and for reasons that seem to be associated with the attitudes of the superintendent or the school board. Again, some examples:

> No, we don't meet regularly. I've asked for that kind of thing. The
> problem is that I don't think we're at the point where we can talk
> together in terms of what we can do together to make things work
> better for us. It's not that we're not cordial to each other. It just
> seems that whenever we do meet, I just hear a lot of complaints.
> The more this happens, the more an expectation develops that I
> will have to do something, and a lot of times I can't do anything.
> So, if anything, you can get yourself into a deeper jam.

> We have a very formal and extensive contract, and yet I feel
> pressure from the union that it should all be very cooperative. I
> find that a difficult concept to work with. My predecessor spent a
> lot of time with the union president, and they became good friends.
> I find that difficult. He expects that he can come in one half-day,
> Monday and Thursday, every other week, and we can solve all the
> problems of the district. I have trouble divulging confidences to the
> union president.

> Of course, I have to deal with problems as they arise, but we don't
> meet regularly. If we did, then it means that they would become
> coarbitrators, co–decision makers, coadministrators, and that's
> very tough to deal with. My board would view that development
> very negatively. They would view it as capitulation—educator
> hobnobbing with educator—and they would think their source of

strength had been washed out. I think I would start to lose the support of my board.

It is an interesting range of responses, then, from superintendents whose pattern of working with the teachers' union does not include a regular meeting of focal people. There is the man, for example, who would like to engage with the union regularly but doesn't, because the latter's agenda doesn't seem to include the kinds of things that he sees as central to the problems of education. "Why expose yourself to all that crap?" he said at another point, while referring to petty gripes that seemed to be central to the union's concern. He wanted to engage with the union on larger issues of school life, but it seemed to be mostly concerned with minutiae, at least from his point of view. Dealing with minutiae on a regular basis was just not what he wanted to do.

Another perspective comes from a superintendent whose difficulty seems to be more conceptual in nature. That is, the union in his district, through its contract, has developed a highly formalized code that governs the relationship between the administration and the teachers. But, according to him, the union also wanted a more informal, cooperative relationship, and the two concepts don't seem to fit well. He seemed to be saying that the union can't have it both ways. They have a lot of power and control through the contract and now seem to want more through meeting in more informal settings. Further, and this seems to be a matter of personal style, he was reluctant to build a friendship with the union president as did his predecessor. The reasoning is obvious. Friendship induces an element into work relationships that may create problems down the line. Better to hold the union president at a distance; that way you avoid personal entanglements that can be embarrassing.

The third comment noted above provides an insight into the organizational complexity that may become involved when consideration is given to what seems a simple question: whether or not the superintendent and the union leadership should hold regularly scheduled meetings to consider problems associated with the schools. It is not surprising, given much of our previous discussion, that questions of power and authority relations should once more come to the surface. In this case, the issue seems to be the need of the superintendent to avoid giving the board the idea that he is yielding power to the union by meeting with them regularly. The board hired the superintendent to make decisions for and run the school district. Teachers are assigned a different role, and for the superintendent to give even the impression that he is taking teachers into his confidence about decisions or consulting with them is too risky a venture for this man in this situation. This is one of the sadder results of teacher unionism. In some situations the trauma that many school boards feel about having to deal with unionism has created such a climate of distrust that it becomes difficult, or politically unwise, for professionals in different positions to talk with each other.

Another thread that runs through this discussion has to do with the character of the relationship that develops between the superintendent and the head of the union. As we have seen, this relationship may be very formal, informal, close, or distant. But there is more to it than that, because the relationship is also inevitably political. In certain cases the superintendent may even have a stake in seeing to it that the union president is voted back into office in the next election. We have one illustration of these circumstances, which, though serious and important to the superintendent, has its decidedly amusing side.

> Well, there was a union election coming up, and the president wanted to be reelected. We had a good, healthy working relationship but, unfortunately, because of this she was seen as sort of Uncle Tomish by the teachers. She wasn't militant enough to suit them. So what happened was this: There was a demand for reopening bargaining the day before a holiday weekend. I knew it was coming, and one night I got notice of a piece of certified mail, return receipt requested, that was at the post office for me. My family got all upset. I refused to accept it, and sent one back which she refused to accept. This went on for a while. It was the battle of the unaccepted mail. I knew what was going on, and so did she. The result was that the teachers started to see her as a fighter, and she got reelected.

This anecdote is worth a smile, of course. But the humorous side of it gives way to the side that is quite serious. For this superintendent, it was quite important to try to keep the president in office, and in order for this to happen, she had to be seen as more militant. So, in a rather unplanned way, he helped this perception develop. More than that, though, the situation is illustrative, once more, of the intricacies of the relationship that may develop between a superintendent and the union leadership. It is not merely a question of matter of factly abiding by the contract. Much more is involved. In some districts, the question is: Who will control things here? In others, the question is: How can we work better together? It should be clear that which questions get raised and how they get answered will vary from district to district and will be dependent upon the mix of attitudes and behaviors that characterize the superintendent, school board, and teachers' union. But the superintendent seems focal to it all.

The concerns and problems that superintendents confront in dealing with teachers' unions go far beyond the issues involved in negotiating and meeting with union representatives. They involve grievances, arbitration cases, and, always in the background, the specter of a strike. They involve self-protection, the school board, the community, and, quite clearly, the youngsters in school and the integrity of the school program. It is not our intent to pursue these aspects of the relationship here. Indeed, a thorough consideration of them could well be the subject of another volume. Instead, the concluding section of this chapter deals with the character of the emotional conflicts that occur and the costs that inevitably need to be paid by the superintendents as they deal with unions.

The Emotional Costs of It All

One can be sure that when a superintendent gets a call from the union president to request a meeting, the aim of the meeting will not be to discuss the weather. A problem will have come up, something will have to be resolved, trade-offs will have to be made, faces saved, and people protected. And, as one may readily infer, all this will cost the superintendent something. Sometimes the conflicts and costs will be major and sometimes minor, but they will always be there.

The interview excerpts that follow present the reader with some sense of the inner thoughts and feelings that may develop as superintendents confront their adversaries in a range of different circumstances. I certainly have no intention of casting teachers' unions in a poor light or of describing them as playing the villain's role. It will be recalled that most of the interviewees saw the advent of teacher unionism as necessary and long overdue. Nonetheless, whether or not the superintendents psychologically put out the welcome mat for the union, the appearance of the union meant that new conflicts and costs were inevitably added to the job. Some examples follow.

One of the superintendents reflected on his experience and feelings when a strike was threatened and was only averted at the last minute:

> I found my behavior changing from that of an educationally oriented leader to that of an army sergeant—or an army general. I operated the schools in strict military fashion. I had a war council. . . . I knew I had to do it, but I didn't like myself for doing it. I hated it. I actually hated it. It's a terrible way to operate. And when we finally settled, three minutes after the strike deadline, every member of the teachers' association broke down and bawled. And I think the board and I felt the same way.

A very extreme situation this was, indeed. And certainly it only occurs in a small minority of schools, though it must be true that every superintendent dreads the possibility. This man paid a high cost, in that his only option, as he saw it, if he wished to maintain the system, was to assume a role that he detested. Not only did he hate the circumstances that were apparently forced on him, but he didn't like himself for the behavior in which he engaged. This experience led him to talk later in our interview about the superintendency as a position. He said that the job was a killing one and wondered how long people in it would continue to punish themselves by doing it. Though there's excitement and challenge to it, quite related to his recent "military" experience, he said, "but, boy, what it costs you in terms of your family life and your emotional stability." And, "Yes, the union has increased those costs."

What seems to happen much more frequently than the type of incident just related is that superintendents, as they deal with the new structure of school system relations engendered by unions, wonder about themselves, their own sense of integrity, and, at times, their competence. Here is the way one man described his feelings after a meeting with his board over the salary settlement in a new contract:

> I have to agree with them. I have to talk their line. And I also have to convince them that what we did was to make the salary schedule competitive. At the same time, I felt that maybe they [the union] did get a hell of a lot they should not have. There are times when I feel that I'm defending things that I know are wrong.

On some level, of course, all of us are engaged, at one time or another, in Janus-like theatrics where we put on one face for a situation but the face that is hidden displays a very different set of feelings. It is part of the politics of every organization's life, and in that sense superintendents aren't different from the rest of us. The problem in this superintendent's situation, though, as he went on to say, was, "I know that a lot of teachers leave early, and I know they don't always have the best interests of the kids at heart." He was forced to live by the politics of the situation, and he didn't like himself for it.

A different type of emotional problem emerged as one superintendent talked about what took place in his district when the union became formalized:

> It was like Future Shock. There was nothing sacred anymore, and for a guy like me who came through a different era, it was a hard adjustment to make. I remember, heck, the guys I used to play golf with, the guys I played poker with, my good friends. As soon as the union came into being, they wouldn't talk to me. I went through personal hell 'cause I couldn't understand how people could change overnight. I've been deprived of friendships, and I've also been deprived of the opportunity of really being more open with some of the people I wanted to be. And because of this, I don't get the immediate feedback I used to get.

Things changed when teachers' unions came into being, then, and not only with regard to legal contracts. For one person, at least, and probably many more, there was a change in personal relationships and friendships, as well as a newly developed inhibition over one's ability to be open with colleagues. So, once more, the role of the union in the school setting exacted its price from a superintendent, this time relative to his need to be friends with and deal openly with educational colleagues.

It scarcely needs to be said that the leaders of teacher unionism did not set out to destroy friendships among school people or to prevent new ones from forming. But when new structures are added to any organization or existing ones are altered, the character of interpersonal and work relations among people in the organization will be affected. When the new or altered structure has as its basic tenet the formal legitimation of adversarialism, one can predict, between the newly legitimated adversaries, a distancing of relationships. Protagonists or potential ones, it seems, cannot get too close to people with whom they see themselves having to do battle with in the future. Though there may be some paranoia attached to this thinking, the political realities of the circumstances suggest that such distancing is prudent.

Our final example involves the attitude of a superintendent whose district, shortly before our interview, had emerged from a very traumatic strike in which he was a central figure, not because of his actions but because of the position he occupied. Teachers' strikes, as we have said before, are not frequent occurrences, though the publicity they receive may tend to create that impression. The comments that follow, then, should not be construed as illustrative of the common experience of superintendents. They are included because not to include them would be to suggest that "It can't happen here." Obviously, it can.

> During the strike, I learned a bit about who I am and what it's possible to be on the job. What it's possible to be is a rubber ball. You can be a terribly courageous guy and say, "I don't give a damn. I'm going to take this position, and that's the way I want it to go." Chances are you're going to lose, and lose badly. You may lose your job, because you've offended your employing board or created the impression that you've betrayed them. And you can lose the teachers, too, because they see you behaving in an unnatural way, and you lose your credibility. You're going to be in the middle. You can't win. And you find out after a while that you don't try to appease teachers who are organized to strike or win a collective bargaining issue. The logic of the position doesn't matter much. What matters is the maintenance of the union's organization and their own power needs. The power of the superintendent isn't the only issue we're talking about. There's power in lots of other places that's vulnerable, or in jeopardy, or must be exercised. The

guy who says only *his* power is vulnerable or in jeopardy is naive. Decisions made by the union executive committee may be made, perhaps, because of their own needs. So you can't win. You have to find out who you are, and I clearly found out that I'm not one of the teachers anymore. I found out I really gave that up a long time ago, but it didn't dawn on me with such force until the strike. I can't go home again, and that hurts. But I've had to realize that that's the way it is.

These are very sobering thoughts, and their message is so clear that they need little elaboration. But the conflicts that this superintendent experienced during the strike had the effect of boldly clarifying for him what he was as a superintendent, and, to some extent, as a person. The process was a difficult one, and what he learned from it was painful, but probably rewarding, too. It hurts to understand finally that you can't go home again, as he said. But also, it's probably better to experience that hurt than to continue to live under the illusion that the circumstances are otherwise.

I want to close this chapter by repeating some points made earlier, to prevent any misunderstanding. I did not write this or the preceding chapter from an antiunion point of view. The arena of superintendent–teachers' union relationships is a very senstitive one. Unions were not formed to extend a cooperative hand to superintendents and school boards. Equally, they were not formed just in order to fight, but their very being mandates that their relationship with superintendents will involve conflicts. Since people react much more forcefully to their experiences of conflict than to those that lack it, it is absolutely to be expected that when a superintendent is asked to talk about how he perceives and reacts to teachers' unions, he will reflect on the conflictual situations into which he had been thrust by them. Sometimes these are exciting and challenging, too, of course, and we have noted that some superintendents enjoy the fray. Whatever his attitude, though, as these two chapters have shown, teacher unionism is an important factor in the reality of a superintendent's work life, and he must learn to deal with it.

8
Emotions and the Superintendency: Some High-Stress Situations

The previous three chapters may have given the impression that the work life of a superintendent is almost totally consumed by his dealings with, and feelings about, the school board and the teachers' union. This, of course, is not the case, though it is obvious that both of these groups function as central forces in a superintendent's thinking. Continual contact must be maintained with the school board, since it is his major source of political, and sometimes emotional, support. And there are times during the school year, either during negotiations or when particularly troublesome grievance or arbitration proceedings develop, when his concern about the union assumes major proportions and takes up what appears to be an inordinate amount of time.

The leadership and administration of a school district, though, involves a superintendent in a host of other activities besides those that focus directly on his relations with the school board or the teachers' union. A list of these activities could be very lengthy indeed. It would include things such as convening meetings, attending other meetings, holding conferences and counseling with the staff, meeting with parent groups, going to ritualistic functions, being seen at athletic events, disciplining teachers and students, attending conferences, testifying at legislative hearings, and on and on. Some of these activities are routine and boring; some are stressful, while others are not so. In combination, they occupy a great deal of a superintendent's time. This chapter is concerned with some activities that seemed to have special emotional meaning for the people who were interviewed as they thought about their work.

Analysis of the interview transcripts revealed four such activities. They concerned planning and presenting the budget; dealing with incompetent teachers; making decisions about expelling youngsters from school; and developing satisfying relationships with the news media. In no way do I think these activities are ones that every superintendent would find compelling.

But the fact is that over and over again, with one odd exception that we shall come to shortly, the interviewees mentioned them as things they had to do that had a powerful impact, in one way or another, on their sense of emotional well-being. Thus, I discuss them here with the idea of adding more insight into the human side of the superintendency.

The School Budget

We deal first with what, on the face of it, appears to be the odd exception referred to in the last paragraph. Probably no single activity in which a superintendent engages has more importance for the welfare of the schools than the preparation and presentation of the school budget. For many of us, the need to think about any type of budgeting process is a dreary, if not mystifying, exercise. Not so for superintendents, or for any other executive officer of an organization, public or private, since the budget represents the implementing tool of policy. It reflects priorities, as well as sacred cows. It has implications for the relative state of peace or conflict in a community, since its "bottom line" directly affects the community tax rate, and the size of the tax rate mandated by school budget increases has been responsible for many more than one taxpayers' revolt. This has held particularly true in the recent years that have witnessed inflation and a downswing in the economy.

   In what are known as fiscally independent school districts—mostly cities —school budgets receive their final approval in the legislative chambers of the municipally elected lawmaking body. In smaller communities, which constitute by far the greater number of cases, though, school budgets are submitted directly to the electorate for a vote. There are thus in these latter cases many more implications for the superintendent's role than in the former. In small communities, what the superintendent does, how he presents himself and the school program to the community, and the extent to which he is seen as a man who has a concern not only for the schools but for individual taxpaying citizens as well will have an important bearing on the way the budget proposal will be treated by the voters. It is not so much that it is *his* budget that is the issue. Indeed, officially the budget is the legal document and proposal of the school board, not the superintendent. But, in the eyes of the public, he is the embodiment of the schools. Further, of course, the budget is *his* in that boards tend to adopt and change both its outlines and details on his recommendation. While it represents the school board officially, it also represents him and his best judgment about what is needed in the schools for the coming year.

   Like almost everything else that attaches to a superintendent's work life, budget preparation implies the need to think strategically, particularly in terms of school program requirements but also in terms of the political and economic configuration of the community. One superintendent put his strategy in matter-of-fact, very rational terms:

> I try to get the board to determine beforehand what their priorities are, before we even start fooling around with dollars and figures. What do we want to accomplish in the next year? And that all begins in August, getting ready for the vote in the fall. We develop a series of objectives for the year, long-range goals, and some short-range goals. And the budget we're building now is going to be based on those documents and some of the things the board said it wanted to do.

The strategy implied here is one in which the superintendent's goal is to create a sort of psychological ownership of the budget by the board, in addition to its legal one. The idea is that if the board truly sees the budget as its own and therefore has a stake in it, its members will be in a better position to urge its approval in an election. That all seems reasonable enough, and one would expect no undue problems of budget passage resulting from it. However, two years prior to our discussion, the budget had been defeated in that district, since both the board and the superintendent had failed to adequately judge the political and economic tenor of the community. It was the year in which Proposition 13 was passed in California, and its contagious effect was felt in a good-sized suburban community in New York.

Another interviewee, whose strategy differed from the one above in that it was the school people who took the budget initiative rather than the board, likened the process to the production of a stage play. His prefacing comment was that the budget, first, must be seen as a document that represents conflicts and their resolution. And, then, in a somewhat amused tone, he said,

> You begin to prepare budgets, and you prepare for a public vote. It's show time, and the curtain goes up pretty soon. It's just like preparation for a Broadway play. So you put everything together. You have all the actors. You have to direct the whole production. You have an assistant director of this and an assistant director of that. The pieces begin to fall into place, and ultimately you take a look at this instrument you are going to give to your board of education and then to the public, and it's a big, big production. You put everything together, and you look at the whole score, the words, the music, the people, the actors who are going to play a part in this whole thing, and you get ready for the day you present the budget. The night I present the budget, I'm pretty well prepped. I have all the material at my fingertips. I have all my

people out there to help me in case I get stuck. They can prop me, but I generally have enough knowledge to do the job. Sometimes we are very successful in all this. We put on a tremendous show. We get everything together, and we have all the answers. And sometimes it's still a box-office flop!

You may recall that in chapter 3, as we discussed the metaphors that superintendents applied to their role, a distinct theatrical impression emerged. The terms *producer* and *director* were used, for example. The theatrics of the situation, as it may apply to the budgeting process, certainly became clear in the excerpt that has just been quoted. It's as though the person who related this scenario was almost sitting back and chuckling at himself as he described his image of this situation. He was almost saying, "Look at this elaborate game I have to play during budget time!" The game, of course, has more than one purpose. It is partly designed to communicate to the board and the community that the superintendent is on top of his job, that he takes things seriously, and that he knows the answers to sticky questions. Thus, it is a means of building credibility. The game is also played out in a way that encourages staff involvement so that the budget doesn't become the superintendent's personal document but represents the best thinking of concerned and hardworking professionals.

There is, however, a possible third function to the game: it may serve as a protective device for the superintendent in case the production is a "box-office flop"—defeated at the polls. If this sounds a little cynical, note what this person also said: "The only thing you have to realize is that you can't take it too seriously. Life will go on even with a budget defeat. Sure, it's important; in many ways, the most important thing you have to do, but the world doesn't end if the budget goes down." So in the event the budget isn't initially approved, if one thinks of the whole process as a dramatic production, one may, to continue the metaphor, cut out a scene here and there in order to get more audience appreciation. But a central issue, according to this individual, is for the superintendent not to get too personal a stake in the specifics of the budget. If the proposal is defeated, it is important for him not to see it as a setback for him as an individual.

This sentiment was echoed by several other people, even though one of them noted that at budget time, "Again, you parade out that little bit of yourself in front of everybody." The underlying issue, though, is not to internalize the situation and not to have too much of oneself riding on the outcome of budget decisions. This is not merely aimed at preventing personal distress and aggravation. It also represents a view concerning who takes responsibility for the schools in the total scheme of community political life. One superintendent put it this way:

> The big thing is not to take responsibility personally for the budget. I do not accept responsibility as a superintendent, nor do I accept responsibility as a person. It belongs to all of us.

Thus, when the people speak at the polls or through their representatives, they must live with what they said, and so must the superintendent. And though he may experience some frustration at the outcome, as one person said, "If they vote down a budget, they vote down a budget. I might have a few beers that night, but why worry about something you can't change?"

All of this sounds rather straightforward. In fact — and I include the humorous references to the "Broadway play" — it sounds a little too straightforward, too pat, as though dealing with school budgets was for the superintendent a matter-of-fact function that had no ripple effects on him as a person. It is hard to believe that there is not another side to the picture and that a decision that has such far-reaching effects can be dealt with so impassively. Indeed, a cue that this may not be the case came from another superintendent, who, referring to the time when the budget is in question, said, "I'm edgy; I don't sleep well. I can't avoid it, and it goes on for a number of weeks."

His reaction may be somewhat extreme, but if I understand anything at all about the politics of school budgeting, this reaction may be a more reliable clue to the emotional reality of the situation than the matter of factness of other comments. One can't help wondering: Why concentrate so much energy on producing a "Broadway play" if one is not highly and personally involved in its outcome? Why teach oneself to avoid getting personally committed to a budget if not for self-protection? These comments seem to express a need to develop a hard shell about such matters, at least in public. What may well be the driving force is the need for superintendents to maintain a cool analytical posture with the community—an energy-consuming behavior in itself. After all, when a superintendent doesn't sleep well, the public doesn't know it.

The Incompetent Teacher

Schools, like any other work enterprise, have people who are more skilled or less skilled at doing their job. There are a few teachers in every school system whose teaching expertise is so great as to attract wide, if mostly informal, recognition. Most teachers are certainly adequate or more than that, but there are some in every district, regardless of its wealth or prestige, who have no business teaching. They are incompetent. The teachers know it, the principals know it, and so does the superintendent. If the person is untenured, he or she may be terminated quickly, and with little trouble as a rule. If the person involved is a tenured teacher, the case takes on a very different complexion and is a source of no small amount of irritation and frustration for a superintendent (and principals, too, of course). The reasons for this are common knowledge. The procedures that must be followed to dismiss a tenured teacher are long, involved, and complicated. They include legal or quasi-legal proceedings, and through one means or another, the task of proving incompetency rests with the school district. No superintendent looks forward to the process. It is burdensome, trying, and unpleasant, so much so that sometimes the superintendent makes an informal cost-benefit analysis and decides that trying to dismiss the teacher is too risky, time-consuming, and too costly to be worth the effort. He tries to bury the problem in the recesses of his mind and go on to other things. The rationalization is, of course, that every system has its incompetents who can't be terminated or won't resign. One simply has to live with it all. But there is some emotional fallout, since the situation makes the superintendent feel relatively helpless— an uncomfortable feeling for people who tend to see themselves as being in charge of things.

The superintendents in this study were able to respond quite readily to this problem area of their work lives. A sense of their feelings is abundantly evident from the following:

> It tears me apart. It really does. We try to work with it. It's hard to prove incompetence, as you know. Almost impossible. If we had more full-time supervisors, we could do something. We try to help them by sending them to conferences. We go with them. And some of them have made some improvement, but it all really tears me apart.

> I cry sometimes. I bite my tongue. It bugs the hell out of me to see incompetence in the classroom. And you can't get at it. You're almost powerless by the laws of the state. There are loopholes, but to get through them costs a fortune of time and money. So you have a win and a lose column. Sometimes you lose, sometimes you win. But it really is frustrating.

> It's one of those things that you tear your hair out about, but you have to live with it. You're damned if you do, and damned if you don't.

The potential emotional impact on superintendents of having to tolerate incompetent teachers in their schools—and pay them as well as excellent ones —is shown in the words they chose to describe their reactions: "It tears me apart"; "I cry sometimes"; "I bite my tongue"; "You tear your hair out." These are not wild, impulsive phrases. They represent deeply felt frustration.

The root cause of the frustration, in addition to knowing that youngsters may not be getting the education they deserve with a particular teacher, is that many times it is a "no exit" situation. As one person put it, "You have to learn to live with the failures of other people." It is not a pleasant prospect to wake up to every morning, and so, as was suggested earlier, sometimes these circumstances are just buried in the consciousness. Noting this, a superintendent said, "I can't do anything about it, so what the hell. Early on I made a decision never to get frustrated about things I can't fix."

There are, though, some things that superintendents can do to deal with incompetent teachers, even if what they do does not create a permanent "fix." The strategy is based, as is much of their work lives, on another cost-benefit analysis. It involves placing the person in a job where, in the best judgment of those involved in making the decision, he or she can do the least damage. This is, perhaps, too coldly objective a way of looking at things, at least in the eyes of a compassionate observer. But sometimes the alternatives are so limited that, as one superintendent said, "You try to get them with people that they will hurt least. It's about all you can do. It's minimizing the effect of a bad situation over which you have little control."

Control does exist at times, however, and it may exist in a subtle or not so subtle manner. An example of the latter was recounted by one person. After talking about how uncomfortable he felt with the legal procedures used for documenting incompetency and saying, "I can't hide behind the door and catch them," he said of one incompetent teacher, quite shortly, "We bought him out." That is, the superintendent, with the board's support, of course, made a deal with the teacher whereby he agreed to resign for a certain monetary consideration. Not all school boards are willing or have the resources to do this, but when they are willing and do have those resources, it removes the problem in a hurry. Needless to say, it would have to be a most pressing situation.

Another example of superintendent control that is more subtle emerged in the following anecdote:

> We had a situation last year. It was in the high school. There was a teacher who just wasn't good, and we couldn't do much about it. Well, there was a combination English and reading project that I pushed and got accepted. It meant raising standards and creating higher expectations for teachers. It meant she was really going to have to confront her own practice. She resigned. And there was a home economics teacher who refused to integrate her classes, boys and girls, in spite of school policy. I pushed the principal to put the screws to her, which he finally did. She decided to get out. I don't know if I did this consciously with the idea in my mind that she'd resign, but I know the thought ran through my mind.

So the control of the superintendent is there, though the outcome of the actions that he takes, in cases such as these, is unpredictable, to say the least. More frequently, as we have seen, the efforts to deal with problems involved with less than able teachers is to put them where they can do the least harm. It sounds cold-hearted and manipulative, but for many superintendents it's the least painful of all the alternatives.

Expelling a Student from School

Every school superintendent has been placed in a position where he had to decide whether or not to expel a youngster from school. The problems involved relate to the student's disruptive behavior in school or infringement of school rules. What we are interested in here, though, is how superintendents react to these circumstances. What does it mean to a man when his best judgment tells him a young person should no longer continue his or her education in that setting? There were two broad categories of reactions in the interviews. One was a rather matter-of-fact response that suggested that tough as it may be, this was another fact of life. These superintendents were saying, "Well, we tried. Nothing worked. That's the way the ball bounces." It sounds like a hardened perspective, but it is perhaps made necessary by a person's need to protect himself from the trauma of knowing deep down inside that somehow, some way, something just hasn't worked right. And that something is a system for which he has more than a modicum of responsibility.

The second type of reaction was anything but matter of fact. It involved some very deep-seated feelings about the superintendents themselves and what they were doing. The character of some of these reactions stands out in boldface.

> I constantly go through a double-edged sword situation. Have we done enough to help this kid? If we had more resources, could we have done something else? It's a tough decision. I guess I'm constantly searching for an answer. Have I just made an expedient decision, or have I made the decision I had to make? That's the gut-wrencher.

> It tears me to exclude a kid from school, and yet I have to go by the record. I have doubts about myself. It's like playing God, 'cause I know I'm making a decision about this kid's life.

> I guess the day I'm not concerned about a youngster I have to expel is the day I ought to leave. I look at it as our failure. I find one of the toughest days I have to face is the day I know I've run out of string on a youngster. It's a very, very tough day.

It's one of the hardest decisions to make, to drop a kid from school. Because you're acting like God, and I don't think anyone has that right. Because you never know, tomorrow he might change. So I sit there, and I weigh everything, and I really get torn as I look at this kid and try to figure out what's the best thing for him.

It scares me to think of that kind of power. I'm not talking about something momentary. I've never thrown a kid out of school permanently, simply because I can't bring myself to do it.

The thoughts of these superintendents speak for themselves, sometimes eloquently. Deciding whether or not to expel a youngster confronts them directly and inescapably with the implied failure of the schools and the fact that their decision may well have a long-term effect on the student. Playing God may not be uncomfortable when it is concerned with bestowing favors. But when it means meting out long-term penalties to young people, and one thinks about it as these superintendents did, the degree of discomfort is sometimes major, as we have seen. It is so major and the potential consequences so great that one of the respondents could not bring himself to expel someone permanently, a position that some of his colleagues might call naive.

The curious thing is that of all the different conflictual situations that have been discussed thus far in this book, this is the one that puts the superintendent in the most direct emotional contact with the educational experience he supervises. The case of the incompetent teacher has some of this coloration as well, but seemingly not to the extent that we have just witnessed. Most of the other conflictual situations had, at their base, underlying system-oriented political considerations. While there is occasionally a political side to expulsion proceedings—pressure from principals or teachers, for example—most times that is not the case. What is the case is that he must make an educational decision about a student that may have far-reaching effects. And he and he alone must make it. Thus, the questioning of self superintendents seem to go through, the searching for an answer, the intense concern to be as right as they can possibly be, all make sense—in a troubling sort of way.

Relations with the Media

If a person ever has any doubts that school systems are public enterprises, he or she only needs to pick up the daily newspaper. Hardly a day goes by, certainly not two, when an item relating to one or more of the local public schools does not appear in print. It may be a news report, an editorial, or a letter to the editor. It may be laudatory or condemnatory. It may have to do with school budgets or bond issues, collective negotiations, controversy over a school closing, competency testing, drugs, an innovative art class, school busing, or what have you. Next to crime—a curious commentary—it might be fair to say that the schools take up more newspaper space than any other single local subject. Certainly, if they are not in second place, they are way up high as a continuing focus of the press.

Quite naturally, superintendents are concerned about the way their schools are treated by the newspapers. Their relationships with reporters are important to them because they have little control over what a reporter will write, what slant will be given to a particular problem, or how the report will finally appear in print. Both the importance and delicateness of their dealings with reporters, in particular, and the press in general, will become evident in the following remarks. The issue underlying all of the comments is, "How will we be treated?"

We deal with two metropolitan newspapers. The problem is they put their neophyte reporters on the education circuit. You can never be sure the reporter you talk to today will be there tomorrow. They're looking for controversy because they want to sell newspapers, and they will tell you that. A good positive story is not good news for them. People don't read that stuff. So, in many cases, they will attempt to create conflict.

I have great concerns about the power of the press. The problem is that many times reporters don't understand the issues they are reporting on. They haven't done their homework. A couple of years ago, we had an extremely positive report on a state audit, but a reporter got ahold of it and lifted out a couple of things we got our wrist slapped for but [that] were extremely unimportant in the long run. The headline writer wrote a negative headline, and we were fighting that issue for six months. It was a very difficult six months for me. I was really ragged. I finally demanded and received an apology from the editor.

You cannot alienate the newspapers. If you do, you've lost the game. You cannot fight the press in any way, shape, or manner. You have to give them the facts, be honest with them, and hopefully, they'll do a good job for you. It's all out of your control, so the only thing you can do is be accommodating. You have to make their job a little easier because if you make their job hard, they'll get you.

The education reporter and I have an agreement: You write it the way you feel, but be accurate. Treat me fairly. You don't have to be complimentary, but don't slander me. Don't write what you write just to sell newspapers. If you do that, then I have to play defensive.

If one forgets for a moment that these were superintendents of local school districts talking, the imagery that gets created takes one into a much larger political sphere. One can almost hear political figures of every stature in almost any governmental entity making similar remarks about their relationships with the press. How odd it is, it might be thought, that people whose training and career goals have all been concerned with occupying positions from which they could provide a higher quality of education in the public schools speak as though they were the press secretaries to powerful political figures—or those figures themselves. It is odd, until one considers again how political the job is. Superintendents seem rarely to be free of either the internal or external political consequences of any decision they make, and, we infer from their comments about the press, reporters are always ready to seize an opportunity to write about problems in the schools or apparently, on occasion, to create mountains out of molehills.

Good news does not make headlines. And so it is that the press must be treated with a great deal of circumspection, with particular attention being paid to cultivating cordial, if not friendly, relations with reporters. There is, then, an ongoing tension that accompanies a superintendent's relationship with the press that is characterized by caution. One person described his reactions this way: "It all makes me very cautious. Too cautious, probably, but I feel I have to be."

One superintendent commented on his inability to control the headlines that accompany news stories about the schools—as distinct from the stories themselves. Reporters may write an accurate account of a school situation that treats an event quite fairly and objectively. But reporters don't write the headlines for the story. This job is left to others who have little or no relationship with the superintendent. The task of the headline writer is to attract the reader's attention, and as this person put it,

> The headlines are what kill us. Most people read them, and we
> have no control over what they say. Even the reporter has no
> control. The person who writes headlines in our local newspaper is
> a sensationalist. He loves to give things big, flashy headlines which
> have nothing to do with the article. So the headlines kill us.

As was suggested earlier, then, the problems and conflicts that are created for a superintendent by the press involve circumstances over which he has little control, and it is frustrating to have little power over circumstances that may affect one's job. It is not so much that newspaper editors and reporters are malevolent toward the schools, though some of them are, as it is that their goal is to sell newspapers, something about which school superintendents could care less. This point, too, leads to a curious sort of conflict. Two institutions—the schools and the press—whose basic goals are widely variant must relate to each other in situations in which the superintendent is at a distinct power disadvantage—an unusual situation, to say the least, when compared to other facets of his job.

9
Emotions and the Superintendency: The General Picture

Superintendents tend to be good at analyzing and conceptualizing the nature of the problems and conflicts they face. Indeed, those are two skills without which they would probably not last long in the position, since the effectiveness of their decision making depends on how well they understand and think about issues that confront them. They seem to be good analyzers, then, particularly of situations that are complex and that demand that the individual who would work in them figure out how their parts fit together. Superintendents often epitomize the practical thinker's thinker: the cool, analytical person who never loses his composure and is somewhat immune to his own feelings, if, indeed, he acknowledges having any.

Much of what has been written thus far belies this image. Superintendents, it turns out, are quite human after all. Though they don't talk in public about the emotionality that attends their work, they most certainly do have feelings about their work life. Preceding chapters have made this quite evident.

In this chapter, moving away from a concern with particularly stressful activities, we focus on what might be called the generalized emotional condition of the superintendency. Our aim is to discuss the unavoidable emotional consequences that the people interviewed felt being a superintendent had for them. Much of the chapter will consider feelings of distress—for want of a better word—that these superintendents encountered in themselves as they did their work. But this point should not mislead the reader, since they were not implying that the job itself was an emotionally negative one. Far from it: they liked what they were doing, felt challenged, had fun, and often were simply quite excited by their personal and professional prospects. Each of them, though, without exception, was able to talk at some length about the job's emotional toxicity (Levinson, 1973)—conditions that were somehow draining of their energy, fatiguing, stress-inducing, or personally troubling.

To use a word that has appeared several times thus far, these conditions were seen as elaborating on their descriptions of the "territory."

As in the previous chapter, we attend to several central categories of response that occurred with some regularity in the course of the interviews. These categories had to do with frustration, caused by the slowness of the decision-making process; boredom; loneliness; feelings of inadequacy; concern over the compromise of ethics; and feelings of personal stress.

The Slowness of Decision Making

Decisions of consequence, and sometimes minor ones, are slow in the making in school districts. As the following comments illustrate, this slowness is debilitating to action-oriented superintendents.

> The thing that is probably most depressing about this job is that by the time you accomplish something, you could care less. There's no victory in it anymore. It has taken so long between the time you set something up and when it's achieved that there's no enjoyment. It's not like finishing a nice piece of woodwork. You get an idea, you start; you get a final product. In this business, by the time you get a final product, you almost forget even what you started it for.

> The thing that really bugs the hell out of me is the time it takes to get a decision made, even when you know what the decision's going to be and that it will be in the best interests of the district. To have to back up and go through all the bullshit when you think you're at the point where something can be done—that really gets to me.

> It's my own impatience with the time it takes to do things. There are issues in the community that have been there so long, it'll take ten years to change them. And I think, God, I can't wait that long. It really bothers me.

> The work load itself is not debilitating. But it's the lack of a sense of productivity because of the time it takes to get things done. The job has become terribly complex, so that the time mandates to reach a solution are not compatible with the time requirements that are necessary to achieve a solution. You can't push a rope. You can't force a tree to grow. You can't force a staff to recognize faster than it's capable or willing to recognize the need for change.

Probably most organizational executives, especially those in the private sector, are oriented toward action and occasionally become frustrated because things move slowly. In this sense, the above comments reflect a common concern. But to belabor the point just a bit, there is a difference here, I think, that is symbolic of the core of the superintendency: its essential politicalness. Things move slowly in the schools for a variety of reasons. But central to this slowness is the system of decision making and decision implementation in which superintendents must engage. It involves the gathering of support, mobilizing coalitions, coaxing, sitting through seemingly endless meetings. Most of all it involves time. The metaphor of his role as that of a trout fisherman that one superintendent applied to himself (chapter 3) makes sense in this context. He is engaged in a slow, delicate process of matching wits with something over which he exercises little direct control. The metaphor doesn't hold completely, of course. When the fisherman lands his catch, he can see it and eat it. Little interferes with his enjoyment of the prize. Not so, though, for the superintendent, from the perspective of at least one person, who felt that the time it takes to get something done in the superintendency makes its achievement much less valuable than if things could happen more quickly. It was as though he scarcely recognized what he'd achieved after he'd achieved it.

An interesting sort of conflict gets created then, and it is one with which all political figures must live. On the one hand, they tend to be people who want to do things. Superintendents, for the most part, want to be in that role so that they can have an impact on schooling. On the other hand, they are part of and give support to the democratic and necessarily political character of the educational system. Their action instincts tell them to "do something," but their political acumen tells them that whatever they want to do will take time. It is a built-in stress circumstance that one superintendent, in a very brief reference to the seemingly endless number of meetings he attended on various issues and the seemingly endless character of the meetings themselves, described as "exhausting." And another superintendent who was very troubled by the intensity of the action–time conflict expressed himself in these words:

> Sometimes I wonder what the hell I'm wasting my time for. To be honest with you, really, I'm too young to get burned out going through all this crap. The excitement of the challenge? Who needs it? You have to wonder if all the time you put in is worth it in the end. It's something I struggle with.

A Sense of Boredom

There is a curious other side to this image of constant and time-consuming interaction in which superintendents find themselves, and which seems to exact its emotional price from them. At times they find the job boring. At first glance, given the things that have been considered in previous chapters, that statement may be startling. But life in the superintendency is not all action, nor is it totally concerned with political things that require a superintendent to put his best wits to work. The organization also has to be administered, sometimes in a very routine fashion. In addition, there are sometimes brief periods when there are no large decisions to be made and things are running so smoothly, the work becomes boring and unpleasant. We have some examples of both types of situations:

> Most things, on a daily basis, get handled pretty well through the organization we've set up. Sometimes it works too well, and I get bored with it because of the lack of excitement. Things are too easy.

> The only thing I find that's debilitating is that I like to be busy, and sometimes I'm bored. I just have a need to feel active, and sometimes I go through periods when there isn't a lot going on. I have to create things to keep me interested.

> I think what happens to me at times is that I just don't want to work on ongoing projects. I basically sit back and wait for things to come, and I become bored. Maybe I'm not working hard enough. Or it's that I just don't want to write that report today. And I sit there, and I'm bored.

> I get very bored when the problems are very small, or when it's a day-to-day maintenance operation. The bigger the problem, the more I get stimulated. It's the crappy little thing—a bus problem, this and that—that really does it for me. But then, I am prone to getting bored, especially when things are too peaceful.

Perhaps raising the issue of the boring parts of a superintendent's life on the job doesn't warrant even the small amount of space that it has been given here. After all, it is not as though the job is a boring one intrinsically, nor, one can assume, that the periods of boredom are of long duration. The fact, though, that a number of interviewees mentioned their feelings about these times provides some insight into the job and the people who occupy it. They seem to be a restless lot, mostly happy, but also worn down when they are contending with complex human and organizational problems. And when the system, through its natural workings, doesn't provide these problems, it is almost as though some superintendents start to initiate them on their own. Underneath is another type of conflict—that between the system's pervasive value of keeping the school scene peaceful and the superintendent's need for meaningful activity that goes beyond routine administration, important as that may be in the service of peace. How one defines "meaningful activity," of course, is an individual matter. For one superintendent, it may be trying to initiate curriculum reform or a particular staff development program with teachers. Another might be concerned with teacher evaluation or trying to improve the school communication network. Whatever the substance, the point seems to be that the people who become superintendents, as a rule, are not content to merely take care of things. It is a boring state and to be avoided. We have an interesting anecdote about this need for action that came from a man who happened to be the oldest of the 25 interviewed and indeed could have retired any time he wished. He was speaking of the frustration he experienced as he saw norms for achievement in the schools becoming lowered. He said:

> I had a colleague call me the other day, and he said, "Gee, you're catching hell in the newspapers again," and I said, "Yeah." And then he said, "When are you going to learn not to change things?" This is a 40-year-old guy saying this. And I didn't say anything to him, but I thought to myself, "Here's a 40-year-old guy who has given up." To me that same guy could be sitting on top of a cesspool with the roof about to fall in, and he simply says, "To hell with it. Let it fall in. I'll move."

Obviously, the 40-year-old man in this case is an exception to our suggestion that superintendents tend to search for action if it doesn't simply occur. Life has become peaceful for him, and he likes it that way. But exceptions are just that. More often, the interviewees expressed a need to be doing something more than maintaining what already exists. And the more complex that something is, the better, even though, as we noted earlier, the combination of complexity and time required is in itself a stressful situation for some.

Lonely at the Top

It is probably endemic to the position of every top executive of an organization that a certain amount of loneliness attaches to it. As we shall see, this is clearly the case with superintendents. While not all of them thought of their job as being a lonely one, the vast majority of them did, sometimes in rather poignant terms. Their words best describe the condition:

> Yeah, it's very lonely. You know why? Because when it comes down to it, if something blows, it's yours. I can't dump it on anybody, 'cause I have a problem with that. I think it's a very lonely position, even with the board. They expect you to solve problems. That's what they pay you for, and of course they're right. Big issues are really mine alone to decide about.

It's lonely at the top. I have friends and a social life, but it's not connected with school at all. I can't be friends with the people I work with or with teachers, or even the principals. No, I don't have friends among the staff. They're not going to trust me enough to be my friend.

It's very lonely. I deliberately avoid getting social at work with colleagues. It's very hard to demand certain things of a friend, and I think the longer you stay on a job, the more difficult it becomes. I do my best to keep arm's distance, and I find that my social life stinks. When I was assistant superintendent, I was a confidante to the superintendent. Now, I miss "me."

One of the problems, as far as I'm concerned, is finding someone I can really talk to. It's lonely. It's not difficult, of course, to find someone just to chat with. It's what you can talk about that's the problem. You can't go home and unload on the guy next door. School superintendents just can't do that because of the public and political nature of the job. You have to watch yourself all the time.

There have been times that I've stood totally alone, you know, totally alone. Sure, I can talk with my staff about lots of things. But even then I'm not sharing that part of me that is still holding those problems at the top.

There was a school thing that turned into a personal attack. I was very much alone. I didn't know where to turn for help. I could turn to a minister or somebody like that, but all they'd do would be to console me. You know, "Be brave my son, and you will have your victory." Well, that's bullshit, because I was hurting right then, and I wanted someone to sit down—and I don't know what I was looking for—someone to work with and give me some support.

The superintendency, then, creates a type of isolation for the person who occupies that position. It's odd, because, as one superintendent suggested, there are lots of people to talk with, but in another sense there's no one. It's not an unusual position for executives to be in, but there are particular aspects of being a superintendent that make the situation different. There is, of course, the commonsense notion of the loneliness connected to being "the man at the top." It's the type of loneliness that attaches to the idea that at times, and particularly when the problem is of major importance, the individual stands alone with the decision. It cannot be unloaded on anyone else, and superintendents tend to feel separated from others at such times. It is a familiar scene: all of us have images—sometimes they are actual pictures—of a major political figure pondering a decision all by himself. *Lonely* is indeed the word to describe it.

Let us turn, though, to some of those more or less unique parts of the superintendency that, as it were, pile loneliness on top of loneliness, in spite of the fact that there are a lot of people around. We have, for example, the idea that one does not, or finds it very difficult to, become friends with staff colleagues or teachers. It's an old adage that the boss does not become friendly with his subordinates, and we had one superintendent who said just about precisely that. "Don't mix business with friendship," is the dictum, and it is not a bad one. The problem is, though, that the administrative staff members and teachers are all colleagues of the superintendent in the very real sense of the word. Further, practically every superintendent has been a teacher, and every teacher can aspire to be a superintendent, a condition very unlikely to prevail in other types of organizations. Most corporate executives have never been assembly line workers, and there are very few of the latter who even faintly aspire to being the executive. But superintendents and their colleagues are cut from the same cloth. If they wanted to, they could speak the same language to each other. As we noted, however, they don't. The distance created by organizational position also creates social distance, and perhaps it is just as well. But it does make for loneliness, and the social distance seems to be characterized by a tension system that can be described as "I would like to be friends with some of my coworkers, but it will be better for both me and them if I'm not."

The loneliness of the superintendency, it seems, is partly a result of the political side of the job. As one man said, "You just can't go and unload on the guy next door . . . because of the public and political nature of the job. You have to watch yourself all the time." So another tension system is created between a superintendent and people who *are* his friends. One must be careful of what one says, even to people who may be close. The possibility, through casual conversation with a neighbor about the superintendent's job problems, of something becoming public that should remain private is too great a risk to take. Every political figure recognizes this possibility and tends to guide his or her behavior accordingly. Those who elect to take the risk are apt to regret it, superintendents no less than public figures in the grander world of public affairs.

We have a final example of the loneliness that attaches to being a superintendent. It has to do with what happened to one superintendent when controversy over an educational issue turned into a vicious personal attack. The words quoted in the last excerpt cited above really don't need much elaboration. The man was the focus of much verbal abuse from a far—right-wing political group in his community. Issues of his partisan politics and his religion were raised, although the latter was dealt with very subtly. Regardless, he was alone through it all, and though he could get lots of sympathy, he had to deal with his loneliness by himself. Again, his words tell it best: "I was hurting right then, and I wanted someone to sit down—and I don't know what I was looking for—someone to work with and give me some support."

He finally did get his support, he went on to explain, through what he described as the American tendency to side with the underdog. Once the community sensed that he was standing alone in the face of an overwhelming force, it came in on his side of the battle: "As the tide began to turn, help came in from all sides." But it didn't come before he was forced to face a lonely period of feeling under siege.

Feelings of Inadequacy

By and large, of course, superintendents tend to feel competent to meet the demands of their job. They seem to have few doubts about themselves and their ability to deal well with things—which really means, publicly, to satisfy the board that they are in control of the complex politics of the enterprise. Occasionally, though, this self-confidence is misplaced. Superintendents do get fired. Usually, when this occurs, it involves either a value conflict between the board and the superintendent or a situation in which the latter has just not proved able to keep the conflicts inherent in the system under control. There are times, too, when the firing of a superintendent occurs less because of his inadequacies than because of the community's need to find a scapegoat for its own inability to resolve its problems. Superintendents are handy and visible targets, even when they are not the focus of conflict.

Feelings of their personal inadequacy to meet job demands, then, did not emerge with much force during the interviews. It was as though these people felt they had a pretty good handle on what they were doing, could anticipate problems that might arise, and could think through and mobilize the resources needed to deal with them. But there was no sense of arrogance or condescension about this, nor was the idea that the job was a "piece of cake." Each seemed, instead, to feel a sort of quiet confidence that he was up to handling whatever situations might arise. It was not that they had the immediate and correct answer to a problem but that given time they would arrive at it. Further, there was also a sense of feeling that they could move on to another, more complex school district and perform equally well.

There were a few times, however, when some feelings of inadequacy found their way into our conversations. They seemed not to be deep-seated and certainly not immobilizing, but they were there nonetheless. A few examples will suffice. One of them felt inadequate when faced with the need to discuss new subject content for courses, instructional processes, or new technology. He said,

> There is simply much more that we know now about everything.
> It's impossible to keep up with it. No way. And I know I feel

> terribly inadequate on those occasions when we get into substantive discussions of instructional programs. I don't know which way to go, which direction to take. I'd like to be able to say that I have the expertise, but I know that I don't.

Certainly, every executive has confronted situations where he feels a lack of personal knowledge concerning a decision he must make. The usual strategy is to rely on one's subordinates to provide the information and to suggest alternatives. No organization could function without this consultative process. What makes the superintendent's position unusual, though, is that in the eyes of the lay public and the school board he is "supposed" to know. After all, he was employed as the educational leader of the local schools. That is the popular image of him, though, as we have seen, one would be hard put to conceptualize his actual work as that of educational leader or statesman. Still, it is the image that people have of another that guides their expectations of his behavior. And so it is that superintendents, aside from their own feelings of wanting to be better informed, may also sense expectations from others that the education business, in all its forms, is something they should know about. They are the ones who make the decisions, and they are the ones who are held responsible. One may speculate that those times of "not knowing" are among the ones that Burlingame referred to earlier as encouraging mystification and cover-up. It's no wonder that they lead potentially to a sense of inadequacy, and we suspect that that feeling is more widespread than most superintendents care to admit.

Another superintendent, relatively new to the position, felt quite comfortable with instructional concerns. It had been some time, though, since he had worked with problems of union contract administration, and he was somewhat uncomfortable about that, but he was learning. What he felt most inadequate about was dealing with the state department of education, particularly as he had to learn the ins and outs of a political and financial sphere far removed from his own day-to-day concerns. "How do you get a handle on that amorphous complex in the state capital?" was the implicit question. It is an interesting query, especially since superintendents arrive at their position through the educational system, not through that of municipal or state government. It is a foreign world, and one with which initially, at least, most superintendents are ill prepared to deal. But they learn, and in fact the responses of most of the interviewees concerning their relationships with state and federal agencies expressed more frustration than inadequacy. They knew how to do what they had to do but were frustrated by the need to do it and the slowness with which things happened as a result of their efforts.

A different perception of his inadequacy was expressed by another person, who was also relatively new to the superintendency. While he felt comfortable with instructional and program issues, he felt quite at sea in dealing with issues that involved power politics, particularly when the board itself was in conflict or its positions were ill defined. Experienced superintendents will probably smile at this last sentence as they observe a newcomer to their ranks going through the political initiation rites, as well they might. They have all been through the situation, where, having been interested and concerned educators, they quickly had to learn to shrug off some of their concerns about school programs, or put them on the back burner for a while, and learn what it meant to manage the politics of their job. But smiles were not the order of the day for this person, whose concern was his feelings of inadequacy.

The last example of feelings of inadequacy comes from a superintendent who was at home with both the politics of his job and the instructional and program problems that confronted him. His sense of being less than competent had to do with his inability to get his secondary school principal to be willing to learn the skills, and put them into operation, of leading his school as a total educational enterprise. As he put it:

> The principal is oriented to nuts and bolts. It's always, "How can we fix things?" and not the central educational and organizational issues of the school. I used to think I could transfer high-level skills to others, but now I'm not so sure.

This man, then, was questioning some of the skills that he used to take for granted and was wondering if he was really up to the job of retraining his secondary school principal. This particular feeling of inadequacy may be seen as relatively inconsequential when set against other functions of the superintendency about which a person may feel utterly competent. However, this superintendent may be confronting a central question that many of his colleagues have shunted aside — the question of the personal ability of any superintendent to make a direct impact on the character of the schools in his charge. It is a very difficult task, and if one is serious about it he will indeed have reason to wonder about his adequacy for that particular part of his job. Perhaps, in the world of school affairs, as in most other sectors of public life, one has to learn to focus one's energies and skills on that which is possible, and simply put aside that which isn't or which would call forth too much conflict. One has only to read the daily papers to understand that this process is constantly occurring in just about every sphere of political life.

The feelings of inadequacy about their ability to do the job that superintendents have from time to time, it is probably fair to suggest, are emotionally toxic. They seem to call forth subtle kinds of questions that remain undiscussed and possibly undiscussable in the ordinary circumstances of their lives.

The Compromise of Ethics

It would be hard to imagine a superintendency, no matter how large or small the school district or whether it is a generally peaceful scene or one that is prone to community conflict, that does not on occasion confront the incumbent with ethical problems. Political crosscurrents rarely subside. Conflicting demands are constantly evident. Many of them, perhaps most, can be and are resolved through the objective consideration of alternatives in the context of the particulars of each situation. Compromise is the essence; in the schools, as in any other institutional form of public life, no one gets everything he wants. This is the central condition of any type of participative governance. From time to time, though, circumstances arise when the type of compromise that a superintendent confronts involves a demand on him, public or private, to act at variance with some of his own values. They present him with an ethical dilemma in which the "compromise" of oneself that he is called on to make involves, according to *Webster's Dictionary*, the making of "a shameful or disreputable concession." The conflict, then, is with himself.

There was a time when situations such as this commonly occurred in relation to hiring. School districts were highly politicized, in the negative sense of the word, and teaching jobs were often given as a form of patronage, regardless of whether the prospective employee was qualified for the job. Superintendents, it appears, were relatively helpless in these conditions, particularly if they wanted to keep their jobs, and there can be little doubt that a great number of "shameful concessions" were made. By and large, those types of demands have disappeared, and superintendents seem rarely called on to make hiring decisions on the basis of favoritism as opposed to competence. We have some examples, though, of other situations that raised value questions for individuals and in which they had to decide whether or not to make a concession of which they would not be proud.

First, though, some of the superintendents talked a bit more generally about being faced with problems that might involve a compromise of principle on their part. The comments they made had to do with their behavior over time and how their experience over the years almost forced the development of an "Is it worth it?" attitude. The following comment provides a good overview of this process:

> When I was younger, my principles really were out front. Boy,
> when I tangled I would bitch and scream. But I guess there's been
> a mellowing process. I guess I'm willing to sacrifice a bit more of
> my principles now simply to keep things steady. Or maybe I've
> realized there is no black and white and that much more of life is a
> grey area. Maybe my principles are slipping, or I can find more

justification for looking at both sides. But there have been a few
times when I've had to sweep things under the table.

Certainly, if a superintendent sees himself dealing differently over the
years with matters that involve his own ethics, it is not a function of time
alone. Other things intervene. One of them might simply be learning to
acknowledge which things are worth fighting over—the process of "mellowing," as it was called. And this, in turn, seems to be connected to the desire
simply to keep things steady, to avoid a conflict that will not have an educational payoff. The other side of it, though—learning that matters are rarely
black and white—has a couple of possible interpretations. First is the undeni-
able reality that much of life, for superintendents or anyone else, is more
shades of grey than anything else, particularly in human affairs. There is
probably no better guideline for a superintendent's behavior than this. On
the other hand, having learned this, the "shades of grey" principle can serve
as a personal protection device to help him rationalize those times when he
ignores an ethical value he holds.

The process goes something like this: When a person is called on to act
in a way that violates one of his values, he experiences some internal dissonance. He knows he should be doing one thing but may find himself
ignoring what he "knows" and behaving in the opposite way. It is an
uncomfortable situation to be in, and depending on the depth of the problem
or how dearly the value is held, can result in some unpleasant moments. The
dissonance—the gap between what one's values mandate should be done and
what one does—must be reduced. One way to do this is to take the "shades of
grey" position, or, as this superintendent put it, "find more justification for
looking at both sides." As one does this, the dissonance tends to dissipate.
I'm not sure there's anything terribly immoral to all this, though if the
process is engaged in over and over again it probably takes its emotional toll
in the long run. As one person mused about just this type of circumstance:

> I wonder if the only way you get into the superintendency is by
> learning to compromise yourself. Sometimes I feel that I'm at the
> point where I don't give a damn for anything. I just do my own
> thing. I'm kind of wondering about that.

This superintendent went on to voice some concern about what was
becoming of him as a person as he was learning to compromise himself. He
said, "Yeah, sometimes I think I may be digging a hole for myself to the point
where I might say, 'To hell with everything.' That kind of worries me."

Not everything is compromise, of course. Superintendents do stand up
for what they believe, sometimes in the face of strong pressure from powerful

opposing forces. Here is an example that involved the use of sick days by a teacher for purposes other than being ill. In this case, the teacher had taken a sick day to go hunting, and somehow this became known.

> Well, he and I had a meeting about it. We talked about working with youngsters, and he said, "Well, I teach my children that sometimes it is better to lie, better not to tell the truth." Now, how can I close my eyes to that? That's why I think it's worth fighting. How do I close my eyes to those things? Do I play ostrich? Or "Isn't it my responsibility," I keep asking myself, "when I know this, to pursue it?" Do I forget it, cross it off, and make that group of teachers who are angry about it my friends? If I do, I will be saying that anyone who wants to misuse a day should go ahead because it's okay with me. How do I ignore if it I know it?

There's a certain comedy to this, although for the superintendent involved it was far from funny. The comedy is that it is common, though not public, knowledge that the sick-day provisions of teacher contracts are routinely abused, sometimes with the active cooperation of building principals and sometimes not. Every teacher, every principal, and every superintendent is aware of that fact, though situations rarely arise when it becomes an issue. There is a fairly ready acknowledgment that this is the way the system operates — via benign neglect, as it were, to avoid conflict. In the above case, the abuse did indeed become public. The superintendent's position was not to avoid the conflict and, indeed, to make an ethical issue of the fight not only for himself but for the school district. He would not have to deal with internal dissonance, since he had not said, "To hell with it." The fight was not over at the time of our interview, the conflict having made its way into the courts. Even if the superintendent wins, the victory may be a Pyrrhic one, since he violated informal organizational norms in favor of his own ethics. People in organizations have long memories.

Another superintendent spoke of a value problem he encountered that had to do with the school program, not the violation of system norms. It involved the special education program. He worked in a very affluent community that prided itself on both the quality of its schools and the academic prowess of its students. Part of its implicit value system was to ignore the needs of handicapped students, except in a peripheral way. Such students were simply not part of the image that the community and the board had of itself and its schools.

> The closest I've come to having to compromise my values was with the special education thing. It was the most hurtful thing that's happened to me since I've been here. Now, I don't carry a torch for

special education, but what really distressed me was there were some children here who needed something, and this very wealthy community was saying, "You're not going to get it." That was equivalent to racism. It's bigotry and snobbism. It was a moral issue. I fought it and won.

It takes a strong-willed superintendent to engage in this kind of battle. The issues involved deeply held attitudes, not legal constraints as was the case in the incident involving abuse of sick days. It also implies a concept of the superintendent's role as guardian of children's educational needs. Some people may regard this as sentimental, but in the long run I think it is not.

In more of a practical political vein, another superintendent described an ethical problem he had experienced and the problems that arose from it:

We had a set of parents who were unhappy about our English program and became very political about it. It was a very difficult spot for me to be in because I agreed with them. Yet I chose publicly not to agree with them because I felt, in the long run, it is better to maintain good employee relations and not indicate that I sided with the parents. I chose to defend the staff, and that has caused me problems. It was a compromise of my own values, and it's very difficult for me to do, personally. They are the most nagging kinds of problems.

Everything that is gained costs something. In this situation, what was gained was an avoidance of staff conflict. The costs for the superintendent were the loss of some parental support and, maybe more important, having to live with the knowledge that he had taken a position in which he didn't believe.

Superintendents, then, perhaps more frequently than they are willing to say, encounter circumstances that require decisions that put them in conflict with their ethical values. They treat them differently, of course. The guiding principle for action, as one person put it, seems to be, "I try to weigh my personal stake in it. Maybe learning that is part of the rites of passage from teacher, to department head, to principal, to superintendent."

Some Stress-inducing Conditions

Much of what has been discussed in this book suggests the stressfulness of the job of superintendent of schools. The reader will recall that one of the interviewees spoke of one aspect of his work as "killing" and of his being "torn apart," not words that are typically associated with positions in which tension and conflict are not prominent (being a college professor, for example). In addition to discussing the various components of his work, each of the interviewees was asked to select a factor in his job that was a continuous source of stress for him. Each was also asked if he employed any particular coping mechanisms to deal with it. The responses, as can be well imagined, varied—different strokes for different folks.

A number of comments associated an ongoing source of job stress with the sheer pace of activity and the fact that there was no "down" or relaxed time. One man said, for example:

> There are times when I feel like I have about 15 balls in the air at one time, like a juggler. It's *so* many things. A committee working on this, a committee working on that, a dozen things going. Trying to keep abreast of all of them. Trying to know what's happening. And the potential is always there for something to get away from you, not in a control sense, but that something isn't going to work as well because you haven't had enough time to study it.

A condition of this superintendent's work life that is stressful, as he sees it, is the seemingly never-ending demand overload and information glut. Things are always happening. Committees are continually being formed, and of course they meet, thus creating demands on his time. And there are things to be read and studied—but there is not much time to do the reading and studying, so it is possible that the best decision or recommendations will not be made. All of us, certainly those of us who are engaged in professional or managerial work, have experienced the frustration and stress that accompany the work condition of simply being overloaded, and having too many things to do too quickly. It is a different circumstance from having to work on a single subject, like writing a book, over a long period of time. By and large, this type of activity is not stress-producing because it is a single task to which a person can devote himself or herself in a single-minded fashion. Not so the superintendency. Single-mindedness, though a quality to be admired in many situations, is inappropriate to the person who would be a superintendent, the comment above suggests. In fact, if we can speculate a bit, a superintendent who can work on only one or a few tasks at a time would probably induce increased stress in the system. Some things that demanded his attention would be allowed to slide until he was up against a no-win deadline. So it is necessary to be a juggler, and a good one at that.

Another superintendent referred to the continuous pace and variety of activity in terms of no "'down' time, absolutely none." As for the summers, "That's really one of the toughest times." His neighbors, of course, don't believe him; they say, "If school is out, why not you?" He also mentioned "the constant night meetings. You're going from seven in the morning until midnight. It really isn't a very healthy routine."

The continuous activity, the very extensive demands on one's time, and the need to keep track of a large number of things at one time seem to be givens of a superintendent's work that are stress-producing. Certainly, though, these conditions are not unique to the superintendency. Most corporate or government executives would probably mention the same stresses, although their evenings may be spent doing paperwork carried home in their briefcases, rather than in attending the seemingly endless round of meetings at which a superintendent's presence is required.

In order to pinpoint more specifically the types of situations that were found to be emotionally taxing and stressful, the interviewees were asked what it was they worried about and "took home" with them at night. As we shall see in the next section, some reported that they were simply able to "turn off" the happenings of the day when they left the office. Most, though, were able to identify types of events, or series of them, that were sources of worry and tension. Again, of course, responses varied. This is quite to be expected. Things that people worry about, the tension that they feel, and the depth of that tension tend to be more a function of individual predisposition than of the environment. What follows, then, is an effort to present the reader with some sense of the range of things that superintendents find worrisome in their jobs, rather than a set of categories upon which there is some agreement.

One superintendent, using the phrase "emotionally tied up," spoke of his concerns in this fashion:

> The thing is, we're continually dealing with people on very gutty and grinding problems, and therefore we get emotionally tied up. And no matter, as aloof as I try to be, and I do stand back—I have to, because otherwise I become too deeply enrooted in some of the decisions I have to make—I begin to lose sleep. I begin to think about how some of the things I have to do affect individuals. Like the time we had to let a teacher go who had been with us 15 years. She cried on my shoulder for an hour and a half. But she needed more help than I could give her, and putting her back on the job was not the answer. Anybody who says that doesn't affect them is crazy, because it does.

Firing a person, particularly one who has been on the job for as long as 15 years, is never an easy task, no matter what the context. Is there something that makes this case different and particularly characteristic of the superintendency? We could probably get answers on both sides of the question. It seems to me, though, that in order to understand this superintendent's story, it has to be seen in the light of his first sentence, where he talked about continually having to deal with people on "very gutty and grinding problems." The essence of the job for him—both its joy and its tragedy—was the most essential humanity that attaches to it. Schools are not engaged, after all, in turning out transistors. Their only mission is to deal well with people, whether they are young or old. And from time to time, for this man, the necessity of dealing with such deep human issues results in his being "emotionally tied up," and worried about the decisions he makes. He takes these worries home with him.

Another superintendent said that his major source of anxiety was his interpersonal conflicts with kids. Sometimes, though not usually, disciplinary problems reached his office. What he said was:

> If I have a real run-in with a kid, really get angry with him, I worry about him. I don't worry that he may throw a rock through my window. I just worry about him, in general.

This short comment, and the previous one as well, may upset some stereotypes held of superintendents as heartless bureaucratic figures. They are, of course, bureaucrats, almost by definition. But they are a curious subbreed of that general category, because, as we noted earlier, just about all of them were teachers at the beginning of their careers. This suggests that some rather basic attitudes of caring about youngsters are deeply imbedded in the makeup of most of them. My interview observations tended to confirm this suggestion, and for one superintendent, as we have just seen, it was this caring about kids in traumatic situations in school that touched off his anxiety. Another superintendent reinforced this point by using the metaphor of a machine as he spoke of the bureaucracy. The illustration is perhaps vivid enough not to require any elaboration.

> You know, the system is all set so that somehow the wheels turn. It's when a human body gets caught between two wheels that I have a problem. It's okay when some paper slips in and the things stall, but when a human body slips in, then I really have a problem. That's when I take things home. What do I do? How can I get the kid out with the least damage?

For another man, the condition that was most bothersome was what he saw to be the board's and the community's lack of concern about school programs. Somewhat colorfully, and with obvious anger, he said:

> What bothers me most is that everybody gets upset about nitpicking bullshit, but nobody wants to get upset about something really serious. In the last board meeting, all that they talked about was the fact that we haven't won any basketball games. Why don't

they ask me about the new reading program? They never ask anything about education, but they really get bent out of shape about basketball. Nobody gives a shit! It's ridiculous!

Tension and stress are produced here, it appears, as a result of the expectations that the superintendent had for a part of his job that was not being met. The implicit question might go something like this: "Why was I hired to run the schools if the people don't care how the schools are run?" It's possible that there are some superintendents who would be exceedingly pleased with these circumstances. They would be let alone to do as they wished, as long as things remained peaceful. The man we have quoted here was clearly not pleased but was most upset. He felt that since the board refused to engage him on matters of educational concern, it was telling him that those matters are not very important, a hard point of view to stomach for a person whose life focuses precisely on those matters.

Our final example of tension and stress-producing situations has to do with school board meetings. The anecdote is a rather long one, but reading it will enable the reader to crawl inside this man, so to speak, and feel his tension with him.

> I can't eat before I go to a board meeting. I'll have supper, but it isn't enjoyable, and I love to eat. Sometimes [the meetings] last till 1 or 1:30 in the morning. They're tense. You can never tell where the shots are coming from. It's hard to tell what's going on out there. Most of the community comments are critical. They are rarely complimentary. And they can get very personal. They produce tension, in the sense that you put a little bit of yourself in every recommendation you make. So you fly a part of yourself in front of everybody constantly. I've come out of board meetings where I've seen one member attack another. Or, I've seen a recommendation that should have gone through 9–0 get tabled. I get home, and I'll eat, and then I'll go to bed at about 3 or 3:30. It takes me a long time to calm down. It's not that I worry, so much as it is that the adrenalin starts flowing at about 3 in the afternoon and doesn't stop until the wee hours. Monday, board meeting day, is a terrible day because I know I'm running into the process—kind of running the gauntlet—that night. Tuesday is a super day!

I certainly wouldn't claim that this superintendent's response to school board meetings is typical. Far from it—but whether or not it is typical is not central to the discussion. Earlier, the point was made that what superintendents find to be stress-producing on their jobs, what consumes their emotional energy, is probably a function of the individual more than anything else. This certainly seems to be the case here. For this superintendent, the anticipation of having to confront an argumentative community and occasional conflict on the board resulted in a high tension level. Others might approach the same circumstances with equanimity, although without doubt all of them have had their share of meetings under fairly raucous conditions. In this particular situation, though, the superintendent could predict that each meeting would involve some unpleasant wrangling. The school board, to use a term coined by McCarty and Ramsey (1971), was a factional one, reflecting splits in the school community. The school district, which had been formed by consolidation of socially disparate smaller districts, had a long history of conflict. It has almost become a way of life, and this particular man, who truly enjoyed his job, had nevertheless to confront the reality that at least once a month he would be going through a period of high stress. It seems not to be a pleasant prospect, but after all, being a superintendent was his choice.

A final comment about the personal stressfulness of the superintendency is in order. The people who hold this office seem to be becoming increasingly aware of the emotional costs involved. Several mentioned retiring at age 55. One referred specifically to his being too young (40) to get "burned out." And they know that the severe physical problems experienced by some of their colleagues have, rightly or wrongly, been attributed to job stress. For example, one man referred to two colleagues, one of whom had suffered a heart attack and the other a stroke; the reference may have indicated some latent anxiety he felt about his own health. In further discussion, he saw the primary strain as resulting from the continual battles that superintendents wage, without a "victory that they see as satisfying to them." He went on to say, "When you see these things happening to your colleagues and friends, you begin to wonder whether it's all worthwhile."

If this seems a depressing note on which to end this chapter, we can remind ourselves that certainly all of us have wondered from time to time, about ourselves and our work, "whether it's all worthwhile." We should also note, however, the implicit hypothesis that being a superintendent means a condition of life where one may continually have to settle for "half a loaf." This, of course, is frequently what a politician's life is all about. It is a publicly acknowledged part of the political world and something that every would-be politician learns from the outset of his or her career. This is not so true of superintendents, though, whose early training and work as teachers had little to do with the life they must lead in their position. The clash between their early value system and the one they must learn in order to survive as superintendents is an obvious one. And it may well be a hidden and pervasive source of stress.

10
The Superintendent as Public Property

The previous chapters have all been concerned, in one fashion or another, with the conflictual characteristics of the work life of superintendents on the job. This one shifts focus. It is primarily a discussion of their off-the-job life as it is affected by the fact that they are considered by the school community as "public property" and that most of them see themselves in that light. The idea, of course, is not that they are chattels of the public — that they are owned by it. Rather, two things are suggested by the phrase "superintendent as public property." The first is the public perception that he is and ought to be accessible, regardless of time, place, or occasion. The second is that somehow, because of both the publicness of his position and his position as chief among the educators of the community's children, his personal life should be above reproach. In sum, as we shall see, the fact of being a superintendent seems to create a condition of personal and family life rather unlike that which most of us experience.

We are not concerned here with the readily observable publicness of a superintendent's life—the ritualistic demands to attend senior citizens' meetings, community service club luncheons, Boy Scout banquets, or sports events. We are examining (1) the perception of the superintendent as public property, which seems inevitably to result in situations where public intrusions into his private life and that of his family are unavoidable; (2) the way in which both on and off-the-job demands affect his relationships with his wife and family; and (3) the role that his wife may play as a person to whom he may turn in times of stress, simply for support or counsel.

Being "Public Property"

With one exception, the superintendents who were interviewed gave ready assent to the idea that their job implied that they were public property. Here is the way some of them talked about it with regard to their visibility:

You really can't ever leave the job. I took a young lady out to supper at one of the local restaurants. It was reasonably quiet. They have a banquet room in back. We sat down, and we weren't there 10 minutes when the bowling team from the school district started walking through. Of course, everybody shook hands and said, "Hello." It's all really very, very visible.

It's my perception that being a superintendent means living your life in a fishbowl. Even if I think I've left the affairs of the day in the office, when I take my kids out shopping that evening I am very sensitive to the fact that I am still the superintendent of schools and everybody knows it. I know I feel that pressure. I can't walk away from it. I can't be just another guy on the street.

It's a fishbowl life. I think that's generally true. Especially, in smaller school systems, which is where most of my experience has been. Everything you do is out in the open. I don't care whether you read *Playboy*, or go to church, or have a fight with your kids or your wife. It's a matter of public issue.

Yes, I'm public property, but I think I feel it less than some of my colleagues. One of the things I think I do, though, is sometimes to overreact. That is, because you're a superintendent you're supposed to be a model of behavior. So what I do sometimes, because I don't like the idea of having to be that kind of model, is, in a social setting, to use somewhat profane language, just to prove I'm not public property. People get angry with me, and my wife says, "Why do you do that? You don't do it around the house. What are you trying to prove?" I guess what I'm trying to prove is that I'm me, and I'm not going to be like a minister because I'm the superintendent of schools.

The following remark comes from the only woman in the sample of superintendents who took part in this study. Her comment is separated from the others because, for the first time in our discussion, it seemed to reflect reactions to her job that were based on her being female and unmarried.

I know I'm a public servant and, therefore, their property. Because of that I have to lead an honorable life, which I think I do anyway. But I can't go out carousing. My social life, I decided, has to be outside of this community. I have to be very careful with whom I'm seen when I'm not at work. I was watched very closely for the first eighteen months I was here. I was even followed by some of the citizens.

The question of whether visibility is a problem, then, is really no question at all. It's a taken-for-granted part of the life of a superintendent of schools. There are, however, different types of reactions to the fact that one is continually visible and that it's difficult to hide from being constantly onstage, even though the drama is not of one's own making. The "audience" is an uninvited one. In one case, the audience's reaction is benign, perhaps even pleasing. The superintendent takes out a friend for supper and is recognized by members of the school district bowling team. It is not exactly a case of public property as we have defined it, but it certainly involves the problem of not being able to hide from the public eye, since teachers are part of that public. In two other cases, the reaction is not so benign. There is, first, the mere feeling that you are being observed differently from others, even when you take your youngsters shopping in the evening. It is the sort of pressure that comes from knowing that you cannot remain anonymous even when you engage in behavior or play a role that ought to be accompanied by anonymity. One can only speculate that if the superintendent happened to purchase his young son a particularly colorful or outlandish shirt, for example, news of the purchase would not remain as information between the salesperson and the superintendent. Private life is not private. And this seems to be the impact of the other not-so-benign reaction that a superintendent's life was, implicitly a public issue, even with regard to what he reads or whether he goes to church.

The man who used profanity from time to time in social settings presents a different view of the visibility problem. He seems to feel that the office of superintendent places demands on him to be something he can't always be—a model of propriety. As these demands get placed—perhaps not explicitly— they also have the effect of saying to the superintendent, "You can't be like the rest of us. We look to you as the intellectual and the moral model of what educators should be." Regardless of whether such expectations are overt or covert or whether they are only hazily formulated, they may inhibit a superintendent from being the kind of human being he wants to be, even in situations that are not connected with the performance of his job. All of us, of course, conform to norms of social behavior. Few of us feel the need to epitomize those norms. So, for one person, at least, the way out of that discomfort was to deliberately break a norm from time to time in order to maintain the picture of himself that he preferred—that of just another human being. One can almost hear him chuckling after the fact.

The reaction of the woman superintendent to being public property and highly visible is similar to the others, but a very different dynamic is attached to it. Two factors seem to be involved. First is the traditional, though now apparently changing, bias against women as school administrators on levels above elementary school. Irrational though the attitude may be, women who aspire to the superintendency are probably viewed with considerable suspicion as they attempt to invade what for most intents and purposes has been a male domain. The second factor, particular to this case, was that the woman was unmarried. The reader will need little reminding to recall that in our culture it has traditionally been "all right" for a man to remain unmarried, but that women in that condition have been viewed with the thought, "Isn't it too bad?" Bachelors have sometimes been the object of envy by other males; unmarried women have rarely been so viewed and have more often been seen as objects of pity or perhaps suspicion.

So it was, then, in the situation at hand, that the female superintendent felt that her public life must be above reproach. And the only way, it appears, that her social life could be a satisfactory one was to make sure it was removed from her school district. Doubting eyes could not be permitted to see her in other than professional circumstances. It is indeed a fairly heavy burden.

Being accessible, for superintendents, is the companion to being visible. It is not only that they tend to be easily recognized by people in the community when they are engaged in ordinary matters of living—shopping, dining in a restaurant. It also seems to be perceived as appropriate at those times of public recognition for individuals to approach them with questions or comments about the schools or, in some cases, about individual problems. Here are some remarks about the visibility-accessibility linkage:

> I feel that I am public property every minute of the day, except when I take a week's vacation once a year. But even going to church, very, very infrequently am I able to get into and out of church on Sunday morning without responding to some question, inquiry, compliment, criticism, or whatever about the schools. Very seldom can my wife and I go shopping without running into someone and having some remark about the schools come up. It holds true for our social life as well.

> In my community, I'm reasonably well known. So it frequently happens that when I'm out marketing, for example, parents will come up and introduce themselves and start telling me a problem right in front of the meat counter.

> I think that most people perceive the superintendent of schools as fair game wherever he can be found. Like in the supermarket, you're liable to be confronted by a parent who says, "Do you know what the hell Mrs. Smith did with my son in English?" And, of course, there's a very clear expectation that you will make a mental note of that and get [back] to them the next morning. My reaction to that is that I am terribly jealous of my own time. I'm tempted to say, "Well, I'll be happy to talk to you about that, but you're going to have to catch me at my office." I don't, of course. I have to leave them with a sense that I'm not simply dismissing them out of hand.

Perhaps the last sentence is the clue to the problem. Being approached with school problems by people you don't know, in all kinds of ordinary living situations, surely must be at least a minor irritant for superintendents.

As one of them said earlier, "You can never leave the job." But the irritation, while possibly being momentarily upsetting, doesn't tell the whole story. Even in circumstances such as have been described, the superintendent is under subtle pressure to be political, in the sense of behaving in ways that will maintain his community support. It is the counterpart to the "pressing the flesh" that politicians do when they are on the campaign trail. In our case, the "pressing" takes the form of listening to the parent or whomever it may be, even though it's the last thing the superintendent wants to do at the moment. It should be noted, though, that not all superintendents resent such intrusions into their private lives. We will shortly note a couple of cases where they were welcomed. But whether they are welcomed or not, the key point is that such intrusions "come with the territory."

Being public property also means that a superintendent's home tends not to be seen as inviolable by at least some people in the community. He may receive some phone calls at home from parents. Sometimes they are angry ones, but this is not too frequent an occurrence. One superintendent who was not particularly upset about getting parental phone calls at home had a good bit of anger when the news media invaded his domestic privacy:

> Those bastards will call you anytime, anywhere. Like after a board
> meeting when a representative of the press has been present. I may
> stop with a board member to have a drink. This guy will call my
> home at 11:30 or midnight and wake my wife up. I may not be
> home, and that's not a problem. It's simply that they infringe on
> your privacy, and you can't afford to tell them off. You have to let
> them know you're human, but you can't turn them off entirely.
> You have to swallow a lot of things, or you're not going to survive.

One's home, then, may not be a sanctuary from the political side of a superintendent's work life. He is always onstage, except, as one person noted previously, during those times when he and his family physically separate themselves from the community by going on vacation. These are the times when, if they desire it, as most of them appear to, they can achieve the kind of anonymity in their private lives that most of us not only take for granted but see as our right.

Not all the superintendents who were interviewed were irritated by phone call intrusions into their homes. Though most saw the circumstance with an air of resignation as something they had to put up with, there were a couple who welcomed them. In fact, they did not see them as intrusions at all.

> I don't live in the district, but I have put a phone in my home so
> that it is a direct, not long distance, line. People can contact me at
> any time, and they do, at all sorts of strange times, including

weekends. I don't get as many calls as people might think, but I always respond to them.

Well, it's not unusual for me to conduct conversations at home over the phone during dinner [or at] 11 o'clock at night. Whenever the public is moved to call. Personally, I love it. If I had my wish, I would wish that each resident of this district, if they needed an answer to a question, would feel free to pick up the phone at any time. If I could get parents to believe and act on that, I'd never lose an election.

It seems to be, once more, a case of different strokes. Superintendents are, like the rest of us, all different people. But, as we have seen, they confront similar situations in their work lives. How they feel and react to these situations becomes a function of their own value systems and set of priorities. For one person, being confronted in a public place or on the phone at home becomes a matter about which to be disturbed, and perhaps frustrated. The guide for his behavior is to try not to upset the intruder, lest there be some untoward political or image-detracting fallout. For another person, though, contacts such as these are not seen at all as odious. They are welcomed and can serve to enhance one's image as a concerned educator, as well as being used to build a more solid political base for school district operations.

There are superintendents, of course, who set very strict limits on the extent to which they permit the public to enter their private lives. One of them did it by simply going to his second home in the mountains every weekend. Another one said, "I have established that I will give up every Monday through Thursday, days and evenings if need be. But stay away from me on Friday evening, Saturday, and Sunday." Perhaps, though, the root of the whole issue of the superintendent's being public property was expressed by the person who said,

Maybe what it's all about is this: they have a better insight into your life than you have into theirs. It certainly isn't a two-way street. I don't have the advantage of knowing where they work or what they do. But they sure know where I work, what I do, and where I live. Right?

Wives and Families

That the wives and families of school superintendents are affected by both the on- and off-the-job conditions of their work lives should come as no surprise. It could hardly be otherwise, since this is true of any person whose career makes him or her a central figure in public life, regardless of the community context. In the case of the superintendent, two things about the demands of his work seem to induce sometimes severe pressures on his relationships with his family. The first is the time that the job requires. The second thing, because the superintendency seems to be a position that almost totally encompasses one's life, appears to be the need of the wife of a superintendent somehow to separate herself from being defined as the "superintendent's wife" and to seek an identity of her own aside from what that role implies. There has, of course, been a thrust among women in general in our society, in the last 15 or 20 years, to find an identity that fits them as people, aside from being so-and-so's wife. In the case we are considering, though, what seems less the issue is finding one's identity attached to a person and more to the role that person plays—the superintendent of schools.

There is a third condition of some superintendents' work lives that, while not applicable to all, does affect the families of some—those who move fairly frequently from one community to another, career-bound superintendents (Carlson, 1972). Several of these were numbered among the interviewees, and their comments will be considered.

The time demands on a superintendent are very heavy. It's probably a little hard for most of us who lead more typical work lives to relate to what a superintendent, and thus his family, consider to be part of the whole game. About three nights a week out, and frequently more, seems to be the rule rather than the exception. As an extreme case, consider the following:

> I'm usually out 4 night a week, sometimes with double meetings. There was one stretch from the beginning of October to Christmas when I was out every Monday through Friday. At least 2 nights a week I'd be out for dinner, and sometimes I'd have 2 meetings after dinner. So I'd leave home at 6:30 A.M. and wouldn't return until 11 [or] 11:30 at night. My wife definitely doesn't like that. I think, in order to survive as a family, we simply take our weekends and get out of town. We travel a lot, or we go up to our cabin.

This particular person was superintendent in a medium-sized city. He was confronted with many, and seemingly never-ending, demands on his time that could, one would suspect, pose a danger to his physical and emotional well-being. The situation that he confronted may be somewhat atypical. But then, consider the following remarks from the superintendent of a relatively rural district:

> My wife's a teacher, and of course her days are full, and she comes home somewhat tired. She is the one who puts the kids to sleep and has to explain to my son how come his father can't [play] catch with

him. She is the one who had to explain to my daughter why I don't sit down and read with them. I think if she had her druthers, I would be back in the classroom. I think she's sorry she ever went along with this. Sometimes we've had some real arguments about my going out.

And these thoughts from the superintendent of a good-sized and rather affluent suburban school district:

My wife is a low-keyed person and very supportive. She thinks I'm nuts to be in this, that I'm burning myself out. I'm going every minute. I'm never home at night. I think she sees me going through things like school closings and wondering why the hell I'm killing myself. She'd love to have me leave tomorrow, but she also knows I'm happy.

From another suburban superintendent, these words:

I'm seldom home at night. There are always things to be done. And there are anniversaries that are never celebrated because of a board or PTA meeting. It all takes a toll, and occasionally the family becomes bitter about the job and the demands it makes. My wife has said that it's the job and not the family I'm married to. But I think I've mellowed and that I'm getting there after all these years. We've begun to solve some of our problems at home.

We should not conclude from this that because of his work the superintendent's family is grim. Far from it—the superintendents and their wives that I know do not see themselves as leading grim lives together. But if one is interested in understanding the superintendency as a job, one cannot neglect its implications for family life. The time demands that it places on the superintendent are severe and unlike those experienced by any other role occupant in public education. His family needs to understand this, as most of them seem to, and be willing to share him with the public. It certainly is not an easy task and, as they all said directly or implied, their wives found themselves at times less than happy with the bargain they had struck. One can, of course, respond that there are many jobs that require the husband or wife to work very long hours and to be away from home evenings or even days at a time. True enough. There are few jobs, though, in which the demands of the public seem to mesh with one's private life in quite the same way as they do for the superintendent.

The situation, then, is one with which superintendents, their wives, and children have to learn to cope. This seems to be particularly true with regard to relationships with the youngsters. Numbers of the men interviewed, for example, said that because the amount of time they spent with their children was so limited, they had to try very hard to make this "quality" time. That is a bit of an oddity in itself. For most of us, the time that we spend with our children is simply time that we spend with our children, without any special significance being attached to it. Not so for many superintendents, who seem to sense, correctly or not, that such time cannot be spent in simple, ordinary living. It has to be "quality" time—special time, free of family conflict, and purposely made enjoyable. Feeling this way about one's time with one's children constitutes a pressure. As one man said, "It's silly to think of putting a strain on yourself to have a good time with your kids, but it's something you really have to attend to." It's almost as though one cannot be an ordinary father. Not only must the time be special—but so must he.

Some superintendents spoke of special customs that had developed in their families to help them and their wives deal with the situation. One man, for example, talked about taking his youngster with him when he got his car serviced simply because it was an opportunity to spend time with him, to talk and find out what was on his mind. He also said,

> It's quickly becoming a tradition in our household that father is responsible for breakfast on Saturday morning. It's a disaster in itself sometimes, but I think one of the things it does is get me time with my kids.

Another man spoke of having developed a personal life-style to complement the job. It had two rules:

> First, I have never taken a job anywhere that I haven't said, "Five days a week I am your servant, your slave. On Saturdays and Sundays you just don't see me." And that happens still. The other rule was, when our children were small, we would all have dinner together, because I was out every night. Developing that personal life-style was a matter of salvation for me to cope with the loneliness and frustration of the job.

These are but a few examples of the special thoughts that the superintendents found it necessary to give to their families and their life-styles. Most of the other interviewees, interestingly enough, were also tied to the notion of the family eating together regularly. It is not particularly odd for a family to have a norm of everyone having dinner at the same time, nor is there anything particularly odd about a husband and father ritualistically having responsibility for a particular meal during the week. What seems to differentiate these rather ordinary family customs from hosts of similar ones is not the custom or practice itself. The difference here is that these customs seem to have been developed specifically to help the family cope with the strains that the work life of a superintendent of schools places upon his relationship with his family.

The problem of a superintendent's wife needing to establish her own identity as a person will be dealt with in some detail in the next chapter. Suffice it to say, at this time, that the superintendents interviewed seemed also to recognize the need for this. Undoubtedly it was not always this way, since school districts, particularly smaller ones, have been prone to think of themselves as hiring not only a superintendent but also his wife, asking themselves, during the hiring process, "What would she be like as 'Mrs. Superintendent'?" As we noted earlier, this situation is changing, helped on in no small measure by the women's movement. The pressures are still there though, apparently, in many school districts.

One superintendent reflected on a discussion he had heard at a gathering of his colleagues when the talk came around to wives and families. There was complaining about community social pressures on wives and the fact that they "had" to do this, that, or the other thing. What he said during our interview was,

> My wife never did that. She always did her own thing, which I think is very good. She never entertained, as I hear about the way some of my colleagues' wives do. We had one party, and that was about it. And she has done her own thing, tried to and has been successful at establishing her own identity as a professional person. I just think that's extremely good.

Whether or not all superintendents, in those increasing numbers of cases where their wives resist the role of "Mrs. Superintendent" and start to initiate their personal quest for identity, will view the circumstance as "extremely good" is an open question. Again, the politics of the superintendency intrudes, not the politics of manipulating conflicting community forces but the politics of dealing with community expectations (particularly those of the school board, one suspects) concerning the role that the superintendent's wife should play in the community.

Moving from District to District

One of the things about this country that makes it different from most others is the fact that a good number of American families, perhaps mostly those in which the breadwinner may be classified as managerial or professional, move a great deal. In times of economic growth, in particular, there is great movement of families from one locale to another, as corporations, for example, shift their personnel. So whatever problems attach to the uprooting of one's family in order to further one's career are not unique to "career-bound" superintendents. Further, as Knezevich (1971) has reported, superintendents of schools tend not to be the highly mobile group that the popular myth describes. Nevertheless, there were some examples of highly mobile, career-bound men among the interviewees, and we deal briefly with their thoughts as another example of the way the work life and, in this case, career aspirations affect problems of family living.

One rather unusual case involved a superintendent who had moved four times in eight years. While he was in his third position, his wife established herself in a business in which she was quite successful and that she found very satisfying. Nevertheless, she agreed to make the move with him—to another state and about 300 miles away—leaving behind one of their three youngsters, who enrolled in a residential prep school. The problems of adjustment proved to be difficult for both the wife and one of the children. "My wife just couldn't take it," said the superintendent. So, after about six months, it was decided that she, with their younger daughter, would move back to the community which they had left, leaving him with his son, who had come to like his new home quite well. Their marriage, though strong, has become a commuting one, once or twice a month. The effects of the separation, though, he saw as being traumatic for the two younger children. In addition, the situation has affected the way he now views his career. What he said was,

> I'll either stay here or go back to a district someplace around where my wife is. Ultimately, I'll be limited to those choices. I guess any hope I had of going to a school district in the Southwest, for example, is an impossible one. A superintendent today is still supposed to be a solid family figure. That hasn't changed.

People do have to make choices, sometimes with fewer degrees of freedom than they might wish. And, though this man's situation seems to be unusual, or perhaps extreme, it is possible to learn about the ordinary from the extreme. The dynamics are much less subtle, but they are similar to what typically takes place. When a superintendent moves, his wife and children frequently need to make radical adjustments to their new living conditions. What does this new community expect the wife to be? What will it be like here to be the children of the superintendent of schools? Are they seen as special or just like other kids? How will the wife establish her own personhood in this new community? The questions could go on and on, but they all point to the tension that develops in a superintendent's family when he moves, because the superintendent is no ordinary newcomer. He is a central figure, and, to repeat, public property. For him, it hardly needs to be said, the problems of adjustment are much less pressing. He has a built-in welcoming community, his work, and his work relationships. Not so his family.

Two other examples provide additional insight into the family problems encountered by career-bound superintendents. The first is from a man in his fifties who has moved several times, rarely staying in a community more than five years:

> It has been tough on my wife. She had to make the moves. She now says she never wants to move again and that she cried every time it happened. But she has learned how to survive through it all. She felt she had to do it, and she did it. But, of course, she paid a price, and I understand that. So the last couple of moves were easier for her. The first was devastating to the point where we had problems concerning the survival of our marriage.

Feminist readers might react to the comment with dismay. It seems clearly a case of a man's career taking precedence over the woman's desires, and possibly her well-being. But if it is a stark case of male chauvinism, the issue here is not to judge it. People make choices, and what we are concerned about is that the career choices a superintendent explicitly and his wife implicitly make may have unanticipated consequences for the character of the family life they develop. And this is true, I suggest, mostly because superintendents are not ordinary members of the community in which they work.

Our last example reveals a somewhat different sensitivity to the family problems of career-bound superintendents. It involves a man whose wife is also a professional educator and who, like her husband, holds a doctoral degree, but of more recent vintage than his. They have two school-aged children, one of whom was in high school and the other in sixth grade at the time of our interview.

> I was more insecure this time in terms of the kids fitting in and settling in. That's worked out well. I was also concerned about my wife in terms of her finding another position, career. It was touch and go for almost a year, but that's worked out well, too. I guess I'm still very optimistic that there is a way of integrating your own career with the other's life space, so to speak. But it's becoming more and more delicate. There are now more definite parameters. My daughter has two more years in high school. She's got to finish it here, so I can't think of moving for two years. She keeps telling my son, "Don't worry. You'll never graduate from Central." It's that kind of thing. I guess I'll take things as they come.

What to make of it all, then? Perhaps not much beyond what already has been said. Superintendents and their families who move frequently confront some problems that are similar to those of their colleagues, and some that are vastly different. Some of the problems are related to personal life-styles, career choices, and learning to live in a new community, problems that huge numbers of Americans face every year. Others are directly connected to the superintendency, not only as a work career but as a position that places unusual demands not only on the superintendent but also on his family. For those who move around, a new dimension is added to their lives that can be frustrating and conflictual and, at the same time, probably exhilarating.

The Superintendent's Wife as Therapist

The final section of this chapter deals with a less direct relationship of a superintendent's job to his family life. A superintendent's wife may play a role in school affairs through acting as a sort of therapist or alter ego for her husband. As we shall see, though one might expect this role to be almost a universal one, such is not the case.

Some superintendents say that when they leave the office in the late afternoon and go home, they also leave their problems there. They compartmentalize their lives so that there is no overlap between work and family, or so they say. Most of their colleagues doubt the truth of such statements. For example, one, in thinking about the fact that he is unable to "totally . . . divorce myself from the turmoil of the job," went on to say, "I think everybody *says* they don't take 'stuff' home with them at night." The implication, of course, is that what people say is frequently different from what they do. It may be important, in order to present an image of oneself as a person who has control over one's life, for a superintendent to behave as though he can shut things off. And perhaps he does. In our sample of interviews, one person maintained that that was precisely what he did.

For the others, though, the question arose concerning whether or not their wives functioned as "therapists" to help them sort out problems, or as a means of catharsis, or simply to offer solace. Certainly, it would not be unusual to expect this. At least part of the lore of marriage involves the idea that the couple will share all sorts of problems with each other in order to get advice and comfort. And, as we have seen, there is much in a superintendent's life that suggests the need, or perhaps the demand, for such help. However, much as it might have been expected that the people who were interviewed (with the exception of the one who maintained that he shut things off completely when he left the office) would say that their wives functioned as therapists for them, they didn't. In fact, more of the group said they did not get such help than said they did. In addition, there were a couple who said, "Yes and no. It depends."

The primary reason that those who spoke of using their wives as therapists gave for depending on them in this way was what might be expected. The wives were seen as agents for a needed catharsis. One man, though he said that it was only rarely that he had trouble sleeping at night because of job problems, went on to say that he thought there would have been many more of those nights had he not been "able to unravel with" his wife. "But once I've done that I've found it to be great therapy." Another said that when he had a particularly trying day, "I go home and bitch to my wife. I can talk to her for an hour. She doesn't give a damn. She just listens, and I'm extremely fortunate that she does." Still another superintendent conceived of his relationship with his wife as of crucial importance to his ability to perform his job well.

> It's a crucial thing for me. My wife happens to be most supportive of the superintendency and of my professional career. She's a real therapist. She knows the ups and downs, and we really don't even have to talk about them. I don't go for a day without unloading a problem. We both find it great therapy for ourselves.

So much for that. These are the kinds of comments to which most people can relate. They speak to the very heart of the human condition, insofar as it is concerned with people's need to find understanding and compassion for the problems and conflicts they confront. But if this is the case, how can we account for the fact that more of the men said they didn't use their wives for "therapists"? The answer, once more, seems to rest with one's personal preferences concerning the relationship between work life and family life, as the following interview excerpts illustrate:

> I try not to use my wife that way. Probably that's one of the things that frustrates her. I don't tell her all that stuff simply because what she doesn't know she can't speak to anybody about. There are some things she's better off not knowing or speaking about.

> No, I don't talk to her about things. I get rid of it in other ways. I've never talked with her about my problems. We have a serious labor dispute going on right now, but I never mention it to her. Because, so what? That's the story of my life. I don't share those problems.

> [My wife] loves to talk about her job. I mean every night. I don't want to talk about my job. I really don't. I think she has come to

recognize that, but we had some real conflict at first. I really don't want to talk about my job at home. It's almost an invasion of my privacy. I will wake up at 2 in the morning with something busting my ass and work on it that way. I process things myself, internally, and emotionally. It works out well for me. I really don't get much out of talking things out.

I'll touch base with her sometimes on major issues of substance, but not often. Especially, though, I try not to vent my frustrations when they involve other people, and that's where my major frustrations come from. I don't want those kind of tensions to carry over into the home. I want to try and keep that all separate. I don't want to influence her perceptions of people about whom she might feel differently than I do.

It's a little difficult to find a common thread in all this. For one man, it was a case of trying to make sure that his wife would not inadvertently say something embarrassing in public. Apparently he avoided bringing problems to her as a way of protecting both of them—a position that some people might find hard to understand. For another man—well, this was just the way he was. Sharing work problems was not his idea of what ought to happen in the conversations between husband and wife, period. A third saw using his wife as a therapist as an invasion of his home privacy, even though he, not a third party, would be the agent of the invasion. He felt that finding his own solutions to problems worked better for him, even if it involved his waking up at two in the morning. And, finally, there was the feeling of a superintendent who simply did not want to introduce work-related tensions, particularly as they involved other people, into his home. It would be, in a way, another invasion of privacy, though he did not say as much.

The themes, then, are hard to come by. But perhaps themes, in this case, are not the issue. Perhaps these excerpts simply illustrate the varied ways that superintendents deal with the question of relating their work to their home. For some, the relationship is close and ongoing. For others, it seems, the question is dealt with by deliberate compartmentalization of business and home affairs.

Some readers might assume on psychological grounds that the "compartmentalizing" group is in for some trouble, either personally or with regard to their family relationships. "People can't keep things bottled up like that. It all has to come out somehow," one might argue. Perhaps so. But as a point of personal reference, I know three of these four superintendents and their wives fairly well. They appear to be happy and to lead as fulfilling lives as any other couples with whom I am acquainted.

As we have seen earlier, most of the intrusions of the job into family life are beyond a superintendent's control: they simply occur. But the extent to which he chooses to engage his wife in his problems—and thus in a sense facilitate this type of intrusion—is quite within his control. Our examples suggest that superintendents exercise this control in different ways.

This chapter has examined the effect of the superintendent's job on his personal and family life. The next chapter carries the discussion further. In it we deal with data from interviews with the wives of five superintendents who reacted to the general question of what being married to a superintendent of schools meant for their lives.

11
Being a Superintendent's Wife

by Phyllis Blumberg

In the preceding chapter, we have listened to what the superintendents had to say about the effect of their work lives on their private lives. In this chapter, we will see what another group with special knowledge of this subject—the superintendents' wives—had to say about it. This chapter will also explore the question of what being the wives of superintendents, or being married to "public property," meant for the personal lives of the women.

Data for this analysis were obtained through interviews with the wives of five superintendents. Like the talks with their husbands, these interviews were open-ended. Each woman was asked to reflect broadly on the question of what it meant to her as a person to be married to a superintendent of schools and what she perceived to be some of the effects on her family for her husband to be so employed. The interviews lasted about 30 to 40 minutes.

First, a few introductory comments. In *Work, Leisure and the American Schools*, Green (1968) separates the concepts of "job" and "work" by suggesting that "the man who views his career . . . as something that is to be accomplished by him . . . has found a work" (p. 88). To find a "work" implies finding a meaning and purpose in one's occupational pursuits, as opposed to just doing a "job," which may have no personal and intrinsic meaning or purpose for a person. This is not to demean "job" and glorify "work," but merely to suggest (1) that our earlier discussions carry the implication that the superintendency is a "work," something with meaning and purpose for the individual involved, and (2) that this idea may explain why superintendents appear to have such broad tolerance for the conflicts that their position introduces into their personal and family lives. That is, if finding a "work" assumes a high priority in a person's life, then having found it may be sufficient motivation for tolerating negative side effects of the occupation.

The belief that their husbands' position and activities had a worthwhile purpose was reflected in the interviews with the wives. Although they expressed a vivid sense of the stress caused in the family by the husband and father's being a superintendent, they also expressed understanding and tolerance of the situation. It was clear that these women recognized that their husbands had found a "work," and that this work was of high social importance. As with their husbands, it seems, recognizing the value of the superintendent's occupation enabled the wives to deal with its negative impact on them and their families. Judging by some of the comments made by the husbands in the last chapter, however, the ability to understand and tolerate the problems created by their husbands' work life doesn't develop overnight. It takes time and appears to be accompanied, in some cases, by not a little family conflict. And there are some superintendents' wives, as it would be perfectly reasonable to expect, who never are able to see their husbands' job in this light and who do not make an adjustment to it.

Here are some of the general comments the interviewees made in describing the problems and conflicts they faced because of the public nature of their husbands' position:

- You grit your teeth and smile and let the matter run its course.
- The kids are in a 'no-win' situation.
- The first year in a new job is horrendous.
- You walk carefully on the tightrope.
- The superintendent's family situation is terribly stressful. We're under enormous strain.
- He's a very easy, very visible target. He's everyone's whipping boy.
- The children took a lot of heat.
- Everything we did was suspect.

There is an interesting tenor to these remarks. Although they refer to some of the same stresses described by the superintendents themselves in earlier chapters of this book, for the most part, they seem to reflect a deeper sense of the emotional strain under which a superintendent's family sometimes lives. "Grit your teeth," "horrendous," "terribly stressful," "enormous strain," "everyone's whipping boy": these are words that suggest deeply stressful experiences. Of course, each of these comments was made with reference to a particularly stressful situation that had developed in the school community in which the family lived and in which the husband had been a central figure; they do not describe a general state of affairs. But the point remains: the feelings expressed by these wives seem to be deeper than those expressed, for the most part, by their husbands. It might be tempting for some readers to attribute this difference to the idea that women are more "emotional" than men, and let it go at that. I suspect that would be a gross error. A more likely interpretation is that the wife of a superintendent typically lives more closely and intimately with the effects that her husband's job has on their family life than he does. For example, she has more dealings with the family's youngsters than he does, if for no other reason than that he is away from home so much, particularly in the evenings.

All this is not to say that the women interviewed felt themselves to be unhappy or playing the role of martyrs. Though a couple of the superintendents, in the last chapter, spoke about their wives being discontented with their situation, the five who were interviewed did not seem to be. However, they did exhibit a keen sense of the stressful and emotionally draining realities of their lives.

An anecdote related by one of them will illustrate. When superintendents gather for professional meetings, many of which are held at resorts, their wives frequently accompany them. Going along is almost a "perk" that attaches to the wife's role, a brief vacation as it were. Programs are conducted for the women, but in this case, at least, the activities had nothing to do with the husbands' professional roles but were completely concerned with stereotyped "feminine" interests. One woman described her disenchantment with this state of affairs:

> About 3 years ago, I put a note in the suggestion box that said, "You know, I'm tired of coming and listening to how to put on cosmetics or fix up your hair. Can't we do something that's of a more intellectual nature? Can't we go to the men's meetings? I find them tremendously interesting. Why can't we be included, and why can't we have meetings relevant to our own needs?" One of those needs for me at that time was for us to sit around and discuss mutual concerns, our mutual problems. Also, I felt there was a need for us to share with the younger women, so that we could help them. It seemed like some of them were being burned out in a year.
>
> I was overwhelmed with the response to my suggestion. There was such a tremendous need that they wanted to form a group the next day, and we did. I just couldn't believe it. We had 60 or 70 women attending. They talked a lot about personal issues. How do you deal with your husband being gone every night; how do you manage your children while people in the community expect them to be the epitome of everything that's good and pure; what happens when your kids get involved in booze or drugs; how do you survive?

This is both a commentary on being the wife of a school superintendent and also on the superintendency. On the one hand, it suggests a need for superintendents' wives to move out of their own sense of isolation so as to better deal with problems of living. It raises to public view the impact that their husbands' position has on these women. On the other hand, it points very directly at the sense of apartness—of being alone with a lot of people around—that is part and parcel of the superintendency. It is one of the prices that both husband and wife pay for being what they are.

Husbands as Public Property

For the most part, the content of the interviews with the wives paralleled the issues raised by superintendents when the latter spoke about the impact of their jobs on family life. For example, here are some wives' reactions to the idea of their husbands' positions as being public property:

> I guess I do view him as public property. He seems to be the only one in the educational process who doesn't have any rights. Everyone else has rights, but not the superintendent. There is no superintendent advocate. We have teacher advocates, advocates for kids, and for the school board, but none for the superintendent. There aren't many people who will stand up in public and defend the superintendent. He's a very easy target. He's a very visible target.

This woman, who had been a teacher for many years as well as a school board member before she married her superintendent husband, went on to say,

> five days a week, 18 hours a day, and being constantly in the public's eye, no matter what we do. Perhaps that has been the most difficult thing for me to adjust to.

One might think that having been a teacher, and especially a school board member, would have provided her with a lot of insight about what it meant to be the wife of a superintendent. In this case, and most likely in the majority of similar ones, this was not so. And, in thinking more deeply about the circumstances, the reason for the gap in understanding becomes apparent. Teachers seem infrequently to have direct contact with their superintendent. Their lives tend to be circumscribed by the activities of their classroom and their school. The superintendent is a distant figure whom they are more apt to read about in the local newspaper than actually see. What most of them learn about what he does, the demands on his time, the essential politicalness of his job, and so forth may well come to them through the teacher grapevine and not through direct contact, except for those few teachers who are in the union hierarchy.

If being a teacher doesn't bring a person a good bit of insight as to what it means to be a superintendent, surely being a school board member should. The contact, though certainly not day to day (except perhaps for the school board president) is fairly close. For at least this one woman whom we are discussing, and I suspect this is generally the case, being a board member did not provide many clues to the nature of the personal and family demands on a superintendent. Sitting around the table in a formal meeting of the board did not prepare her well for marriage to a person whose job necessitated both publicness and politicalness. She expressed her surprise in this way:

> There's always a guardedness. In public, a superintendent doesn't have the option of voicing his own opinions or his own feelings. There's always the problem of living up to the image, and I guess along with that is the image of the superintendent's wife.

She did not learn about this guardedness and the need to constantly live up to some vaguely defined image until she married a superintendent. The curious part of it all is that the need for a superintendent to be guarded and to present a particular image of himself only becomes manifest *in* public, but not *to* the public. When one is circumspect in what one says and does, it usually is the result of an inner dialogue, not one that is held openly.

This woman's comments were echoed by another who was married to a man who had been a superintendent for 13 years. She first talked about the time demands of the superintendency, noting, with perhaps some exaggeration, that these demands lasted from Monday to Monday and that the day might extend from 7 in the morning to 1 or 2 the next morning. Then she said,

> When you're in a public position, the community's aware of who you are. Whether you like it or not, you're onstage. The superintendent's everybody's property. He's on call 24 hours a day. Most of the time, I'm used to it.

The mere passage of time does seem to be a mellowing agent. People get used to and accept many things as years pass that they have had difficulty with accepting at first. But occasionally, even after 13 years, an additional straw breaks the camel's back, as this woman implied.

In the following case, however, time did not help to soothe ruffled feelings. This woman, like her husband, holds a Ph.D. She was more than ordinarily aware of the role demands on her as the wife of a superintendent of schools. She talked rather poignantly about "being terribly upset about being referred to in the local newspaper as ———, wife of ———, School Superintendent of ———— District." Her point was related to her own identity as a person. Her experience had been that if she made any kind of public statement that was in any way controversial, she was identified as the superintendent's wife, and not as herself for what she might represent. In a rather rueful tone, she added that no one ever quoted what *he* said and identified *him* as *her* husband.

She did not seem to be expressing jealousy or a wish to share headlines with her husband but to be asking, somewhat forlornly, "Who am I?" Must what she is, in the eyes of the public, be restricted to being the wife of the superintendent? Or, somehow, and surely unwittingly, was that part of the bargain that had been struck by virtue of her marriage? She partially acknowledged that bargain by saying virtually the same thing as the woman noted just previously. "The superintendent's wife," she said, "is always onstage. That's a given of the job, whether you like it or not."

The Superintendent's Children

Being the child of a superintendent of schools, particularly a school-aged child, seems to have its own special problems, as their mothers see it. Here are some remarks that make the point quite vividly:

> They really have to develop a good self-image, because they're in a no-win situation. If they do something well or receive some honor, the comments are like, "Well, it's only because your father is the superintendent" or "The teachers are easier on you." By the same token, if someone jumps on top of him or whatever, it's "Well, you know, he picks on you because your dad's the superintendent."

> Our kids are always in the limelight. They can never do anything without the whole town knowing about it. For the most part, they have adjusted quite well. My son is now in college, and it's just as if a weight has been lifted from his shoulders. He is much more relaxed and happier. I think he went to school every day with the attitude that he continually had to watch himself.

Not only are the wives of superintendents onstage, it seems, but so are their children. Further, as one person implied, they "can't win for losing," particularly, one would assume, in smaller communities. If they shine in school, it's because of their fathers. If they don't shine, do get in trouble, or get picked on, it's also because of their fathers. This is not to say, of course, that the children of superintendents necessarily live in a continual state of tension, although the above quote seemed to suggest that in one case at least. Tension does exist, of course, but as one woman put it, "I think that kids are very resilient, and, for the most part, they seem to accept whatever the situation is." And another, in the same vein, noting that her husband's position had taken a sort of toll on her children, said, "It's something that the kids have to live with. I agreed with my husband when he said, 'If the kids adjust, they'll probably be much stronger for it.'"

Another type of problem arises for a superintendent's children and their parents when they become involved in schools as parents. One mother commented,

> I think teachers are terribly threatened at the prospect of having to tell you your children are having problems. In particular, one of the children was having a reading problem, and I knew it. Every report card we got said that Susie was doing fine; there was nothing to worry about. Lo and behold, it turned out, she was going to a special reading teacher, and the only way I found out was that my child told me. The teacher was afraid, I suppose, that she would suffer repercussions if she told me Susie wasn't doing well. It would be almost as though the superintendent wouldn't see her as a competent teacher.

Another mother talked about parent–teacher conferences, situations that teachers seem rarely to look forward to, regardless of who is involved.

> So, who goes to the parent–teacher conference? If the superintendent comes on the scene, even if he comes feeling positively about things, it certainly causes discomfort for the teacher. On the other hand, if his child has a problem in school, that's also very difficult, even if he goes there feeling like [any other] parent to find out about the school welfare of his child. We simply deal with it on a sort of lesser-of-two-evils basis. I go; he doesn't. But even I create problems for teachers, not for what I do or say but for what they think I might do or say.

There seem always, then, to be binds relative to a superintendent's children in school that need to be worked through, for the most part by his wife. The binds appear to be a function of a set of untested assumptions that teachers make about "what the superintendent will do if. . . ." All parties to the situation seem to feel a bit as though they were "between a rock and a hard place." Dealing with the circumstance is not easy, and one suspects that it is dealt with more by avoidance than anything else.

Finding Time for Family Life

Another theme that ran through the interviews had to do with the difficulty of finding time together simply for family life. "How do we manage to get the time?" was the implicit and recurring question. One wife said that her children complained about their father's absence at times, but that it was she who really felt the pressure. It was as though she had to double as mother and father: be a den mother, always be the car driver, and make all the arrangements for special child-centered occasions. The time demands of her husband's job simply didn't permit him to become involved. It is certainly true that this condition is not idiosyncratic to the superintendency, but for this woman, whether or not she was a special case was not the issue. The issue was that for all practical purposes she was the child raiser in the family, days and evenings. The options were very limited.

The effects of time demands on a superintendent are felt in other ways by their wives and families:

> So we have to plan very definite times when he will get away and we can do particular things as a family. Otherwise, the time just slips by, and you lose it. There has to be some point in the year when he just leaves . . . when we can all go and get away so that nobody can get in touch with us.

This is not an unusual feeling: most of us feel, from time to time, that we "have to get away." But another person, talking about the time demands, said,

> We try to find some time just for the four of us in our family or just for the two of us. Sometimes it's just a matter of meeting for lunch. Just trying to schedule some time to talk with each other. Yes, sometimes time is that tight. Summers are good for us because there usually aren't many evening meetings. It's funny, though, many community people don't think the superintendent works in the summer because the schools are closed.

Another person spoke of how her husband deliberately planned certain times at home, usually around dinner, so that he can "spend some time with the kids and find out what's going on in their lives. Plus, he's up early in the morning and always sees the kids at breakfast. We make a special point of it." And still another woman, with grown children and thus more freedom, commented:

> We'll take off on Friday and just go for two days. And it's probably
> the most relaxing situation we find ourselves in, because we are not
> under any strain. You don't have to worry. People understand.

On the surface, statements such as these concerning the need to "get
away" or make sure there is time spent with children "to find out what's
going on in their lives" differ very little from attitudes one might expect from
spouses of anyone in a public or private executive position. However, in
addition to these dimensions of the problem, there seems to be a sense of
urgency about securing and protecting time away from the public eye. One
wife phrased it this way: "We have to get out of town, even if it's only for
dinner, at least every two weeks." Time demands interact with job pressures,
it appears, to create the need to escape, a not atypical condition in American
life, but one, as far as the superintendency is concerned, that seems to have
eluded public consciousness.

Acting as Therapist

One thing that was abundantly clear from the interviews with the five wives
of superintendents is that they were keenly aware of the pressures and
stresses under which their husbands work. It could scarcely be otherwise.
They have had to adapt their personal lives to this condition. But there are
also the side effects to which we have already referred, such as the loneliness
caused by the politicalness of the superintendency and the need for husband
and wife to be circumspect in the public parts of their private lives. They tend
to have many acquaintances but very few close friends, particularly in their
own school locale. As one wife put it, it's necessary for "us to go outside our
community for close friendships." Another side effect, more directly related
to the stress of the job, seems to be a concern on the part of a number of the
wives for their husbands' health. They have all heard about the heart attacks
that have been suffered by their husbands' colleagues and, correctly or not,
attribute at least part of their cause to the stress of the job.

   This concern with the stressfulness of their husbands' position and its
loneliness led quite naturally to discussion of what we have termed previously
the role of therapist or alter ego that a superintendent's wife may play for
him. A broad framework for the enactment of that role was provided by one
woman, who said,

> It's probably one of the only professions where you don't have
> people, on a day-to-day basis, that you can sit down and really talk
> to. An engineer has another engineer. Or a lawyer has another

lawyer. Superintendents don't necessarily always have other superintendents. They're not, in my experience, prone to call up another superintendent if a crisis or a problem arises. They feel that it's their job, that they're supposed to solve the problem. They've been conditioned to survive by their wits and be tremendously independent. It's like they feel they need to be competent regardless of the situation.

This is an interesting comment on the nature of the people who become superintendents of schools and, if correct, distinguishes them to some degree from other figures in public political life. In the history of public executive officeholders, confidants often seem to have played a major role. Such officials seem nearly always to have had figures—sometimes shadowy ones—near them who served as confidential advisers and counselors. For the most part this does not appear to be the case with superintendents. Of course superintendents do consult with their staffs about problems and decisions, but they seem to shy away from intimate and confidential relationships with anyone connected with their work. Enter the superintendent's wife, as therapist, alter ego, or sounding board. The following comments are illustrative of the role:

> It depends what the issue is. There are times when he does not like to come home and rehash what's been going on. That's hard, from my point of view, because I like to know what's going on. But he just says, "It was horrendous enough, and I don't want to live through it all again, explaining it." But then there are instances where he needs additional input and wants to get my perception of situations.

> He uses me as a sounding board and also to vent his frustrations now and then. Particularly this happens in situations where he can't speak with anyone else, because in the role of superintendent, there's nobody to talk to. It's a lonely spot.

> I'm probably his best listener. He confides in me. I know pretty much what's going on in that district. That job is pretty much of a loner one, and I'm sure he feels lonely. He doesn't feel close to anyone on the staff. I don't think a superintendent can. My husband sometimes feels the only person he can talk to and know that it's not going to be misconstrued or passed along is his wife. All the other people he deals with have their own little piece of grass and live in their own little world.

> I can listen to him for hours. But I can never repeat anything to anybody. I mean, in a sense it's like a confidential relationship between a client and analyst.

Perhaps what is more important in these comments than the simple fact of a superintendent's wife playing a therapist's role for her husband is the recurrent description of the superintendency as a lonely position. The point has come up previously, in this and earlier chapters. One may, indeed, wonder about the extent to which the loneliness of the job is a stress-inducer itself and contributory to perceptions of tension and strain that both the men and their wives have of the position. Surely, as we have noted at other times, casual conversations with superintendents or observations of them in public situations do not necessarily reveal any of this. But it does seem to come out in the relationship between the couple.

The superintendent's wife, our hunch is, plays a crucial role for the vast majority of superintendents in helping them maintain their sense of emotional balance despite the loneliness of their work. Some of them, though, are loners by predisposition. We had an example of one in the last chapter who simply preferred not to share his concerns with his wife. This case is apparently very much an exception, as it appears that his colleagues mostly seek out their wives as people to whom they can turn to satisfy the very human need for someone who will listen.

There is, though, a bit more to it than being able to listen with understanding. In the last excerpt above, one wife compared the confidentiality of her discussions with her husband to the "relationship between a client and an analyst." Perhaps this is the crux of the matter, and perhaps, by inference, this is what the wives, and the superintendents as well, really meant when they talked about the loneliness of the job. It is not so much that there is no one with whom to talk as, it appears, there is no one with whom to share confidences. Put another way, the sharing of confidences, such as might be discussed between a superintendent and his wife, with people with whom he works or friends is seen as too risky a venture. To paraphrase a slogan from World War II, "Loose lips get superintendents in trouble." The circumstance seem to be a rather sad commentary on a superintendent's work life, but it is apparently a realistic appraisal of an important fact of that life.

The Problem of Identity

We turn finally in this chapter to problems that a wife of a superintendent may encounter in seeking her own identity—being herself as a person—apart from that self that is identified primarily as the wife of a community's chief educational officer. The reader will recall the anger expressed by one person earlier in this chapter at a newspaper account that gave recognition to her not for who she was but as her husband's wife. This was the public side of things, and though the irritant was of a passing sort, it is perhaps symbolic of the more general problem that these women face in their personal and public lives. While some of the problems they mentioned may seem to be trivial, they had, as we will see, deep meaning for the person involved. Here are some examples, starting with a wife who had developed her own career after having been a housewife for some years:

> Long ago I determined, well, I'm going to have to be my own person. I can't do what everybody else wants me to do, because you can't win that way either. You're suspect no matter what you do, what you wear, what you say, how you act. I had to be me for myself.

Speaking of things that some people might consider to be of relatively minor consequence, another wife said:

> Years ago I decided I was going to be my own person. At first I made sure I wore a skirt to the grocery store, etc. Now, I feel people have to accept me the way I am and the way I want to dress. I guess it took a lot of growing up. I came to realize that people were going to criticize me no matter what I did, so why not be myself?

And this poignant and powerful comment came from a woman who had played "Mrs. Superintendent" for a number of years and had developed the feeling that she was just an appendage to her husband's role:

> When the change came, it was dramatic. Without knowing it, I was propelling toward that point. But when I hit age 40, age 39, and recognized that soon my children were going to be grown, I began to look at myself. I realized I had to do something and do it fast. As I began to venture out into the university and into other areas, I realized how important it all was to me. I was desperate, really desperate to do that. And that—the formation of my own identity during those couple of years—was a crisis time for my husband and me. He had difficulty dealing with the fact that I had to be myself. At times, I said, "No, I don't want to go to that meeting with you. I'm sick of meeting with board people. No, I don't want to go with you to a convention, because that's not my thing. I'd love to go with you on vacation, but I don't want to sit talking to board members, just dealing with their needs and those kinds of issues." So that was a kind of crisis for us. As I began to work, I realized the terrible pressures he worked under. And I appreciate his job more and more and more every day. I don't know how he does it.

We are not implying that the concerns that these women expressed about their own identities are solely a function of their being married to school superintendents. Questions related to a woman "becoming her own person" have been with us for a long time, though they certainly have come to our culture's center stage most forcefully only in recent years. Nevertheless, though the sentiments expressed by these women, and the earlier irritated comment from the one who was identified in the local newspaper as "the wife of ———," are now familiar ones in American society, they have a special character that relates to the superintendency. Note, for example, the constraints these women were operating under even with regard to how they dressed in public. The constraints were related not so much to whether or not they were conservatively or fashionably dressed but whether their public image fitted the image of how a superintendent's wife was supposed to dress.

Was it all trivial? Does whether or not one wears a skirt or jeans to the grocery store fall into the category of being a major problem? Men may think not. For example, they might find it easy to say that the importance of such a question pales in the light of others that confront the women of today's world. But to speak globally of "women"—or of any group—conceals the facts of what may be going on in the life of any particular woman. Decisions about what to wear in public, for the two people who talked about them, could not be made in isolation from the image they felt compelled to project. If, as one person suggested previously in this chapter, a superintendent's children were supposed to be the epitome of everything that's good and pure, would not the same hold true for his wife? And don't goodness and purity, in the public's mind, and particularly when the behavior of the wife and family of a public figure is concerned, at times get connected with the manner in which they are dressed? Whether or not it is a rational viewpoint, it seems to be true that there is or was a value system associated with matters of attire and that these women sensed it, as do the wives of other public or quasi-public figures (e.g., clergymen) who also live under the pressure of having to exhibit model behavior.

Note, finally, the similar language used by the first two women quoted above as they talked about their public behavior and appearance: "You're suspect no matter what you do, what you wear, what you say, how you act. I had to be me for myself," and "I came to realize that people were going to criticize me no matter what I did, so why not be myself?" The point is, once again, that wives of school superintendents live under pressures related to the fact of their husbands' position. The pressures are real. They impinge on behavior and the wives' sense of self, as they, too, become public property.

The case of the woman who at age 40 felt the need to move beyond the role of wife and mother is a familiar one. It, too, had its connection to the superintendency. Not only was it important to her to establish her own identity; in the process she appears to have rejected some of the social expectations for the behavior of a superintendent's wife—as when she said, "I'm sick of meeting with board people" and refused to attend any more such meetings. Certainly, many women have had similar feelings as they have contemplated their lives and embarked on careers of their own. The interesting part of this situation, though, is that as this woman finished her training and started to work as a professional school person, she also developed a different sense of her husband's job and gained a deeper understanding of the pressures under which he worked. Life, it seems, takes many unanticipated turns.

In this chapter, our discussion of being a superintendent's wife has surely offered only a brief glimpse into that circumstance. It has also, in its own way, elaborated on the underlying theme of the superintendency as a work life of conflict. We have powerful and sometimes poignant examples of the conflicts induced on both a superintendent and his wife by reason of the job he holds.

The image of the helpmate wife, often seen as odious by the women's liberation movement, emerges as a necessity of life in the superintendent's family. And this very fact, it seems, causes a conflict, since the women involved, as they pursue their own lives, may find themselves personally and professionally at odds with external expectations about what they should do and how they should do it. Though they acknowledge and act on the necessity of being supports for their husbands and protectors of their children, they also have a sense of needing to do more, to avoid being smothered by the superintendency. They perform their own balancing act, dealing with competing forces that we may infer have much stronger emotional pulls, because of their wife and mother roles, than those with which their husbands deal.

12
Living with Conflict: A Broader View

For the most part, our analysis of the work life of school superintendents has been organized around some central ideas that the people in this study expressed when they thought aloud about the meaning of "being a superintendent." In this chapter, the theme of understanding the superintendency as a position that engages the superintendent in a work life of conflict is approached more generally and not through specific role characteristics. The discussion is organized principally around several anecdotes of conflictual situations in which some of the interviewees found themselves entangled, either by their own choosing or because something just happened and their involvement was inevitable. The cases were chosen to give some picture of the variety of circumstances that present themselves as an integral part of a superintendent's work life. Readers of this book who are superintendents will undoubtedly be able to relate very well to the situations and engage in their own internal dialogue about them. Those who are not will find that their comprehension of the flavor of the superintendency will be enhanced.

The Minority View

It is important to note that not all the superintendents interviewed agreed that dealing with conflict was central to their work life. Two did not. In one case, that of a person in his first superintendency, his work life seemed to be characterized more by placidity than anything else. It was not that he did not have occasional tussles, more often than not with one of his administrators or a teacher or two. But by and large, his life seemed to be rather slow moving, and not because he simply sat at his desk and dealt with routine administrative matters. On the contrary, he was heavily involved in matters of curriculum and instruction, trying to induce change. In these efforts he occasionally had differences with people, but the differences did not seem to be

186

matters of great concern to him. He attributed this relative peacefulness—
sometimes amounting to boredom—to two factors. One was the fact that the
community was a relatively small one, about 20 miles from a good-sized city.
The population was fairly homogeneous and stable, as was the composition of
the school board, only one of whose five members was new each year. The
community and its educational establishment were not exactly a social cocoon,
but in some ways it resembled just that. The second factor was that the district
had "a strong union contract with a positive management factor. We haven't
had a lot of conflicts or erosion of power." This, as we have seen, was atypical.
In statistical terms, the situation in this school district would be an outlier, thus
quite variant from the rest of the sample.

In the case of the other superintendent who did not see conflict as the
main characteristic of his job, the factor responsible for this view appeared to
be his concept of himself in his role, rather than the sociology of his community. He saw himself as "different, in some ways, from what you may call the
typical superintendent or administrator." This difference was, as he put it,
that "whenever a problem arrives, from whatever source, I don't ever find
myself bent on forcing my direction." Whether or not his attribution of this
motivation to many of his colleagues is fair is not the point. He saw it that way
and used that guideline both as he compared himself with others and as he
confronted his daily work. This enabled him

> to operate in the way I think things should happen until I get
> feedback which indicates that someone else thinks differently. And
> then the way I approach the situation is this: I really try to find out
> where that person is coming from. I try to analyze that, because my
> basic mode of operation is to do the right thing, rather than to do
> my thing. In the end, what might be perceived as conflict, or
> nearly, doesn't come across as being conflict. But I will not do
> anything if I feel in my gut it's wrong.

One can argue, of course, that the issue raised by this superintendent is
just semantic. "He deals with the same things and operates like all the rest of
us, but he just phrases it differently," the thinking might be. Or we might
infer that he is a consummate politician, who, standing back from the fray,
prefers to see what others might call the crosscurrent of conflict indigenous to
his job as a series of problems to be solved by smooth rationality and by
persuading others to approach them that way. In any case, he did not see
conflict as a major aspect of the superintendency. "Believing is seeing," Karl
Weick (1979, p. 135) has noted. The perceptual screens of all of us operate in
such a way that we frequently see things as we desire them to be. This is not
necessarily an escape from reality. It may, indeed, be a creature of reality.

The Superintendency Compared with Other Executive Positions

Most of the superintendents, as we have seen, viewed "living with conflict" as the salient imperative of a superintendent's work life. But is this imperative unique to the superintendency? The matter has been touched on briefly in earlier chapters, but let's look into it more closely here. Aren't other chief executive officers of organizations placed in situations where they must continually work with and help to resolve conflict? The answer to these questions is both yes and no. It is yes as far as any broad view of executive leadership is concerned. Executives are expected to provide direction, pay attention to both the internal and external environment upon which their organization's welfare depends, and set in motion procedures for resolving conflict when they are called for. So far, so good. Superintendents are expected to engage in similar activities.

From another viewpoint, though, the answer is no. This position—and it is mine—acknowledges the similarities just noted. But it also suggests that there are additional factors in the superintendency that simply don't exist in the job of the corporate executive and that make a qualitative difference between the essential characteristics of the two positions. Many of these additional factors have already been discussed, though not in this context. They include such things as the public perception of the superintendent as the guardian of a sacred public enterprise, the education of the community's children; the politicalness of the relationship between the superintendent and the school board; the fact that superintendents once held the same job—that of a teacher—as the people over whom they are now expected to exercise authority; the huge number of community and governmental groups with one or another stake in the schools; the superintendent's visibility and accessibility as public property. The list could go on, but the point has now been made.

Two of the interviewees make these points quite graphically. The first compared the pressure he saw himself as facing with that encountered by executives in the private sector:

> I have never been in private business, but my impression talking
> with friends I have is that though many of them work long hours,
> they don't have as many different kinds of pressures [as] a
> superintendent has. I'm talking, for example, about problems with
> the community and with kids. I'm talking about being involved
> with parents or being involved in a lawsuit because of an insurance
> recovery. I'm talking about having to go to the state capital and
> speaking with legislators because bills under construction are very
> poor for education. I'm talking about dealing with curriculum
> matters—sex education, for example—and knowing all the
> ramifications of how the churches feel about it. Or knowing

whether or not it's important to have the same reading series in a
[school] building for all grade levels. Or dealing with the intricacies
of budgeting or the overwhelming number of personnel issues we
deal with. This is a human enterprise. All aspects of it. There are
no material products that we deal with. They're all human. And
this intensifies and magnifies the number of problems.

In more detail still, and with almost machine gun-like rapidity, the
second superintendent described the array of groups or individuals with
whom he had to deal in one way or another:

Well, you always have superintendent–board conflict, particularly
when there are factions on the board. The superintendent's in the
middle trying to balance these. Then there is the administrative
staff, whether it be the principals, assistants, or whatever.
Obviously, there's the union. Community groups all over the place.
Sometimes student interest groups, more of late, but a lot more in
the sixties. The news media is constant. TV, the local paper versus
the city paper. And there are support groups, booster clubs for
athletics, the band, even art. And special interest groups. For the
handicapped, for example. They're coming right off the walls of
late. There are the federal and state mandates. All the titles and
categorical aid programs. The PTAs, the businessmen, the clergy,
real estate interests. Parents with kids with specific problems. I'm
going 100 miles an hour all the time. You always have another
mountain to climb.

The aim here is not, of course, to create the image of the superintendency as an impossible job (though one might get an argument over that) or
the parallel image of the superintendent as a harried, overworked person.
There was rarely, in the interviews, an inkling of a person feeling sorry for
himself. Nor is the interest here to make them out as heroes. None of them
spoke, at all, in heroic terms. But it is important to understand, though, that
superintendents, even as they occupy positions of power, authority, and
prestige, must interact and deal with large numbers of situations over which
they can exert no direct control or even, at times, indirect control. Further,
much of what occurs in this work life is unpredictable. As one man said,

There's always the potential. It's not that you always have
something happening, but you always have the potential that
something is going to happen, this afternoon, for example. And
number 1, you don't even know about it, and number 2, you have
no control over it. It's going to blow hell out of your ears. The
potential is always there for an explosive situation to develop.

All organizations, and therefore all leaders of them, have to deal with uncertainty. A case can even be made that the development of organizational strategy to deal with uncertainty is the primary task of any organization, public or private. But a case can equally well be made for the uniqueness of schools in this regard and for the consequent effects on the people who run them. In a school system, some things—mighty few—are predictable. We know, for example, what the school-age population will be over the next few years. We know that the decline in numbers of pupils will probably necessitate the closing of schools. But we can't predict how the community will react to this, what pressure groups will form, how powerful they will be, or what strategies and tactics they will use to try to influence decisions. Or, to use a different example, any superintendent knows that the introduction of a sex education program or school busing to create desegregated student bodies in individual schools will create unhappiness in some segments of the community. What is difficult to predict is the form that the unhappiness will take. Or, to push our concern with uncertainty and unpredictability in the direction of the absolutely unknowable, there is no way a superintendent can know when an irate parent will physically assault a school principal and school secretary, as happened recently in a school district with which I am familiar. It is an extreme example, of course, and is made only to reinforce the suggestion that there is an uniqueness about the schools in their ability to make their organizational environment more predictable. And part and parcel of this unpredictability is the ever-present potential for "an explosive situation" to develop. School superintendents can rarely be confident that the relative lack of conflict that they may experience on Monday will continue on Tuesday.

This last point suggests that the superintendent's stance relative to the development of conflict in his system must of necessity be a reactive one. Not entirely so, of course, because some general vague outlines of problematical or conflictual situations can be predicted, as we have noted. But some, perhaps many, are completely unforeseeable.

Most superintendents, however, are not people who passively wait for something to happen. It is true, of course, that some do "retire on the job at an early age." It is also true that a common stereotype pictures them as bureaucrats who do very little of substance. One reason for this stereotype, incidentally, may be that much of their work is concerned with long-range projects that consume a great deal of time, but the results are not readily observable in the day-to-day life of school people. A close examination of what they do is likely to reveal that they are constantly on the move, testing here, pushing there, or nudging gently in another direction. Further, as they assume the classic functions of leadership—creating organizational movement, encouraging more efficient and effective productivity, for example—they become at times, as we have seen, instigators or creators of conflict, though usually not for its own sake. It is not a new story. We can predict that when actions are taken to induce change — or sometimes when they are merely contemplated—some type of friction will occur within the organization. The superintendency, in this respect, is little different from its counterparts in other types of organizations.

One superintendent spoke directly about this conflict-creating behavior. He first took note of his reactive stance by suggesting that it "was simply part of his position, part of the whole fabric of American education. You manage these things the best you can." He then went on to say,

> There is another type of conflict that is created by superintendents themselves. That is, you say, "I know if I do this, it's going to create something." For example, when you go into a very tense organization, and you say, "We're going to reorganize the administrative staff." Well, there is a good deal of conflict associated with that that you created that wouldn't be there if you hadn't pressed it, if you had just left the issue alone and said, "To hell with it." But I think I do create that stuff.

It is probably true that as superintendents go about creating situations that focus on changing something, they are also testing the boundary lines of their authority and influence. There is a lot of ambiguity attached to the position, even for those who have occupied it for a long time. The only way one can find out what he can do or what he is expected to do is to do something. A superintendent finds out in a hurry in what areas he can operate with relative freedom and in which ones he will encounter opposing forces.

The several anecdotes that follow describe situations where a superintendent found himself reacting to conflict or behaving in ways that would create it. They will also illustrate some of the thinking that these people used as guidelines for action or as strategies for conflict resolution. We deal first with some conflictual situations that would fall generally into the reactive category.

Desegregating a City School System

> We were under state mandate to desegregate the schools. We had no option, though my value system was congruent with the mandate. We had to deal with it. A tremendous conflict situation development with all sorts of crosscurrents. Everybody thought we had a plan for resolving the whole thing and that we were just waiting for the right moment to lay it on. Well, we had no plan for resolution of the whole business. What we did have, though, based on our study of what had happened in other districts and the problems they had, was a plan for getting everybody involved in

knowing the people on the other side of the issue. What we did was develop this thing called a regional plan, based on areas of the city. It was really a process of getting all those people, the main actors in this whole conflict situation, to come together and realize that there were people on the other side who had genuine beliefs. They were not nasty child molesters and beaters and all that, but they were just people with concerns.

They came together. They spent hour after hour together, and by the time they got through they were talking with each other. They didn't change their ideas in terms of what they wanted to accomplish, but they were much more willing to compromise for something in between. And so they came up with some answers. And most of them who went through the process still don't believe it. They think we were some type of geniuses who had some plan in our pocket for doing this, and we just convinced them where to go. But most of the ideas came out of their discussions. Not in terms of a proposal. But someone would start to talk, and then we'd hear them say, "Gee, this might be something." And then they'd back off because they really couldn't navigate that. And then we'd see someone start to move toward the same idea, so we knew where the common ground was. So we put it all together, and I think that's why things were so quiet.

The conflict was there, and we had to work to diffuse it. Conflict was the underlying problem, and the issue was how to overcome it. Generally, if you take it on as *your* problem, then you've got to come up with the solution. But if you look at the people involved as resources, then it's a different situation. They've got the energy because they are the protagonists in the first place. If you can bring them together, then you have got something. But you've got to look at the payoffs, and you have to know that in the end you may have to make the decision by yourself. But sometimes, by sitting and listening to them argue, you come up with something that will be a compromise. And even though you finally have to make a decision to which they can't all agree, you get a whole new perspective on what might be workable. If you go into it dreading having to make a decision because you're going to have to choose between two sides, God, it's a stressful thing. If you go into it with a sense of adventure, then you may be able to help these two groups to come to consensus that both can live with and support. It's a whole different situation.

The conflict, in this case, was predictable and unavoidable. The situation had to be confronted, as it has to be in school districts across the land. All of us are familiar — too familiar — with the community strife and occasional violence that has accompanied conflicts associated with racial desegregation of the schools. How does it get dealt with? The answer frequently has been by court order, with the courts sometimes assuming the responsibility for implementing the decision. The history of these circumstances is not a pleasant one.

What we had in this city, it seems, was a strong desire to avoid intrusion by the courts into the schools at any level besides that of the very general policy that essentially said, "You must desegregate. How you do it is up to you, but if you don't make the decision, we will." The resolution of the conflict apparently meant invoking the most basic tenet of democratic community life: those people who are involved in the results of a decision ought to have a part in making it. There are costs involved in the process, as there are in any other. In this case, the primary costs were time and emotional energy. Evenings seemingly without end were spent with community groups. And there must have been times when people wondered whether or not it was worth it. The conflicts were eventually resolved, though, at least to the point where the resolution could be lived with, and things have indeed been quiet.

Beneath it all was a point that our superintendent mentioned only in passing but that may be crucial to dealing with conflicts that have deeply imbedded emotionality at their roots. He spoke of creating situations in which all parties to the conflict would somehow, through talking with each other, be able to realize that there were no ogres among them, that they were intelligent people who viewed things differently. In other words, in order to engage in such a process of community conflict resolution, the basic negative emotionality and stereotypes that each side attributes to the other must be dealt with first.

The suggestion here is that this will occur as the superintendent sits and listens, and sits and listens some more. Further, the process cannot be seen by the participants as simply a democratic game, a charade. This perception, too, may well be avoided as the superintendent sits and listens.

Some superintendents may not have the kind of skills and emotional makeup suited to this particular strategy of dealing with conflict within the community. The strategy involves reaching out to people in a way that communicates authentically to them that the community has a right to be involved in the schools; that the superintendent does not necessarily know what's best; and that they are not being convened to rubber stamp a decision that has already been made. Most superintendents would agree with the principle. Putting it into practice may well be another matter, particularly if, at some level, there is an attitude of "leave the driving to us."

Closing a School

Though it may have seen its peak, few sizable communities have been able to avoid the problems and conflicts attached to closing schools because of declining enrollments. The field of public education is full of the lore of expansion. It had no such history relative to contraction. In the anecdote that follows, the superintendent describes the turmoil that occurred in his district when a school had to be closed because of declining enrollments. Like the previous case, this situation was unavoidable; it simply had to be dealt with. It all started with a community vote on the school budget that supported the school board by a very small margin, an unusual circumstance in this district and an indication of developing community unhappiness with, and possibly distrust of, the board and superintendent.

> So we [superintendent and school board] started to talk about closing a school. We went through the discussion without too much of a problem. I was trying to sort out what the power situation was because I knew that there would come a time when they would look to me. They know sometime I'll strike and say, "This is what I think is best." And it's based on good reasons. This time that flash didn't come. I couldn't see the decision. The light at the end of the tunnel didn't shine. There were too many conflicting positions.
>
> The more we got into it, the more communications opened up with the public, the more the conflict grew. It included all parts of the community, the staff, the teachers, the kids, the parents, business leaders, the clergy, and so forth. They all came out of the woodwork.
>
> A lot more things had to be sorted out. No longer was it just a little old decision made by nine people that generally the community forgets about after it's made. Anyhow, we decided to close a building. It was a 9–0 vote on the board. No hassle. Now we had to go through and sort out which building to close. And we set up the process, had a lot of meetings in schools and so forth. Board members attended, people from the community attended. We really researched the problem well. There were a lot of questions, but none really at a gutter level.
>
> Well, then we named a school, and of course all hell broke loose. So, all of a sudden the board was saying, "What the hell happened?" And "What happened to our superintendent? He was saying, 'Close the school, close the school,' and it isn't going like it always does."
>
> There was a split on the board. I guess their confidence in me was a little shaky, and I was a little shaky myself. I should have known it was going to happen. But other times, if there was a difficult decision, we would sort it out pretty well, get all the data, and zingo, make a decision. And it always held and held well. And this was the first one that didn't. There was no question that we could hold to it and pull it off educationally. But that wasn't the problem, and that's what hung me up. That is, if we did that, we'd have the community off the wall.

So that's what I tried to get the board to look at. I started to
drive hard. "Before you change your mind," I told them, "or if you
change your mind, you have to consider the impact, politically, on
the community." Well, I hadn't done my homework well enough
with the board. Though they should be, they're not political
animals. The vote ended up 5–4. First, it was 4–4 with a swing
vote. The vote that was swung was maneuvered a little bit, which it
always has to be. I'd do it again. It was the best decision that could
have been made. But the conflict is still there. It came out very
sharply between and among board members. Almost to the point of
not speaking to one another, not trusting one another, wondering
who the hell was running the store. They started to question
everything I normally did. They started nitpicking. [They'd ask,]
"What about the teachers? What about the union? Are those
teachers going to unionize now that they see that we didn't stand
firm on this? What about the parents? Are they going to think
we're whippy [weak] and defeat the budget?"

A number of things were problematic here. The community, had rarely
experienced any trauma involving the schools. An affluent suburb, it was
looked at occasionally with envious eyes by its neighbors. Suddenly it was not
the object of envy at all. It was wracked with dissension, and who can be
jealous of that?

Several possible explanations can be given for the development of the
situation from what seemed to be a simple management decision about which
school to close into a conflict that became, at times, bitter and highly emotional. That it was sparked by a management decision is a matter of more
than passing interest. The broad policy that something had to be done about
the effect of declining enrollments and that the solution was to close a school
had already been made without much furor. Why not? Enrollment had de-
clined, and tax money could be saved by closing a school. Who is not in favor
of that? But such policies are about general principles; they are not management implementation decisions. In this case, agreement about the general
principle soon gave way to community conflict when the question became
"Whose ox is getting gored?" It is not a very genteel question when we think
about school-related decisions, but an entirely appropriate one when we consider that these decisions are made in a climate of community politics. In
times of growth, the question rarely gets raised. There are resources enough,
and occasionally more than enough, for everybody. In times of economic
contraction, people tend to become protective about what they have. So it
could be said that the conflict and the way it was dealt with was merely a
reflection of the anxiety that people feel when they perceive that something is
going to be taken away from them.

Surely this last interpretation is a little too simple. It is important to note that this particular community had had little experience in dealing with conflict concerning the schools. It had always "been taken care of" by its school board and superintendent. Suddenly, in the eyes of many people, that was not the case. Having little previous experience with conflict, they didn't know how to behave, at least on the level of rational discourse. We add to this the fact that no clear solution had dawned on the superintendent, as it typically did. The handle to it all simply did not present itself to him, and his board, trained by him to expect that handle, was somewhat at a loss when it did not appear. The board's confidence in him became less solid than it had been, and this seemed reflected in its vote split, as close as it could be.

This was a very complex situation, one for which simple answers seem to be less than adequate. One thing that is clear, though, is that the implementation strategy was different from the one employed in the school desegregation situation just described. Parents, in particular, were approached differently. In the former case, parents of affected children were seen as integral to the problem-solving, decision-making process. In the latter, it was as though parents were more of an audience: meetings were held, information was given, and reactions were listened to. But that seemed to be all, initially, at least.

The aim here, of course, is not to criticize. The superintendent and the school board had followed a line of action that had been successful in the past. Perhaps their problem was that they had failed to see the depth of emotionality that can attach to closing a school and the potential conflict that could result. And perhaps they had a prior clue to this that nobody recognized: the fact that for the superintendent "this time that flash didn't come. . . . The light at the end of the tunnel didn't shine."

The Roof Fell In—Almost

The situations in these two anecdotes, although they mandated reaction on the part of superintendents, also afforded the superintendents a small luxury of time to plan, consult, and discuss problems with people. Further, these were educational and management problems. But superintendents have responsibilities that go far beyond educational matters per se. Theirs is the whole ball of wax, so to speak, and included in it, of course, is a primary concern for preserving the health and safety of youngsters in school, quite apart from anything that has to do with their education. In what follows, a superintendent talks about a situation that had occurred in his district that he could not have foreseen and in which things had to happen quickly:

I received a phone call while I was working on the budget: [I'd better] get to an elementary school, because there was imminent danger of the collapse of the roof, and the building houses 600 students. We discovered it inadvertently through a routine examination of all building roofs in the district. My first reaction was that we've got to find another place for the kids. We dealt with architects and consultants, and we made decisions related to being able to keep students in that building until we could find outside facilities for them. We had to be careful, as we got that information, because as the staff saw people walking through the building, poking holes in the roof, word began immediately to filter out. Concern generated, and it got communicated to students and then to parents. So we had to be very cautious during that time not to let anything get out of control or leak the news, because we didn't want panic in the other 11 buildings.

We finally made a decision that we had to make a move that would involve renting a vacant building in a neighboring district. It would cost us between 25 and 30 thousand dollars. We had to have a meeting with parents quickly, so we distributed a letter to the kids to take home to their parents. I was immediately taken to task by the teachers for not having brought them on board sooner. "Why did they have to learn about it through the letter?" I got a chance to explain our problem to them, but they were still in a state of shock about their not being included. There were some parents who were absolutely opposed to the move. In fact, I still receive letters from time to time telling me it was the worst thing to do, and the issue is the fiscal conservatism of the community. The board wavered. Some said, "Let's get on with it," and others said, "Absolutely not. We're going to keep the students inside the district." Well, we finally decided on the move, and the board voted 100 percent to support it, despite the cost, and they stood together in front of 250 irate parents and staff members. It was the first time in my memory that they had been that solid.

It's all an indication, I guess, of the fact that no matter what you do, you immediately begin to infringe upon people's territory. It is really an unbelievable job. The whole job is conflict-ridden. And sometimes the central character in the conflict—the superintendent—ends up being a casualty of it, no matter how rational and reasonable he thinks he's being. Eventually, I think it gets to everyone.

It may seem odd—or does it?—that even such primary issues as those that involve the health and safety of youngsters have the potential to become objects of conflict within the day-to-day life of a school system. One would have good reason to expect that on problems such as this, interested parties

would take the position of "First things first. Make sure the kids are safe."
But it didn't happen quite that way in this case. Parents were upset because
the decision to make a temporary move to a building in another district would
involve extra costs, despite the fact that the buildings in the home district
could not accommodate the children. Teachers were upset because they were
not kept abreast of things. The superintendent did not inform them earlier
because of what he saw as the need to keep information about the problem
within as small a group as possible while the situation was being analyzed. He
became a target of criticism from both groups for the way he handled the
situation.

 Might the superintendent have done things differently, so as to avoid the
conflicts in which he became involved? Or is his analysis correct, that "no
matter what you do, you immediately begin to infringe on people's territory"? Given the conditions of a superintendent's work life, the latter
hypothesis is more likely to be true. It is possible that the superintendent
could have weighed in advance the teachers' possible distress about having
been kept in the dark against the importance of preventing leaks. But these
are judgment calls, and there appear to be few decisions a superintendent can
make that will not be faulted by one group within his constituency or
another. The larger part of the problem, though, as we have so often noted, is
the unavoidably political nature of the job. The superintendent was correct in
his territorial analysis. What he was describing, in fact, was a conflict model
—not an educational model—of the superintendency. There are those who
might wish this model away, but to do so would be to imagine a world that
doesn't exist and that is unlikely to come about. In point of fact, as we shall
note at the close of this chapter, the superintendents in this study, who are
probably not very different from most of their colleagues, seem not to want to
wish the conflict model of their job out of existence. For many of them, it
offers high excitement and challenge.

Some Principles About Principals

Every organizational executive needs to deal with problems that involve other
administrative personnel and their job performance. School superintendents
are no different. In the private sector, although the situations that are encountered may be difficult to resolve, there is a certain luxury in the fact that
for the most part they involve internal organizational issues and are dealt with
without any intrusion from the outside. The same does not necessarily hold in
the schools, particularly with principals, who frequently build up their own
political support system in the community. In fact, they may be encouraged
to do just that as a means of creating good school–community relations. That

this can turn out to be a two-edged sword will be seen in the following situation, which had as its starting point what the superintendent perceived as the development of excessive feelings of ownership of schools by their principals:

> Probably the greatest conflict for me is the *my* syndrome I get from principals. *My* school, *my* kids, *my* teachers. And it isn't. It's *our* school, *our* district, and so forth. That, to me, has presented the greatest conflict. That bugs me more than anything. To try to get at it, I moved all the elementary principals one year. Raised hell with them. But it was the only thing that could happen. There was this one guy who had been there 4,000 years. Couldn't get in his school. Couldn't influence him. No one could. Parents couldn't, and I had trouble getting in to influence. He retired, but there was another guy just like him, and he took the switch very hard. Put up a hell of a fight, which immediately brought on a tremendous conflict. I mean tremendous.
>
> He decided he was going to fight the decision, and he put together a hell of a lot of community support for why he should stay in that school. He had a lot of petitions, had a big dinner, a lot of crying. He broke down, physically broke down in front of one group. It was amazing. I couldn't believe his behavior. Of course, it killed him with the board because they couldn't believe his behavior either. Anyone making $30,000 couldn't move two miles? In the same kind of job? The short end of it was that the committee of people put together a petition with about 200 signatures. They came to a board meeting and demanded that he be reinstated in his old school. The board reacted unanimously that it wasn't going to happen. The decision was made, and it was going to hold.

This anecdote testifies to the different centers of power and influence with which a superintendent may have to deal, even when the issue about which he decides is properly an internal organizational one. Most superintendents have, either formally or informally, an understanding with their board that their prerogatives include the right to make staffing decisions. It is a prerogative that they tend to insist on, since without it they see themselves as relatively powerless to effect organizational change. Obviously, in this case, the principal did not acknowledge that right, which is a rather curious circumstance in itself. He did what anyone with his perceptions probably would, but, as we have seen, he miscalculated the odds. He organized community pressure, one may infer, assuming that the board would buckle under the pressure and reverse the superintendent. What he failed to understand was that if the board had done as he wanted they would, in all likelihood, then have had to look for a new superintendent, since they would have succeeded in emasculating him in the process of soothing the community.

This incident illustrates that even in those areas of school life that are considered the proper province of a superintendent's authority, such authority cannot be assumed to be immune from external attempts to influence a decision, creating situations that may involve deep emotionality. The conflictual circumstances a superintendent confronts, even when they may be properly classified as "in-house" matters, seem impossible to encapsulate. In the work life of a superintendent of schools, there seems to be no such thing as a "containment policy" that works. And trying though that may be at times, it's probably the way it should be.

Superintendents as Creators of Conflict

It is true, of course, as much of the preceding has indicated, that as superintendents react to circumstances that occur in their districts or merely take one type of administrative action or another, they create conflict where none had existed previously. And though they may know very well, as they contemplate one decision or another, that problems within and among groups will result in conflicts with which they will then have to deal, for the most part their decisions are not taken with the intent of provoking those conflicts. It is simply a fact of life.

Occasionally, however, circumstances develop, or they simply may have been in unquestioned existence for a while, in which the superintendent deliberately behaves in ways that he knows may lead to conflict. He does this in order to achieve other goals, or perhaps simply to shake things up in order to force an examination of the ways the schools are operating. We have a couple of examples. The first one is concerned with the superintendent's authority, or "Who's Boss?"

> When I came to Middlehaven, there was a very entrenched teachers' union. Very entrenched, to the extent that they had made alliances with the building administrators. And nothing happened. It was a closed shop. And I created a conflict. I refused to recommend for tenure a guidance counselor who was a strong union organizer and who happened to be the best friend of the principal. It was a borderline case, and I just refused to recommend. It went the route of a board hearing and a commissioner's hearing, and he ruled in my favor. Finally, there was a Supreme Court (state) action, and we won. What I demonstrated to the faculty was that the principal did not have all of that power and that there were ways in which he couldn't control a situation. That would not have happened unless we faced a conflict situation. It was uncomfortable and a bit risky. But I don't

think the authority structure would have ever changed otherwise. They had to know the superintendent was in charge. Else it would have gone on and on and on. The superintendents in the district were always the ones who left. There were something like 7 in a 6-year period. He always was the one who threw up his hands and left, because he couldn't deal with the power structures of teachers and administrators, who were in bed together. The principal left once he realized he had lost power. It was uncomfortable, all right, but it was also satisfying to be able to straighten something out that both the board and I thought was pretty bad.

One can raise questions about the superintendent's use of his power and influence here. Was it appropriate or ethical for him to recommend a denial of tenure so as to disrupt the informal power structure of the system in order to reestablish it along more formal, accepted lines? Some readers undoubtedly, will feel it was not appropriate or ethical and assert that there are other ways of dealing with such situations. Perhaps so. But recall a theme that has run through this book concerning the history and development of the superintendency. It is a theme of power and conflicts over it. Sad to say, when conflicts have their roots in a quest for power, they seem infrequently to be resolved by the parties' agreeing to be nice to each other. We witness this phenomenon endlessly in the daily newspapers.

This is not to say that this superintendent's action was the only thing he could have done. It certainly smacks of Machiavellianism. But the superintendent was presented with a dilemma. He could simply let the situation continue, in which case he would probably follow shortly on the heels of "something like 7 [superintendents] in a 6-year period" who had resigned the position. Or he could take a high-risk action, deliberately initiate a conflict, and hope for the best. If his risk didn't pay off, if he lost the struggle, his tenure in the position would be as short-lived as his predecessors'. But he won, and the power structure of the district was realigned to his satisfaction and that of the school board. In school organizations, as in any other, individuals occasionally become caught in battles not of their choosing, and they get hurt. This seems to be a given. When the conflict is framed in win-lose terms—a zero-sum game, as was this one—the chances of someone's getting hurt are enhanced. It's not a pleasant prospect to contemplate, but not to contemplate it means to shut out parts of a superintendent's life that he occasionally must confront.

Shaking Up the System

It is undoubtedly true that some superintendents are more disposed toward creating conflict in their system than others. They use that strategy as the primary vehicle for change. In the sample of superintendents in this study, there was one man who seemed clearly to take this position.

> One of the women who hired me said, "Are you crisis-oriented?" I said, "What does that mean?" She said, "Are you unhappy when there's nothing to do?" I said, "Yeah." She said, "Do you go out of your way to create problems?" And I said, "You know, that's a pretty severe indictment of an individual. However, there's probably some truth in it." (My wife will say, "For God's sake, that school system is regarded as one of the best in the country. They like it the way it is. So leave it alone.") But I come in and see ways it could be infinitely better, so I put the spotlight on it and, I guess, create crises.
>
> For example, our high school. The principal didn't recognize what was going on. His interpretation of his job was to let the staff go. "They're good people. They don't need me. I'm here to act as a buffer against the parents, to make the schedule, and go out and do all the speechifying." I said, "Bullshit, Jim, you're here to pull this community together." What I had found out was that there were some teachers who were teaching 35 minutes a day and some, the good ones, teaching 4½ hours a day. Some classes in the same subject met 3 times a week, some 4, some 5. There was no rhyme or reason other than teacher preference.
>
> So I did an analysis of the high school and went public with it. The public was very frightened: "My God, you mean there is something wrong with our high school?" I had to go public with it because when I tried to work with the faculty about the problems I saw, they said, "You're right. We've got a problem. You're the problem." They told me that my job was to stay in my office and make sure there was enough money. I told them I didn't see it that way, and while I had to take care of the money side, I was also there to improve the overall operation of the school district. Well, we're getting there. I'm up there at a meeting with them every week.

Every superintendent, of course, has his own view of what changes need to take place in his system, as well as his own theory of how best to induce the change. Most would undoubtedly prefer a change model based on rational persuasion. In the above case, the superintendent started out that way but apparently without much success. The alternative he chose, after being frustrated by the principal and the faculty, was a conflict model. He deliberately initiated a conflict by "going public" with the problem in a community in which such an action was sure to create a disturbance. It was a power play, without question, and he needed a broad base of community support to accomplish what he wanted. As in the situation in which the superintendent denied tenure as a means of initiating a conflict, this one too had its risks. The community could have refused its support and left its superintendent a lonely figure, high and dry with his ideas, with no way to implement them. Fortunately for him—and perhaps for the schools—this didn't happen.

Two more general points connected with these last two anecdotes that have implications for understanding superintendents and the superintendency go beyond a strategy of initiating conflict. The first has to do with the power and authority that are attributed to the office, subjects that have been addressed numbers of times throughout this book. Obviously, a superintendent has the freedom to attempt to influence the schools in many different areas. They include matters of budget, personnel, organizational structure, curriculum, and staff development. But despite this wide range of activities in which he may roam at will, his power to influence matters directly is frequently circumscribed, particularly if the focus of his attention is the normative structure or curricular patterns of a school. If, for example, a superintendent is interested in any thorough-going analysis and possible changes of educational programs, the authority of his position typically does not suffice to engage the committed energies of people directly. His power and influence base must be broadened outside his office. If this can be accomplished within the professional administrative and teaching staff, so much the better. The necessary dialogue occurs among colleagues. If, however, he meets internal resistance and is still interested in pursuing his goals, he must turn elsewhere. The board can be very helpful, of course, through its policymaking function, but the history of educational change is filled with policies that have been subverted or ignored. It is difficult, though, for building administrators and teachers to ignore the community. Thus it is to the community that the superintendent needs to turn at times in order to mobilize a broader and more powerful base of operations. This is precisely what was illustrated above. Whether or not "going public" is the preferred tactic is not a matter for our disucssion. The fact that school communities, if they are mobilized, constitute the critical power base for a superintendent, though, is a major part of what holding that office is all about.

The second point involves the question of the character of the conflicts in which a superintendent engages himself if he has an option of whether or not to join the battle. To oversimplify, the political rule of thumb that might be cited here is, "Don't get involved unless you think you have a better than even chance of winning." It is all much more complicated than that, of course, involving among other things an analysis of the personal risks and time requirements that attach to a variety of courses of action. The rule, though, is still a good one and probably undergirds much of a superintendent's daily thinking. As one man said,

> There are some battles you're gonna have to fight. You have no
> choice. But for lots of others, why spend energy on something you
> can't change? It's like pushing that wall. I can work like hell 8
> hours a day, but if it doesn't move I haven't done any work.

This is certainly not bad advice for anyone, let alone superintendents. But within the educational enterprise, it seems to speak to them more than it does to teachers or principals. The comment just quoted is a restatement of the time-worn but accurate phrase that defines politics as "the art of the possible." It seems clear that a superintendent needs to be a skilled practitioner of that art, particularly when he has to make a judgment on the extent and character of his involvement in the conflictual life that confronts him.

It takes no flash of insight to suggest that how each superintendent deals with that life, in terms of the strategies and tactics he employs, is a function of how he sees himself, the ways he is predisposed to analyze situations, what he thinks is called for in a particular circumstance, and the settings in which he sees himself operating most skillfully and comfortably. But is there anything unique to the superintendency that might indicate that certain ways of dealing with conflict are to be preferred over others? The answer is probably a negative one, although it is helpful to remember that conflict resolution in a school district cannot be productively thought about unless one considers the political and social fabric of the particular community involved. Nevertheless, it is in our interest to listen to the superintendents in this study talk about some of the major premises that guide them as they think both strategically and tactically about conflict as a basic theme of the superintendency.

One prefatory note: Superintendents, certainly those who have survived in the position for a long time, seem to have a tendency to offer prescriptions about what things have to be done in order to perform the job successfully. And why not? They are action-oriented, practical people, each of whom has been through his own private and public battles. The very fact of their survival is testimony to their success. It would be foolhardy not to pay attention to what they say about what has worked for them. But the strategies they offer should be viewed as additional data, not as rules. Three general themes developed. They are illustrated in these comments.

> The main thing is to defuse it as fast as possible, because you have
> a conflict everyday, no matter what you do. The point is that as
> soon as you calm people down on one side, something else will
> pop up.

> You have to try and avoid that which is avoidable. But you also
> have to learn when it is better to avoid and when it is better not to.

> What you do is you anticipate and you plan for all those things that
> seem to be coming along as far as the real conflicts are concerned.

Like what we have done is to take some of the key issues in
education that we can see coming up and have written position
papers on them. So that when anyone comes along and says, "Well,
what have you been doing about this?" We say, "Hey, we're
prepared. We've done the research. Here's what we've found out,
and here's what we're doing about it." Like the problem of
teaching foreign language that occurred in a neighboring district.
We did a paper on that 6 months ago. If you anticipate, that solves
a lot of headaches.

On the face of it, these seem to be rather straightforward axioms. Defuse
things as quickly as you can, avoid conflict when you can, but learn when it's
appropriate to join battle, and anticipate and plan for problems you see
coming up. They are not bad ideas and seem particularly appropriate for any
person who manages an organization whose viability is based on welding
consensus in a climate of competing interests. There are subtleties involved,
however, to which it is necessary to attend.

Defusing conflicts and avoiding them when possible seem to make good
managerial sense in almost any situation. They are ways of dealing with the
need to maintain the school system, as much as possible, in a state of
conflict-free equilibrium. Because the schools and what goes on in them are
so open to public scrutiny and concern, when the equilibrium is upset in
more than minor fashion, the essential business of education begins to suffer.
While it may not be completely true that peaceful schools necessarily mean
good education, it is probably quite true that disruption in schools makes the
provision of good education very problematic. It would be hard to find a
legitimate argument to counter that point.

But note the idea that there are times when a superintendent may and,
perhaps should, make a decision that a particular conflict should not be
avoided. These are times that require delicate judgments to be made. What is
at stake? The integrity of the system? The integrity of an individual? The
values that guide working arrangements? The balance of power between
school management and the teachers' union? The quality of education? But
there may be more at stake than the substance of the problem, because the
times that require such judgments of the superintendent are also the times of
more elevated risk for him. His prestige may be on the line, as well as his
reputation as a person who is able to make sound, politically and fiscally
sensitive decisions. The questions that the superintendent must always try to
answer at times like this are "Is it worth it? What are the chances of winning
or losing, and what will the costs be if one wins or one loses?" No guidelines
provide reasonable responses to all these questions. But their answers, when
they emerge, are found in the idiosyncratic political and social life of the
particular school system and the manner in which a superintendent analyzes
and judges it.

The strategy of anticipating potential conflicts and planning to deal with them, skills that undoubtedly develop with experience, make ultimate sense, of course. This strategy constitutes the heart of rational school administration, much as it does the administration of any other organization. However, subtleties are also involved here. What is at issue is the level of confidence that the school board has in the superintendent as a person whom they trust to guide them. School boards typically do not like to be surprised by events that could have been predicted. As the superintendent predicts, plans, and informs his board, in effect he functions as their protector. In the process, of course, he builds on his reputation for being knowledgeable and as a person who can be depended on in times of crisis. It may well be true that the superintendent who performs this protective role well is the one whose survival on the job is most likely to be guaranteed, a point that few superintendents neglect to think about from time to time.

In picking up the various strands of thought about the superintendent's continual involvement in conflict in this chapter, we have been reminded of the negative aspects of this part of the job. Let's remember, at this point, that for many of our interviewees, the challenge of dealing with conflict was the "juiciness" of it all. The modal response of the majority of the interviewees, when asked to say how they felt about "living with conflict," is reflected in the following brief remarks:

> I look forward to the battle. Absolutely! I get juiced up.

> It's probably the most exciting thing I can imagine doing.

> It's an enjoyable experience. There's just no end to it.

> I love it. I can say I really love it. I love conflict resolution. I'm not a masochist, but I get bored when too much time passes when there isn't a major conflict.

> It's what makes the job exciting. If everything went according to Hoyle, my God, I'd be bored. Every day there's a conflict to be resolved. It's like playing baseball. You've got so many innings in there, and you pitch, and hopefully you win. But baseball games get over. Here, it never stops. It goes on every day, and every day is a test of your wits and your ability.

Spoken, it seems, like the political animals that superintendents, for the most part, are. Though they undoubtedly become weary and debilitated at times, and though they occasionally speak of early retirement to get out of the "rat race," most of the evidence points to superintendents as people who like to play the conflict game—and like, quite naturally, to win more often than to lose.

13
The Superintendency:
Some Dilemmas of Leadership

The "book" on the superintendency is never closed. There is no summary to it. And so it is here that, in this final chapter, rather than concluding with some definitive remarks, we keep the "book" open with a discussion of some central and continuous dilemmas of leadership that are inevitably faced by a superintendent. Dilemmas of leadership in any situation are best understood by understanding the character of the underlying dynamics of that situation. It seems clear that "living with conflict" is the "axial principle"—to borrow a term from Bell (1973)—by which the superintendency may be most fruitfully understood. Though Bell used the term as a device for understanding society and its institutions at large, his definition of it as "the energizing principle that is a primary logic for all others" (p. 10) seems readily transferable to our concern, the work life of superintendents. That is the argument we have made, not only as far as the current work of the superintendent exists, but as it has existed historically.

Unless, however, one is interested only in knowledge for the sake of knowledge (a not ignoble goal), understanding this "energizing principle" of the superintendents' work life, interesting and helpful though it may be, can leave the educator, student, or involved lay person somewhat unsatisfied, as it did this writer. Superintendents, after all, are not employed to be objects of academic curiosity. To the contrary, theirs is a "do something" job. Though the precise nature of the doing varies from district to district, it always involves the exercise of leadership, however that is conceived in any particular situation. Generally superintendents are expected somehow not only to keep the organization running as smoothly as possible but also to influence the character and the substance of educational life in the systems in which they work.

The genesis of the focal dilemma of superintendents as leaders is immediately isolated in these two opposing demands. The pressure to keep the school system organization running smoothly implies a reactive stance. It suggests the need for a superintendent to be continually aware of potential problems in the schools or the community, so that the conflicts emanating from them may be managed with a minimum of disruption in the system. If he is successful in playing out this part of his role, he may indeed gain the reputation of being a manager who is able to keep things under control and who can keep the system out of trouble, or at least keep aggravating problems at a low level. This is a state that school boards would undoubtedly applaud. By focusing on the management of conflict and becoming highly skillful at it, a superintendent will assure himself of a long tenure in his position, if he desires it.

Behaving in ways that maintain the organization as a system with minimally disruptive conflict is one thing. Behaving in ways that change the character and substance of educational life in the system is another. The process of change, almost by definition, implies the development of conflict, and sometimes its deliberate induction on the part of organizational leadership. It is important, though, to recall Burns's (1978) comment in the last chapter. He wrote, pointedly, not of the inevitability of conflict in a political world but of "the function of leadership in expressing, shaping, and curbing it." Burns then went on to say:

> Leaders, whatever their professions of harmony, do not shun conflict; they confront it, exploit it, ultimately embody it. Starting at points of contact among latent groups, they can take various roles, sometimes acting directly for their followers, sometimes bargaining with others, sometimes overriding certain motives of followers and summoning others into play. (p. 39)

Hence the dilemma of the superintendent. In order to maintain the system so that the school board is pleased with its peacefulness, conflict must be anticipated, confronted, and diminished. However, in addition to reacting to potential or actual conflict and dealing with it in his organizational maintenance role, the *superintendent who would lead* must seek conflict out and occasionally promote it. This is much more subtle and requires much more skill than the "bull-in-a-china-shop" image of a conflict-oriented superintendent charging around his district and upsetting things. As Burns, in his discussions of leadership, puts it, "The fundamental process . . . is, in large part, *to make conscious what lies unconscious among followers*" (p. 40). The conflict within a school system or within a superintendent's daily life is overt and easily perceived. But this very overtness conceals motivations, aspirations, and goals that are present in a school community. They exist at a deeper level than is obvious for all to see, and it is at this level that a superintendent may find the primary energy source to guide his work.

It is a tall order to suggest that superintendents, if they would lead as well as manage their school districts through their political skills, need to focus some of their energy on making conscious that which lies unconscious in a community's concerns about its schools. Full of risk as it is, such a strategy runs counter to the dictum of "keeping things peaceful so that the schools may go about their business." Balancing the two demands, one for system management and the other for educational leadership, presents the superintendent with a daily dilemma, whether or not he is conscious of it. He has choices, of course. He can opt for the former, in which case his behavior communicates that all that is required for the schools to perform an adequate task is an atmosphere of peace and quiet. Or he can choose to focus his energy on the latter, thereby encouraging conflict to emerge. In this case, he can probably be assured of a more chancy tenure but also one that poses the possibility of educational change that is more than window dressing. The resolution of this focal dilemma of the superintendency is dependent on the personal needs of the particular individual involved. One's relative needs for security and certainty, and one's ability to tolerate conflict, can tip the balance in one direction or the other.

This discussion of what we have termed the focal dilemma of the superintendency has deliberately been phrased in abstract terms. Much stems from it that is quite concrete, however, and that finds its data base in the problems that were raised by the superintendents who were interviewed for this study. They imply personal decision-making dilemmas for each superintendent as he thinks about his role of manager of the politics of education in his school district. In the balance of this chapter we discuss several of them that have emerged in my mind as I studied and thought about the superintendents I know and the superintendency as an office.

How "Democratic" Should the System Be?

The dilemma here has to do with the character of the decision-making and influence processes that are developed in a school district. This dilemma has a long history: the reader will recall that questions of power and decision-making prerogatives pervaded discussion of the superintendency early in its development. Which powers belong to the school board, the superintendent, the professional staff, the community? How open are or should the district's decision-making processes be to influence from the community, from the teachers, or from other special-interest groups? Which parts of the superintendent's organizational territory should have sharply defined boundaries that separate them from the territory of other groups? Which parts of his territory should have hazy boundaries, so that decisions can be made depending on the particular situation at hand?

Academic answers to these questions are not hard to come by, but a superintendent's world is one of politically oriented action, not academics. He may be employed in a school district in which the board's attitude is that teachers have too much power in the system, so that efforts by the superintendent to involve teachers more deeply in decision making are seen as signs of disloyalty and weakness. Or, feeling that the parent community should have more direct influence on school decisions, he may create a structure designed for that purpose, only to find himself immobilized by the conflicts that emerge, thus inadvertently creating an image of himself as ineffectual. Regardless of the issue at hand, questions of governance of school districts require elegant balancing. It is the superintendent who typically is at the pivotal point in the whole process. Democracy in any political system, let alone the schools, is not an orderly business. How much disorder in its name can be tolerated in a school system, and toward what end? That is the essential question with which superintendents must deal relative to school decision making. It is, perhaps, less a case of being damned if he does and damned if he doesn't than a matter of the character of the political balance that is achieved in the school community as a result of governance actions. The dilemma is a real one. Sometimes its horns become obvious for all to see. More often, perhaps, it lies below the surface of a superintendent's daily life, constituting a substantial part of the political "underworld" of his job.

When Should One's Political Capital Be Used?

A wise old superintendent used to give lectures to graduate students about his "cookie jar" theory of leadership as it applied to the superintendency. The image was that of a superintendent on whose desk there was a jar of cookies. They were his stock in trade, which would be given out in exchange for something he valued. This may sound terribly paternalistic, but it was more the hallmark of a shrewd politican than that of a benign father. This man understood very well that if he was to get the things he wanted from the staff, school board, or community he would have to give something in return. The cookie jar represented what he had to give, and primarily it consisted of time and resources, either fiscal or human. As he gave things, what he received in return became his political capital that he could spend in other ways. Sometimes he traded for personal loyalty; sometimes for extra effort; sometimes for political support.

The dilemma is what to give to whom, and when. In other words, what transactions, at what times, constitute a fair bargain? How these decisions get made is idiosyncratic to each superintendent. That they must be made is without question. They make up another part of the political underworld in which superintendents live, and it is probably true that the extent to which a school community sees its superintendent as able to strike fair bargains will help to determine his success on the job.

For some superintendents, as we have seen, the whole process of compromising and bargaining that makes up any political setting is distasteful. For them, the dilemma takes the form of a decision to join in and be part of— indeed lead—the process or seek a different type of position. That puts it all in a very stark light, but one that portrays a good part of the superintendency quite accurately.

Political Strategist or Educational Statesman?

Given what we've said about the political nature of the job, one might argue that the dilemma posed by this question is no dilemma at all. Being an educational leader, one might argue, is no longer the primary focus of the superintendency. The thinking and decision making that affect the school life of youngsters daily takes place outside the superintendent's office. He no longer, except in very few situations, becomes involved with teachers about their work, and his relationships with principals frequently revolve mostly around their membership in his management group. Further, because he is removed by time and organizational function from classrooms, he can no longer lay claim to being the expert on educational matters.

We have touched many times on the ironic dilemma that develops when a teacher becomes a superintendent. A person who entered his profession because of a genuine interest in being an educator finds himself forced to function more as a politician than as a teacher. What does a superintendent do with that essential part of his self-concept that is "educator" when he deals with what is, in effect, a new career? In a very real way he is in education, but not of education. His professional associations change, as do the problems to which he must attend. Things that get discussed with colleagues are rarely concerned with problems of youngsters or teaching and learning. But he is still an educator and, in fact, has the image of chief educator of his school system. And the psychological home in which he was once welcomed as an integral family member now has room for him only as a visitor or sometimes an unwelcome guest.

Perhaps I am making too much of all this. Surely, most superintendents seem to adapt well to their job demands. But they are also, as we have seen, somewhat lonely in that job, having no friends among people who used to welcome them as friends. They no longer share with colleagues both the joy and pathos of what it means to be intimately involved with the education of youngsters. Further, and perhaps most important, the development of this intellectual and social distance between them and "hands on" education means that they lose credibility as educators among the educational fraternity. The impression I have gotten from talking with teachers is that they don't think that superintendents know much about education, though they may be seen as very skillful managers of school districts.

The dilemma remains. What is the superintendent, and where is his home? How does he play out his role of manager of the politics of education and still maintain, in his own mind at least, the image of a person whose intellectual roots are in territory that is no longer his? I don't pretend to have the answer to the questions. But surely, for many superintendents, they lie just beneath the surface, well repressed in all likelihood, but present nonetheless.

Being the Boss but Not Being the Boss

We have frequently noted the ironic fact that a superintendent has ultimate responsibility for a tremendous number of circumstances over which he can exercise only indirect control. Even his ability to get his subordinates within the school system to implement his ideas for changes in education practices is limited. With the exception of his authority to convene a meeting of his subordinates, there is little of substance that he can initiate and then see implemented without finding that the idea or proposal is altered by another group or simply by the fact of geographical distance between himself and the implementors. School people—though not necessarily in a conspiratorial way — are incredibly skilled at sabotaging the best intentions of their organizational superiors. Teachers, especially if they have tenure, interpret the curriculum as they see fit. Superintendents have little control over that, nor, as a matter of fact, do principals. And principals run their schools pretty much as they wish, sometimes heeding the superintendent's desires, sometimes paying them lip service, and sometimes ignoring them altogether.

The roots of this dilemma are found in the essential voluntariness of the system. Not everything depends on voluntariness, of course. Reports have to be completed and filed, schools have to be open on time, and teachers and principals have to be there. Rules and other norms of operation such as these, though, are simply accepted parts of everyone's organizational work life. Voluntariness relative to them is rarely an issue. However, it most centrally is when a superintendent wishes to influence the more substantive part of school life: the curriculum, teaching practices, or the character of supervisory practices, for example. In other words, when a superintendent tries to influence the structure of educational practice and the enactment of that practice, he must depend on the voluntary motivation of people. Further, though he does have the power to reward individuals through dispensing organizational "goodies" (giving time and money for a teacher to go to a conference, for example), he has little power to impose sanctions, particularly in these days of strong unionism.

Being responsible for the behavior of others but not being able to exert direct control over that behavior, then, constitutes a real dilemma for superintendents who care, as most of them do, about what happens in the schools. Many times they simply have to make peace with themselves over aggravating situations, judging that the costs that are attached to changing them are simply too great. Over the long term, though, the resolution of this dilemma probably rests on one's insight and ability to conceive of the superintendency as a position where one's power to get things done is a function of one's skill in mobilizing support from the groups that don't have to give it.

How Honest Should One Be?

We have discussed the honesty question before, but its importance for the life of a superintendent suggests that the dilemma should be highlighted at the close of this book. On the face of it, one might be inclined to say that this question poses no dilemma at all. After all, most of us grew up under the dictum of "Honesty is the best policy." If you do something wrong or if something is amiss and you are responsible for it, it's said, your situation will be worse in the long run if you don't tell the truth about it than if you do.

Few of us would argue against the abstract value of these statements, and it is probably true that most of us like to think we model them, at least as far as our personal demeanor is concerned. But we need to recall that Burlingame seriously doubted "that honesty is the best policy for superintendents who wish to retain power." What a contradiction we have! It is in the schools that the story of George Washington and the cherry tree first comes to light for most children. Honesty is to be valued, and uncompromisingly so. Yet, we have a serious scholar of educational politics and management telling us that a variance in the personal theme of honesty is probably required for school leaders who wish to retain their power and thus their tenure in office. Something seems out of kilter—or does it?

Two points need to be made that may help us understand the dilemma. First, Burlingame was not advocating lying or deliberately falsifying the facts. Though moral purists might disagree, it does seem that there are various shades of honesty. There is a difference, for example, between not telling the truth and not telling the whole truth in the sense of providing honest responses only to those questions that are asked. Successful trial lawyers are very familiar with this idea. Witnesses in court may be coached only to answer those questions that are asked and not to offer information on their own. It is the opposition whose responsibility it is to probe for the "whole truth." A witness can be indicted for perjury only for lying, not for omitting information for which no one asks.

A superintendent's world, of course, though sometimes it may feel that way, is not a courtroom. It is a fragile world composed of a wide array of conflicting and competing values and forces that need to be held together lest it disintegrate. It is, as we have so often remarked, a political world. Further, it is probably no accident that politics is referred to as a game. The object of playing a game is to win, or at the least, not to lose. One strategy that is employed in many, but not all games is that of deception, and the conditions of a superintendent's political game are that at times he too, must engage in deception in order to play his game well.

This all may sound very distasteful to the reader. But we are not suggesting that a superintendent need be deceitful or underhanded. We are only trying to suggest that his work life is composed of many situations in which wisdom and the demands of the political conflict at hand dictate that he not tell all he knows or that he behave in ways that keep things peaceful by, as Burlingame puts it, engaging in the processes of mystification or cover-up. So the dilemma, once more, is an obvious one and one that is kept secret, as a rule, by most superintendents. How honest should one be? Again, there is no answer. Only the question is ever present.

Surely, any thoughtful superintendent could add to the list of dilemmas. But perhaps the importance of the discussion lies as much in its symbolic value as its substance. That is, this final brief chapter with its concern with some dilemmas of a superintendent's work life is symbolic, I think, of the superintendency itself. It is a position that, throughout its long history, has continued to put its occupants in one quandary after another. Perhaps that's the way it should be—since the process of education itself involves, ideally, meeting and dealing with the dilemmas of life. The work life of superintendents models this process. It is not a bad model, at that.

Why Be a Superintendent?

Given all that has been said in this book about the conflictual and sometimes emotionally traumatic work life of a superintendent, a few remarks are in order that address the questions, Why do it? Why be a superintendent? What's the compensation for being involved in a type of work that confronts a person with what seems to be an unending number of conflicting pressures in one's public and personal life? What makes up for having to be continually on your guard concerning what you say in public or to your friends in private—

or even, at times, to your spouse? The list of questions could go on and on as one reflects on what the superintendents who were interviewed said about themselves and their work.

Some of the answers have to do simply with those things that typically accompany jobs of high responsibility. In this case, superintendents are paid well, at least by standards of the educational world. They are prestigious figures in the community. And, unlike principals and, particularly teachers, they are not building bound. They are free to roam around and set much of their own daily schedule. In the world of the schools, incidentally, this last point is no small matter. But these points don't describe what superintendents find meaningful about their work or what its underlying satisfactions are. So, back to the interviews to help us understand some of the circumstances that apparently provide the basic raison d'etre for being a school superintendent and continuing to want to be one. Here is a fair sampling of the comments that were made:

> It's the completion of something, a project. Something I can see. Something that's tangible. If we can win our busing case before the state Supreme Court, I would get tremendous satisfaction out of it.

> We have a problem with school drop-outs. If we can get the board and the community to buy a work-study program so we can entice these kids to stay in school till they graduate, I'll feel very good about that. But it's going to be hard to pull off, because the district has no history of doing this kind of thing.

> The excitement and enjoyment comes from always having to deal with things that are in movement, with change. It's being able to mix it up with people.

> Having an idea and seeing it through to fruition and not getting credit for it. I guess that's where I get the greatest satisfaction. I've influenced the situation, but no one besides me knows it. That's the greatest reward I can get from the job.

> It's getting people to work together, getting departments to work on new programs together when they had never done that before. It's seeing principals grow from not being managers to really flowering in that role.

> It's continually meeting new situations that require resolution. But interestingly, the most exciting time every year has to do with [seeing] who are the new people voted to the board of education. Because then you have to do a whole job of reeducating people, and that takes some time. Each person and each board is different. That begins to be exciting.

There it is, and it's by no means the whole story. But I think that what these people are saying is this: What makes being a superintendent meaningful is the opportunity to be involved in the whole flow of events that make a school district tick. It's seeing people, particularly adults, learn and grow and knowing that you've influenced their development. It's testing your skills against situations that sometimes seem unchangeable. It's seeing things happen in your district and knowing that, though your role may have been behind the scenes, without you they wouldn't have happened. It may all seem like poor and rather will-o'-the-wisp compensation for "living with conflict." But apparently, it is enough.

For Further Reading
References
About the Authors
Index

For Further Reading

In the preface I wrote that rather than including a typical "review of research" in the body of this book, I would provide a brief bibliographic essay for those readers who might be interested in further study of the superintendency. What follows is necessarily selective. Though three of the books mentioned had their start as doctoral dissertations, for the most part I have paid little heed to the very large volume of research that appears in dissertation form. The fact that most dissertations are notable only for their unspectacular findings suggested this was a prudent thing to do. Likewise, there are numbers of books about the superintendency that are rather dryly descriptive or prescriptive concerning the superintendent's function. These, too, I ignore here and focus instead on several that helped me get a "feel" for that office and for the people who occupy it. Some of them have been referred to earlier in this book.

Two books, Gilland's *Origin and Development of the Powers and Duties of the City School Superintendent* (1935) and Callahan's *Education and the Cult of Efficiency* (1962) originated as dissertations at the University of Chicago. Both deal with aspects of the history of the superintendency. Gilland's work was based on a study of school board documents in 30 cities in the country. It traced the development of the city superintendency from its early days as mostly a "service" function to its mid-1930s status as an office of executive power. His major concern was the set of conditions that he saw giving rise to the transfer of executive power from lay school committees to the superintendent. For someone who wishes to read history qua history, this book will do well.

Callahan's book, on the other hand, seems to carry with it more of a sense of the dynamic nature of the superintendency. His study was originally conceived, as he notes in the preface, as an exploration of "the origin and development of business values and practices in educational administration." This was not a very exciting theme to me. But as I noted in chapter 1, his insights into the systematically derived vulnerability of school people were powerful ones. *Education and the Cult of Efficiency* is a book that should be read and studied by professionals and lay people alike.

In *Managers of Virtue* (1982), Tyack and Hansot, a historian and a political scientist, provide a history of a different sort. The book presents a fascinating story of the development of the public schools through description and analysis of the attitudes and behavior of some focal actors on the educational stage. Many, but not all, were school superintendents. The reader is led to understand—and, in my case, marvel at—the almost messianic fervor with which many of these people approached their task. The schools were, indeed, to be the vehicle through which the experiment in self-government that America represented would be proved successful. If one wishes to understand today's schools, and thus the superintendency, in a way that helps fit things together, *Managers of Virtue* is an indispensable resource.

The superintendency has also attracted the interest of behavioral scientists, whose approach to its study has been more empirical in nature than that of the authors just mentioned. *Explorations in Role Analysis* (Gross, Mason, and McEachern, 1958), for example, is a study whose aim is both to refine the concepts of role conflict and resolution and to develop a deeper understanding of the superintendency and the crosscurrents of forces that affect one's behavior in that role. A detailed review of the results is not possible here, of course. One summary point that clearly emerges, however, is that superintendents must make peace with the fact that they will frequently confront situations in which they will be pressured to make a decision on the basis of things other than the substance of the problem. Professional values often take a back seat to political forces. Or, as the authors comment on the conflict between a superintendent's professional obligations and the expectations of the lay community, "By not yielding to the unprofessional expectations of school board members and key influentials in the community, he may endanger his own position" (p. 259). Touché!—as has been noted in various ways earlier in this book.

Numerous subsequent studies have found their beginnings in Carlson's (1972) *School Superintendents: Careers and Performance*. This book can be thought of as the seminal study of the career mobility of superintendents, but it didn't start out that way. In Carlson's words, "This orientation was, by and large, accidental. . . . My original intention was to concentrate on the way a chief executive new to his post related to the social structure of the containing organization" (p. vi). As a result of this shift in orientation, Carlson developed a typology of superintendent careers relative to patterns of mobility. Two categories emerged: "place-bound" and "career-bound." Both types tend to have essentially similar credentials.

Here the similarity ceases, however. The place-bound superintendent is one who applies for the job in his home territory until it is offered to him. Of course, he may wait a long time, and possibly in vain. Nevertheless, for him the place is the thing, not the career. On the other hand, the "place" for career-bound superintendents tends to be rather inconsequential. For him, the career is the thing. Further, career-bound superintendents are not all cut from the same cloth. According to Carlson, there are three subtypes: "hoppers, specialists, and statesmen" (p. 43). The descriptors are apt. Hoppers are continually looking for their next position. They tend to be very able people, they do things quickly—perhaps too quickly—and then move on. Specialists are just that. They do one thing (business management, curriculum) very well. They move into a school district, "do their thing," usually stay a bit longer than the hopper, but then they too move on. The statesmen's commitment to a community is usually longer than that of hoppers and specialists. They tend to focus on the system as a whole, not a part of it, and they are "never a candidate for a new superintendency; the school boards come to him" (p. 45). One suspects that the "statesmen" constitute the elite of the superintendency, even if the idea goes publicly unacknowledged.

As we have suggested numerous times in this book, questions involving the superintendent and the lay school governing board have a long history. At their roots, these questions have been concerned with power. Two well-known books give attention to the issue. McCarty and Ramsey, in *The School Managers* (1972), approach it through an analysis of community political structure. Their study, appropriately for our purposes, is subtitled, "Power and Conflict in American Education." They posit the existence of four community types (dominated, factional, pluralistic, and inert) and suggest that the character of the school board reflects the community power structure. Therefore the role of the superintendent vis-à-vis the school board becomes a function of the board's structure. The problem is not that superintendents need be prisoners of the community power structure as they work with their school boards. But they can't ignore it.

The concern of *Governing America's Schools* (Zeigler and Jennings, 1974) was with studying the factors that might affect a school board's democratic responsiveness to its community. Though their focus was not directly on the superintendency, they could, of course, hardly avoid it. Further, the words and phrases they use to conceptualize superintendent–school board relations fit well the theme of "living with conflict." "Dominated by superintendents," "opposition to," "challenge," and "board—superintendent contest" are some of the key ones. The book is rich in analysis of the problems of school governance, particularly in its discussion of some factors that may affect the ways in which lay boards deal with the professional expertise of superintendents.

A final suggestion for further study by readers of this book is *Profile* (Feilders, 1982). This is a participant-observation study of "a day in the working life of Robert Alioto, Chief Superintendent of the San Francisco Unified School District" (p. 1). Interesting in the delicate detail that it presents about this one day, it also touches on a number of issues that have been dealt with in more depth earlier in our own discussion. Even the superintendent of the San Francisco schools cannot count on having a completely private lunch, for example: he is recognized and called to as he leaves a restaurant. And his day ends at the close of a school board meeting (at 10:45 P.M.) as "he shakes hands with a supporter, listens as a final critic berates him about his 'overhiring of women'" (pp. 92–93). *Profile* is a short book, but it does give one a sense of the type of action that is a superintendent's work.

The literature of the superintendency, as can be seen from these few pages, is wide-ranging. It is inviting to students who wish to pursue it for academic reasons; to superintendents who wish to get better conceptual handles for their work; and to lay people who simply may want to learn more about those who play a large role in their community's educational life.

References

American School Board Journal. August 1891, *2*, 6.

———. October 1891, *2*, 7.

———. The "czar" movement. March 1895, *10*, 5.

———. May 1895, *10*, 8–9.

———. August 1895, *11*, 8–9.

———. Letters from a country superintendent to his daughter. November 1922, *45*, 36.

———. Letters from a country superintendent to his daughter. February 1923, *45*, 34.

———. August 1976, *163*, 23–25.

Annual Report of the Superintendent of Common Schools of the State of New York, Together with the Reports of County Superintendents. Albany: Carroll and Cook, 1845.

Bacharach, S., and E. Lawler. *Power and Politics in Organizations.* San Francisco: Jossey-Bass, 1980.

Bakke, E. *The Fusion Process.* New Haven: Labor and Management Center, Yale University, 1953.

Bell, D. *The Coming of Post-Industrial Society.* New York, 1973.

Boyd, W. The school superintendent: educational statesman or political strategist? *Administrator's Notebook,* August 1974, *22*, 9.

Burlingame, M. Superintendent power retention. In S. B. Bacharach (ed.), *Organizational Behavior in Schools and School Districts.* New York: Praeger, 1981.

Burns, J. *Leadership.* New York: Harper & Row, 1978.

Callahan, R. E. *Education and the Cult of Efficiency.* Chicago: University of Chicago Press, 1962.

Campbell, R. Is the school superintendent obsolete? *Phi Delta Kappan.* October 1966, *48*, 2, 50–58.

Carlson, R. *School Superintendents: Careers and Performance.* Columbus, Ohio: Merrill, 1972.

Cuban, L. *Urban School Chiefs Under Fire.* Chicago: University of Chicago Press, 1976.

Cubberley, E. *Public School Administration.* Boston: Houghton Mifflin, 1916.

Eisner, E. *The Educational Imagination.* New York: Macmillan, 1979.

Feilders, J. *Profile.* Belmont, Calif.: Fearon Education, 1982.

Gilland, T. D. *The Origin and Development of the Power and Duties of the City School Superintendent.* Chicago: University of Chicago Press, 1935.

Goldhammer, K. Roles of the American school superintendent, 1954–1974. In L. Cunningham, W. Hack, and R. Nystrand (eds.), *Educational Administration: The Developing Decades.* Berkeley, Calif.: McCutchan, 1977, pp. 147–64.

Green, T. *Work, Leisure, and the American Schools*. New York: Random House, 1968.

Griffiths, D. *The School Superintendent*. New York: Center for Applied Research in Education, 1966.

Gross, N., W. Mason, and A. McEachern. *Explorations in Role Analysis*. New York: John Wiley and Sons, 1958.

Hall, G. S. The case of the public schools. *Atlantic Monthly*. March 1896, 77, 402–13.

Heller, M. Ten sure-fire ways to kill a superintendent. *American School Board Journal*. May 1978, *165*, 25–27.

Hess, F. The political dimension of local school superintendency. *Council Journal*. New York State Council of School District Administrators. May 1977, *1*, 125–37.

Iannaccone, L. *Politics in Education*. New York: Center for Applied Research in Education, June 1967.

Jones, L. Politics and education. *Atlantic Monthly*. June 1896, 77, 810–22.

Katz, D., and R. Kahn. *The Social Psychology of Organizations*, 2nd ed. New York: Wiley, 1978.

Knezevich, S. *Administration of Public Education*. New York: Harper & Row, 1975.

Knezevich, S. (ed.). *The American School Superintendent*. Washington: American Association of School Administrators, 1971.

Levinson, N. *The Great Jackass Fallacy*. Cambridge, Mass.: Harvard University Press, 1973.

McAndrew, W. Appraising radical teachers unions. *School and Society*. February 6, 1932, *35*, 191.

McCarty, D., and C. Ramsey. *The School Managers*. Westport, Conn.: Greenwood, 1971.

March, J. American public school administration: a short analysis. *School Review*. February 1978, *86*, 217–50.

Martin, J. A., and S. Zichefoose. As reported in *School Administrator*. January 1980, *37*, 3, 5.

Meyer, M. *The Teachers Strike: New York*. New York: Harper & Row, 1969.

Mosher, E. Educational administration: an ambiguous profession. *Public Administration Review*. November/December 1977, *37*, 651–58.

Nation's Schools. It's a no-win game. March 1972, *89*, 66–68.

Nolte, C. M. How fast is the power of the superintendent slipping? *American School Board Journal*. September 1974, *161*, 9.

Northeast Dubois County School Corporation. "News . . . from the Superintendent's Office." April 1980.

Sarason, S. *The Culture of the School and the Problem of Change*. Boston: Allyn & Bacon, 1971.

———. *The Creation of Settings*. San Francisco: Jossey-Bass, 1972.

School and Society. The Seattle School Board and the Teachers Union. July 7, 1928, *28*, 11.

Sease, D. In the line of fire. *Wall Street Journal*. June 2, 1981, *197*, 1.

Taylor, F. *The Principles of Scientific Management*. New York: Harpers & Brothers, 1911.

Tyack, D., and R. Cummings. Leadership in American public schools before 1954: historical configurations and conjectures. In L. Cunningham, W. Hack, and R. Nystrand (eds.), *Educational Administration: The Developing Decades.* Berkeley, Calif.: McCutchan, 1977, 46–66.

Tyack, D., and E. Hansot. *Managers of Virtue: Public School Leadership in America, 1820–1980.* New York: Basic Books, 1982.

Weick, K. Educational organizations as loosely coupled systems. *Administrative Science Quarterly.* March 1976, *21*, 1–19.

———. Loosely coupled systems: related meanings and thick interpretations. Unpublished paper. Cornell University, 1979.

White, L. D. *Introduction to the Study of Public Administration*, rev. ed. New York: Macmillan, 1939.

Wilson, R. *The Modern School Superintendent: His Principles and Practices.* Westport, Conn.: Greenwood, 1960.

Zeigler, H., J. Riesman, and J. Polito. *Conflict Management.* Eugene, Ore.: CEPM, College of Education, University of Oregon, 1981.

Zeigler, L. H., and K. Jennings. *Governing America's Schools.* N. Scituate, Mass.: Doxbury Press, 1974.

About the Authors

Arthur Blumberg is Professor of Education at Syracuse University. He received his Ed.D. from Teachers College, Columbia University and has served on the faculties of Springfield College and Temple University. Dr. Blumberg has authored or coauthored several books including *Supervisors and Teachers: A Private Cold War* (McCutchan, 1974) and *The Effective Principal* (Allyn & Bacon, 1979). His research and writing interests focus on the character of schools as adult work-settings and the nature of the work life of people who hold leadership positions in schools.

Phyllis Blumberg is Associate Dean, College for Human Development, Syracuse University. She received her doctorate from Syracuse University in counseling and guidance. She is a clinical member and an Approved Supervisor of the American Association of Marriage and Family Therapists.

Index

DATE DUE			